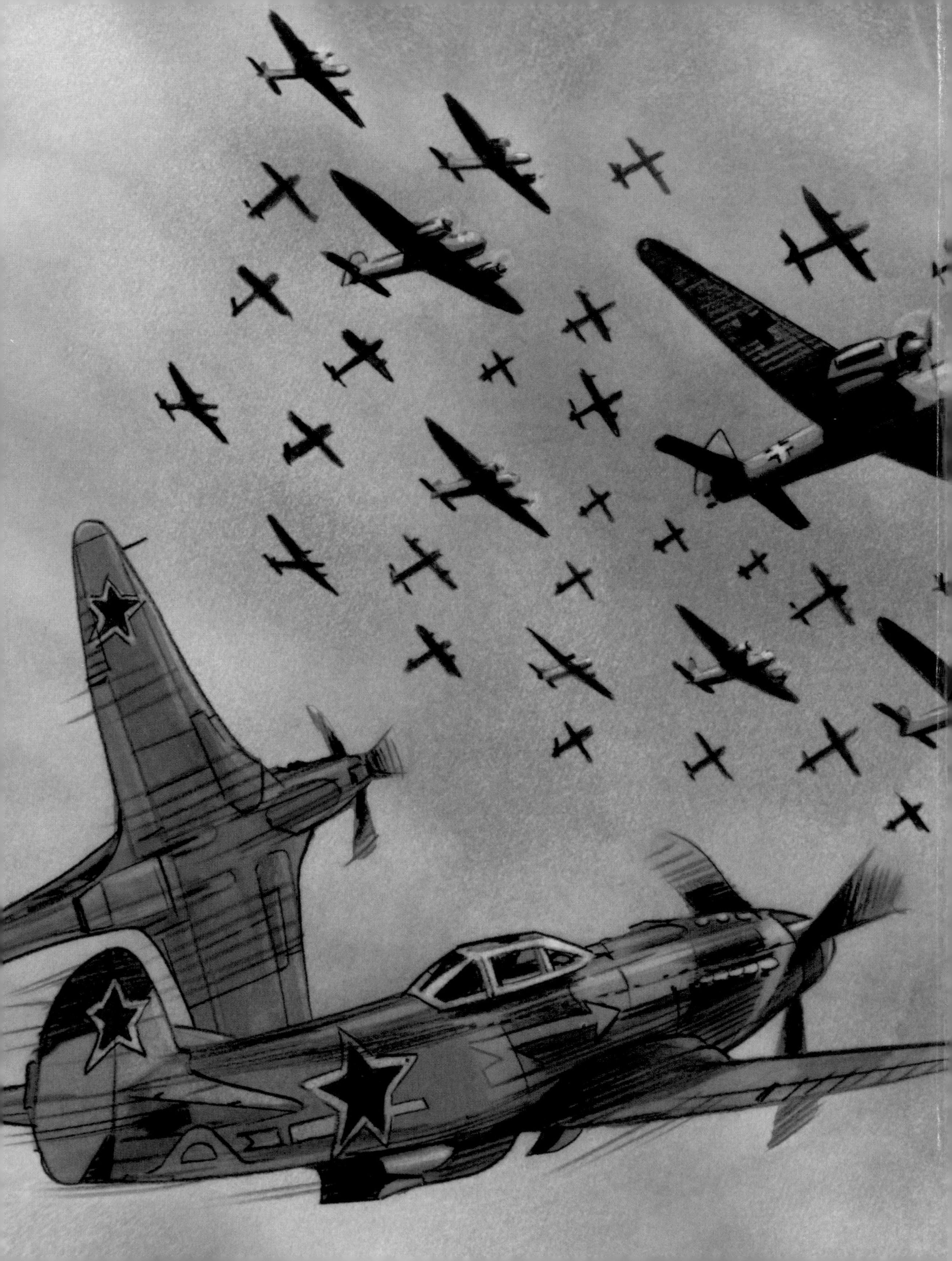

AMAZING WORLD WAR II STORIES

FOUR INCREDIBLE TRUE TALES

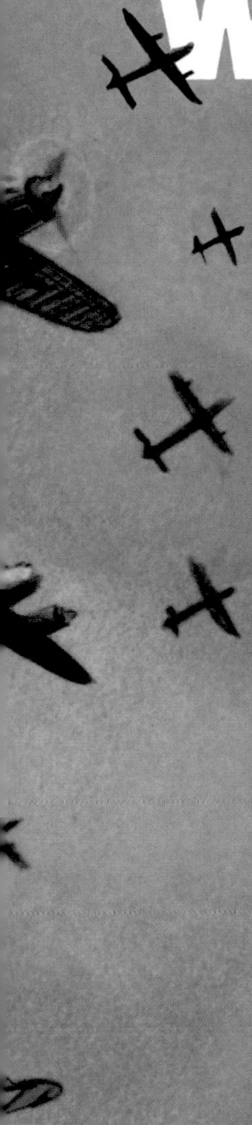

WRITERS
Blake Hoena, Bruce Berglund,
Nel Yomtov

ILLUSTRATORS
Alessandro Valdrighi , Marcel P. Massegú,
Rafal Szlapa, Trevor Goring

CAPSTONE PRESS
a capstone imprint

Graphic Library is published by Capstone Press, an imprint of Capstone.
1710 Roe Crest Drive, North Mankato, Minnesota 56003
www.capstonepub.com

Library of Congress Cataloging-in-Publication data is available on the Library of Congress website.
ISBN: 978-1-4966-6658-1

Summary: In graphic novel format, tells the amazing stories of unsung heroes of World War II who showed the courage to fight the enemy in ways beyond battling on the front lines.

Design Elements by Shutterstock/Guenter Albers

Direct quotations appear in bold italicized text on the following pages:
Navajo Code Talkers:
Page 17: from *Defending Whose Country?: Indigenous Soldiers in the Pacific War,*
 by Noah Riseman. Lincoln, NE: University of Nebraska Press, 2012.
Page 36: from "Remarks by the President in a Ceremony Honoring the Navajo Code Talkers,"
 by The White House, Washington, D.C., July 26, 2001 (https://georgewbush-whitehouse.
 archives.gov/news/releases/2001/07/20010726-5.html)

Night Witches:
Pages 43, 45: from *Wings, Women, and War: Soviet Airwomen in World War II Combat,* by
 Reina Pennington, Lawrence, KS: University Press of Kansas, 2002.
Page 65, panel 2: from "Women Veterans of Aviation in the Soviet Union," by Reina Pennington
 in A Soldier and a Woman: Sexual Integration in the Military, edited by Gerard J. DeGroot
 and C.M. Peniston-Bird. New York: Pearson Education, 2000.
Page 65, panel 3: from "Nadezhda Popova, WWII 'Night Witch,' Dies at 91," by Douglas Martin,
 The New York Times, July 14, 2013. https://www.nytimes.com/2013/07/15/world/europe/
 nadezhda-popova-ww-ii-night-witch-dies-at-91.html

Unbreakable Zamperini:
Pages 70, 71, 72, 73, 90 : from *Devil at My Heels,* by Louis Zamperini with David Rensin. New York:
 HarperCollins Publishers, 2003.
Pages 75, 79, 83: from *Unbroken: An Olympian's Journey from Airman to Castaway to Captive,*
 by Laura Hillenbrand. New York: Penguin Random House, 2014.

U.S. Ghost Army:
Page 99: from *Ghost Army of World War II,* by Rick Beyer and Elizabeth Sayles. New York:
 Princeton Architectural Press, 2015.
Page 102: from *Secret Soldiers: The Story of World War II's Heroic Army of Deception,*
 by Philip Gerard. New York: Dutton, 2002.
Page 121: from *Ghost Army of World War II,* by Jack Kneece. Gretna, LA: Pelican Pub. Co., 2001.

Editor
Aaron J. Sautter

Art Director
Nathan Gassman

Designer
Ted Williams

Production Specialist
Katy LaVigne

Printed and bound in China. 5645

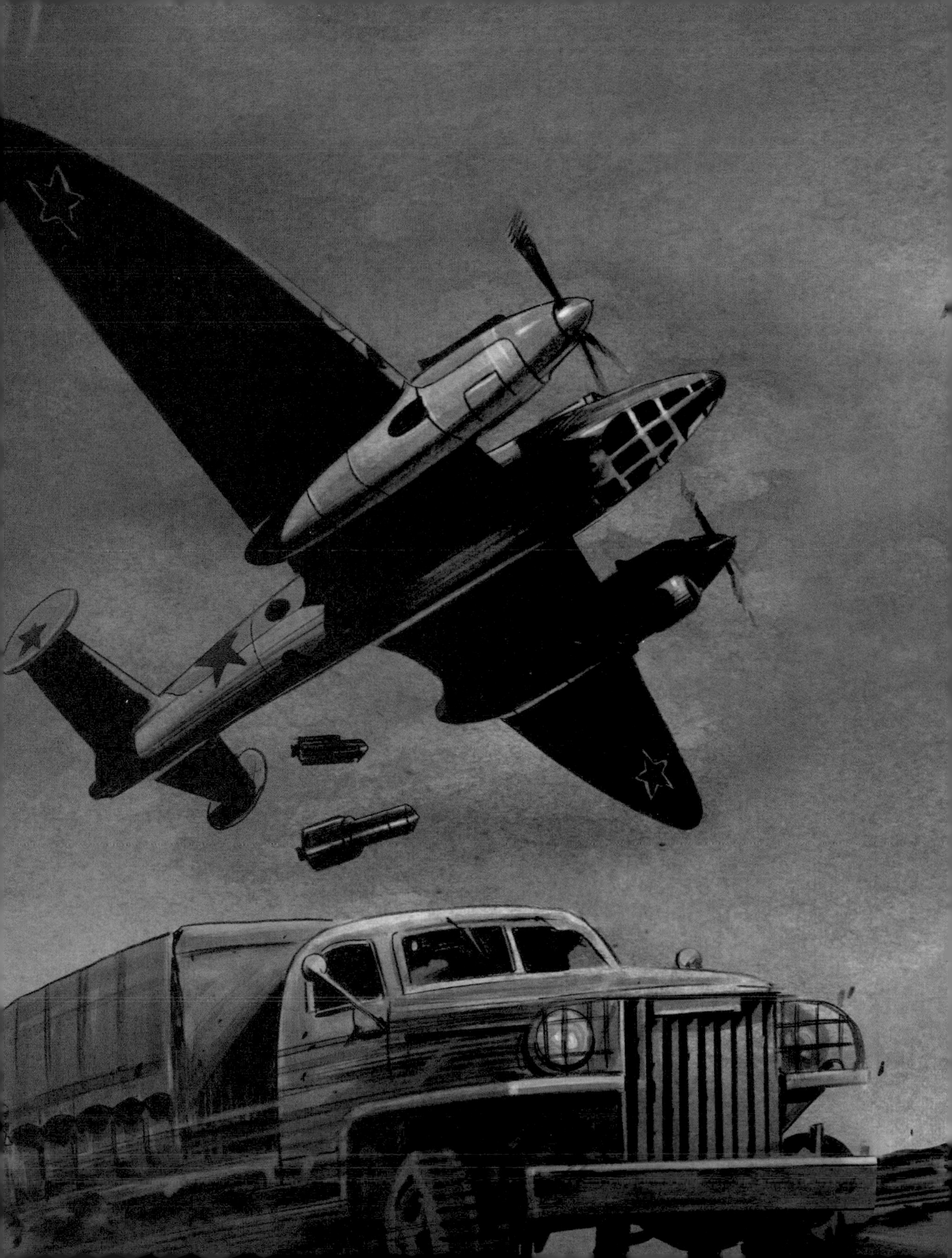

TABLE OF CONTENTS

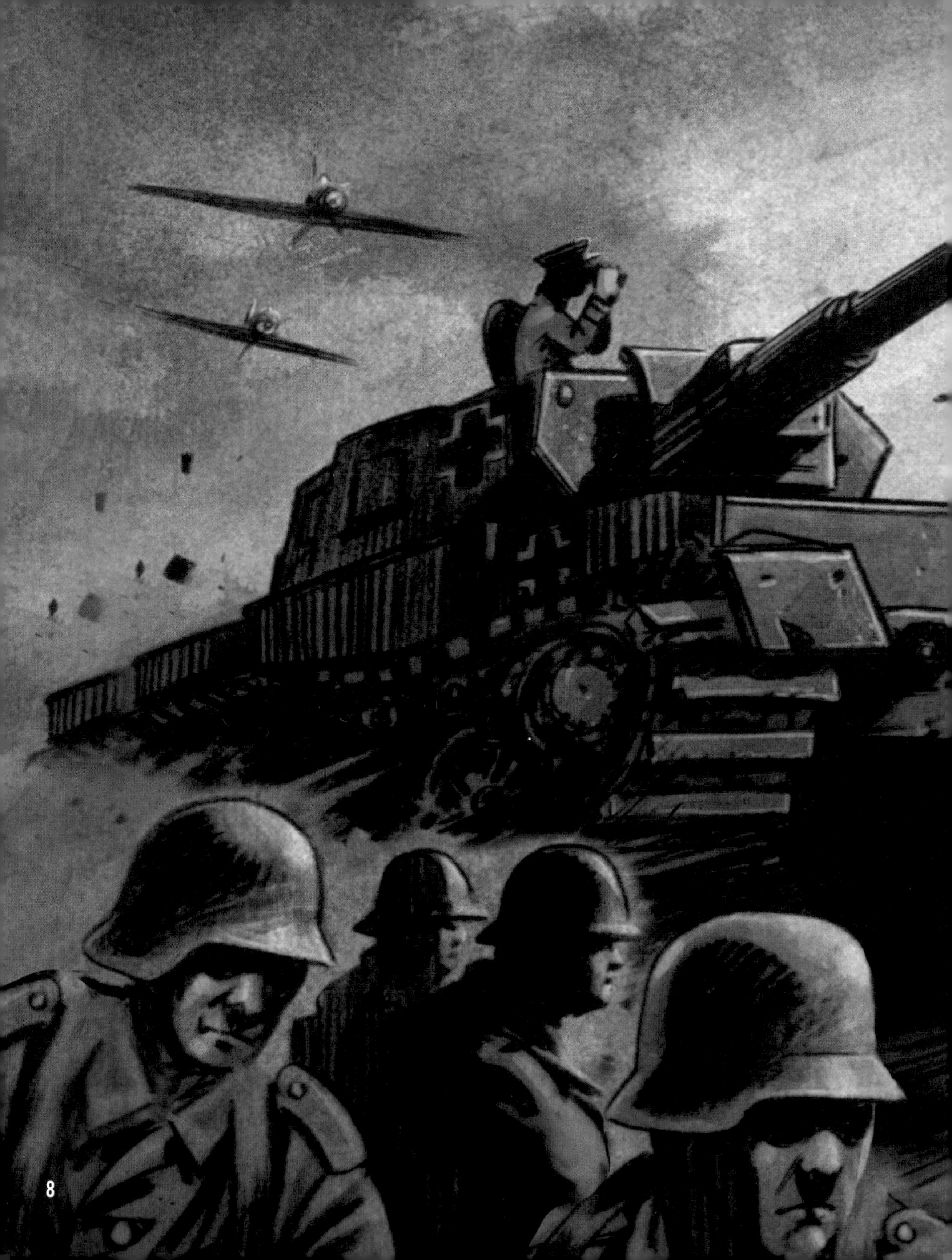

THE UNSUNG HEROES OF WORLD WAR II

Tanks rumbling through muddy fields. Fighter planes and bombers roaring through the sky. Explosions blasting through buildings. The screams of armies charging into battle. These are the sights and sounds of history's biggest and deadliest conflict.

From 1939 to 1945, soldiers fought one bloody battle after the next throughout World War II. German leader Adolf Hitler and the Nazi Party controlled much of Europe. Meanwhile, Japanese forces captured many islands in the Pacific Ocean. Eventually, the United States joined Great Britain, the Soviet Union, and other Allied forces to stop the Axis nations from taking over the world.

Troops on the front lines showed great courage while fighting under enemy fire. But some soldiers showed bravery by fighting in other ways. In the Pacific, the Navajo Code Talkers relayed important messages during battle using their unbreakable code. In Europe, the U.S. Ghost Army created fake camps and illusions to draw enemy fire away from real U.S. ground forces. In the Soviet Union, a squadron of female pilots flew hundreds of daring nighttime bombing missions in old, rundown airplanes. And in Japan, one lone U.S. soldier faced down his personal enemy with only his iron will and unbreakable spirit.

These are the tales of those who fought bravely—but did so in secret. The experiences of these soldiers went largely unknown until long after the war was over. They are the unsung heroes of World War II.

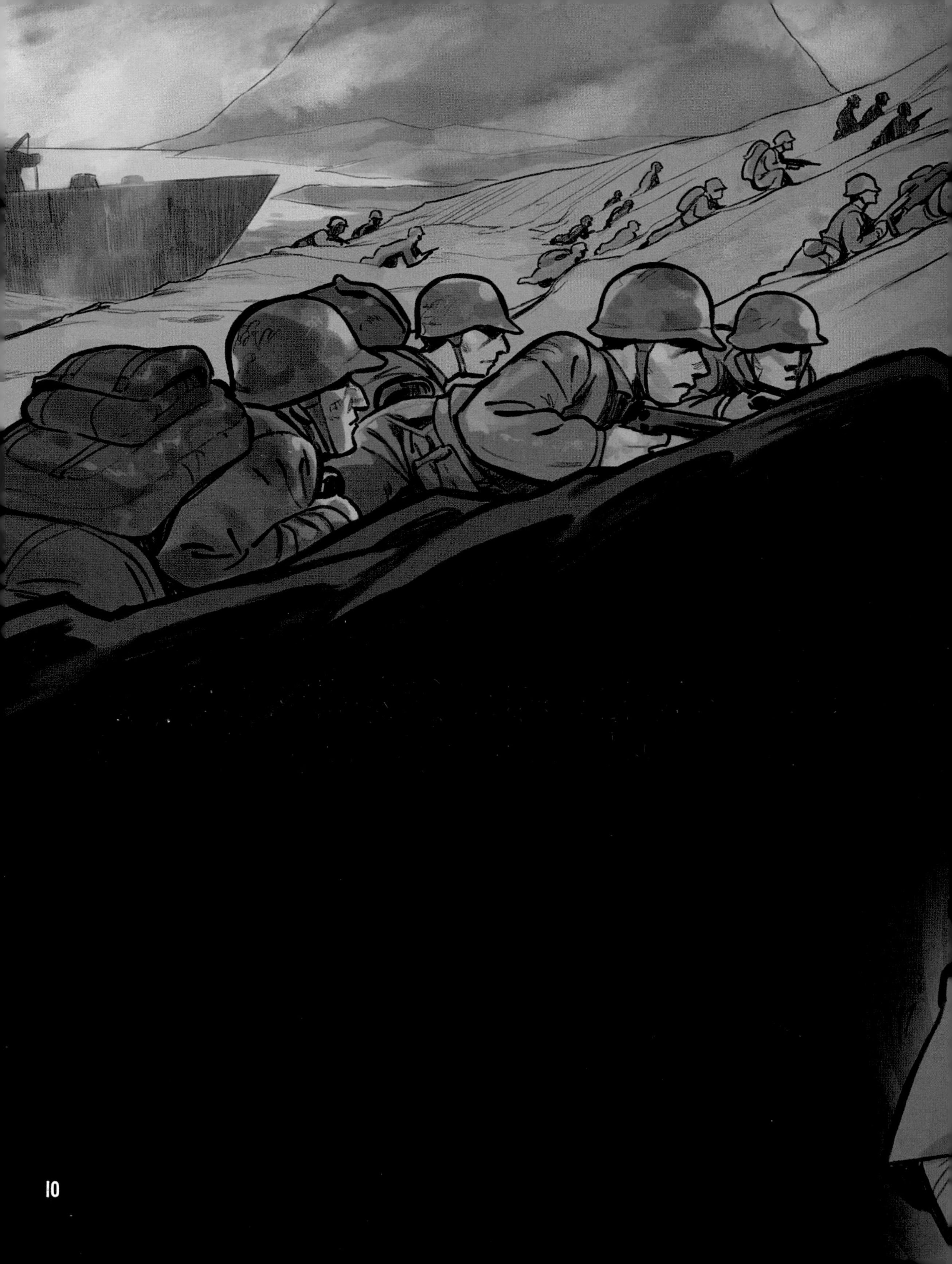

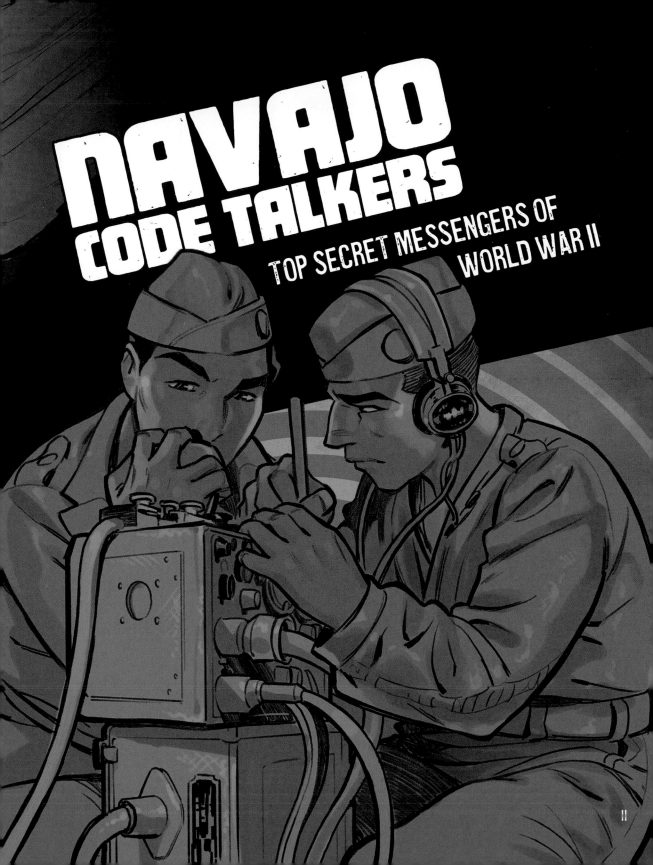

NAVAJO CODE TALKERS

TOP SECRET MESSENGERS OF WORLD WAR II

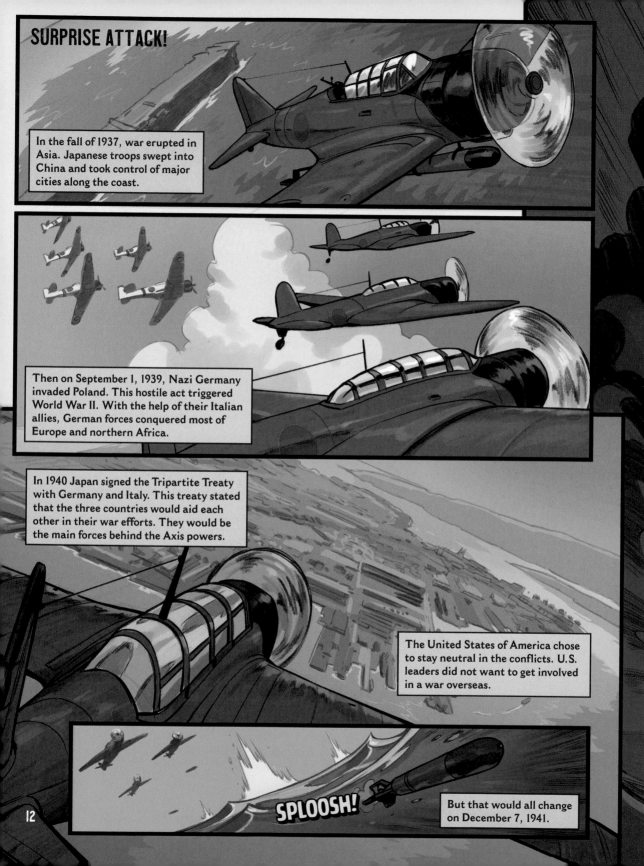

SURPRISE ATTACK!

In the fall of 1937, war erupted in Asia. Japanese troops swept into China and took control of major cities along the coast.

Then on September 1, 1939, Nazi Germany invaded Poland. This hostile act triggered World War II. With the help of their Italian allies, German forces conquered most of Europe and northern Africa.

In 1940 Japan signed the Tripartite Treaty with Germany and Italy. This treaty stated that the three countries would aid each other in their war efforts. They would be the main forces behind the Axis powers.

The United States of America chose to stay neutral in the conflicts. U.S. leaders did not want to get involved in a war overseas.

SPLOOSH!

But that would all change on December 7, 1941.

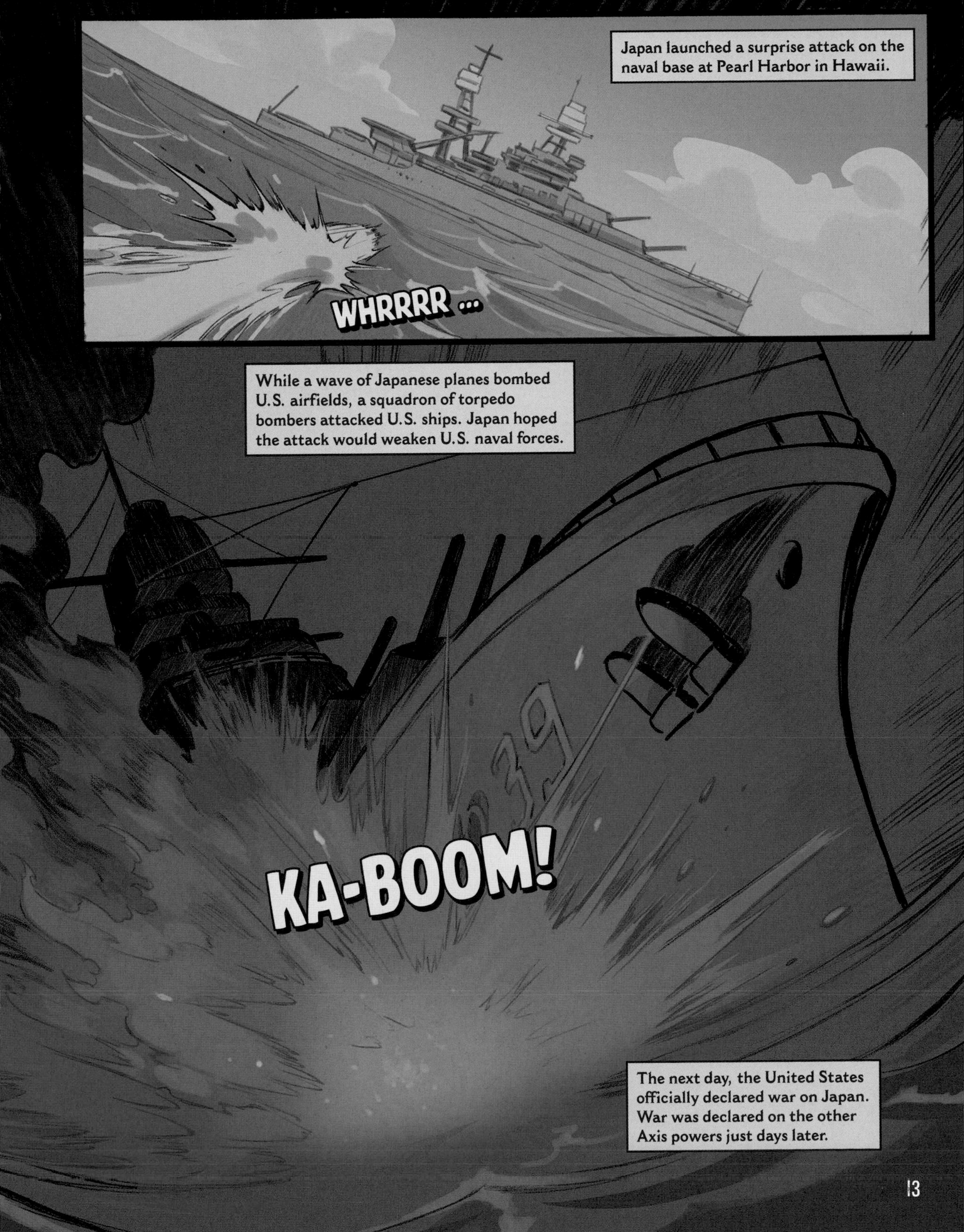

Japan launched a surprise attack on the naval base at Pearl Harbor in Hawaii.
WHRRRR ...
While a wave of Japanese planes bombed U.S. airfields, a squadron of torpedo bombers attacked U.S. ships. Japan hoped the attack would weaken U.S. naval forces.
39
KA-BOOM!
The next day, the United States officially declared war on Japan. War was declared on the other Axis powers just days later.

CREATING A NEW CODE

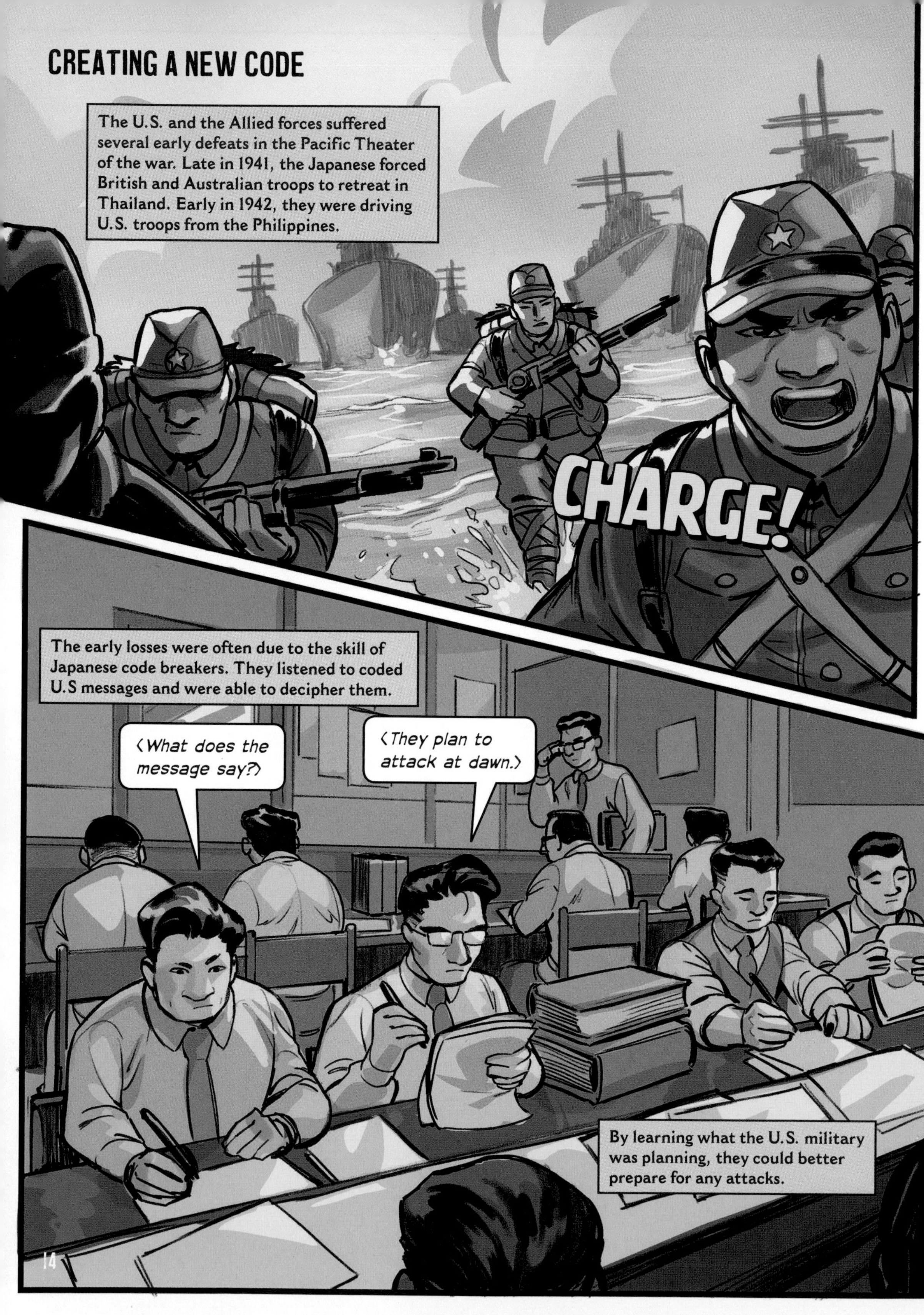
The U.S. and the Allied forces suffered several early defeats in the Pacific Theater of the war. Late in 1941, the Japanese forced British and Australian troops to retreat in Thailand. Early in 1942, they were driving U.S. troops from the Philippines.
CHARGE!
The early losses were often due to the skill of Japanese code breakers. They listened to coded U.S messages and were able to decipher them.
〈What does the message say?〉
〈They plan to attack at dawn.〉
By learning what the U.S. military was planning, they could better prepare for any attacks.

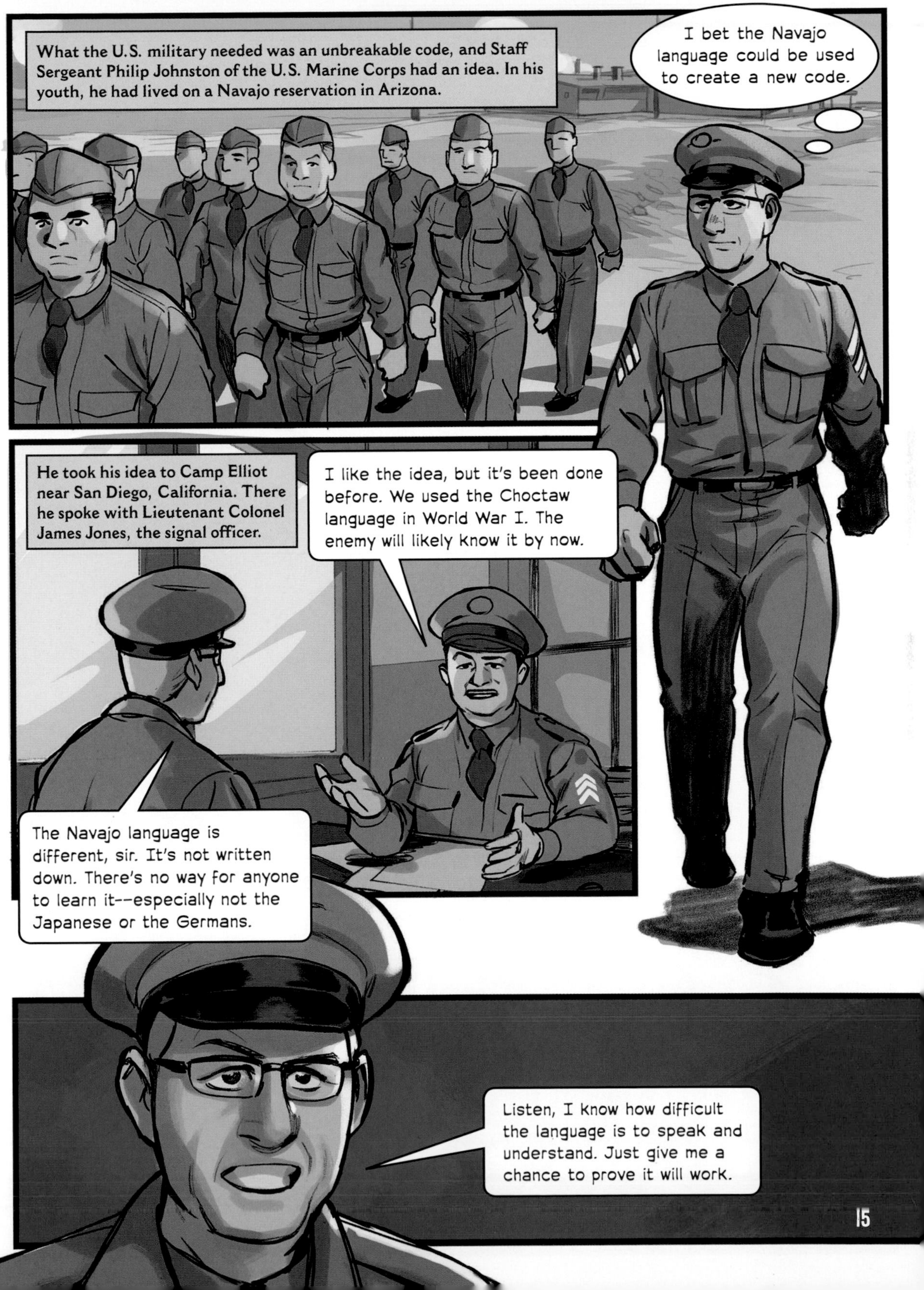

What the U.S. military needed was an unbreakable code, and Staff Sergeant Philip Johnston of the U.S. Marine Corps had an idea. In his youth, he had lived on a Navajo reservation in Arizona.
I bet the Navajo language could be used to create a new code.
He took his idea to Camp Elliot near San Diego, California. There he spoke with Lieutenant Colonel James Jones, the signal officer.
I like the idea, but it's been done before. We used the Choctaw language in World War I. The enemy will likely know it by now.
The Navajo language is different, sir. It's not written down. There's no way for anyone to learn it--especially not the Japanese or the Germans.
Listen, I know how difficult the language is to speak and understand. Just give me a chance to prove it will work.

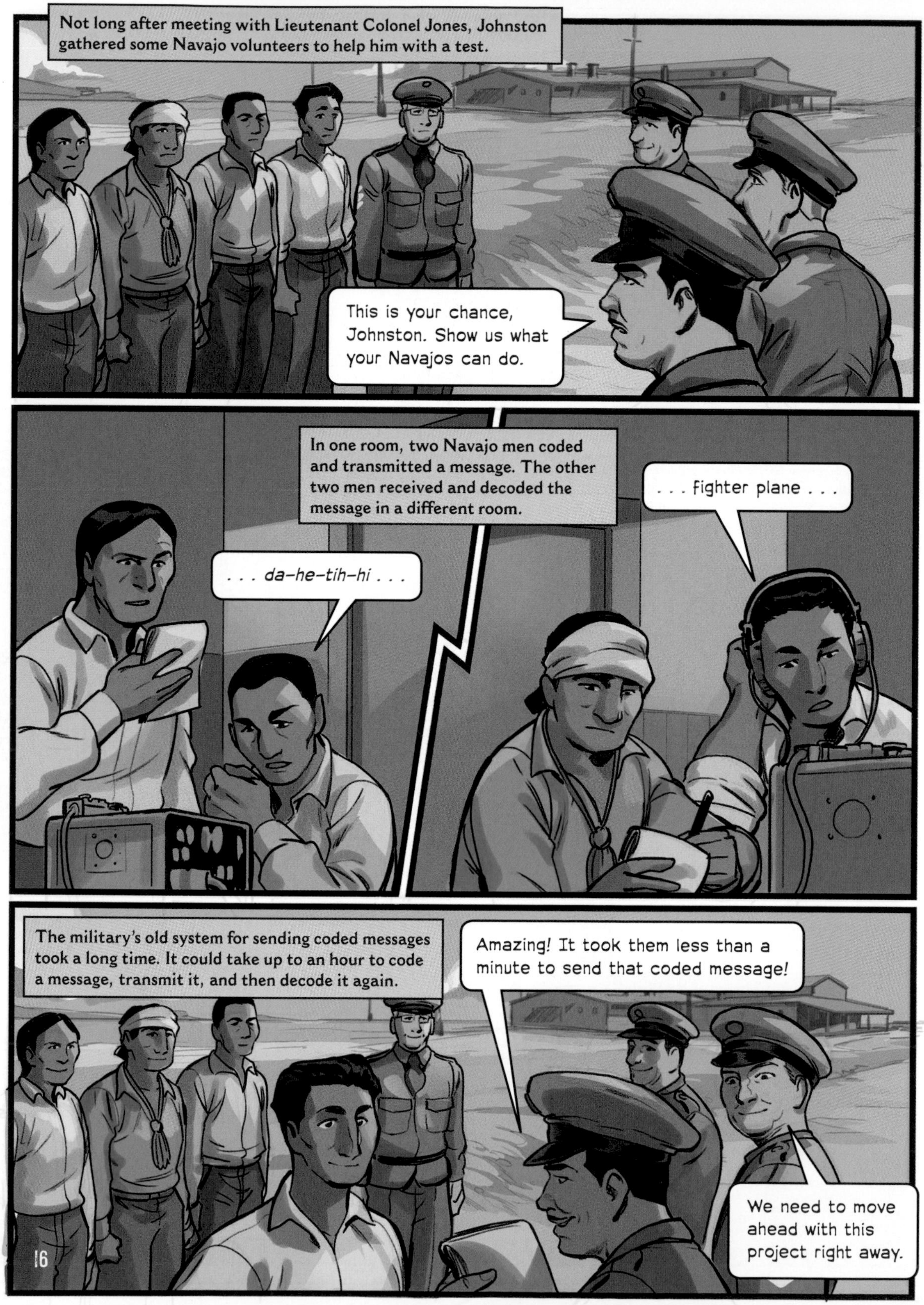

Not long after meeting with Lieutenant Colonel Jones, Johnston gathered some Navajo volunteers to help him with a test.
This is your chance, Johnston. Show us what your Navajos can do.
In one room, two Navajo men coded and transmitted a message. The other two men received and decoded the message in a different room.
. . . da-he-tih-hi . . .
. . . fighter plane . . .
The military's old system for sending coded messages took a long time. It could take up to an hour to code a message, transmit it, and then decode it again.
Amazing! It took them less than a minute to send that coded message!
We need to move ahead with this project right away.

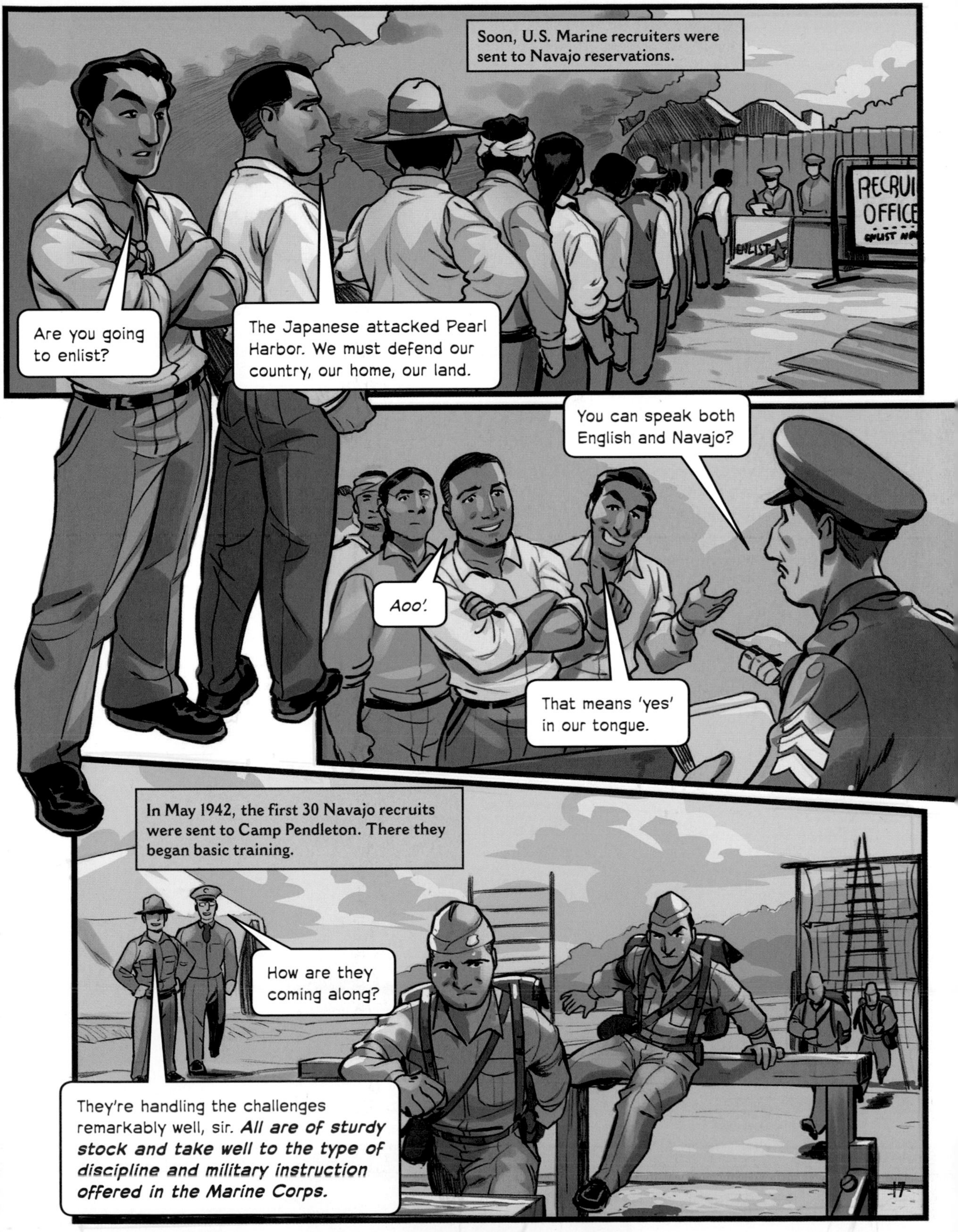

Soon, U.S. Marine recruiters were sent to Navajo reservations.
RECRUI OFFICE
ENLIST
Are you going to enlist?
The Japanese attacked Pearl Harbor. We must defend our country, our home, our land.
You can speak both English and Navajo?
Aoo'.
That means 'yes' in our tongue.
In May 1942, the first 30 Navajo recruits were sent to Camp Pendleton. There they began basic training.
How are they coming along?
They're handling the challenges remarkably well, sir. ***All are of sturdy stock and take well to the type of discipline and military instruction offered in the Marine Corps.***

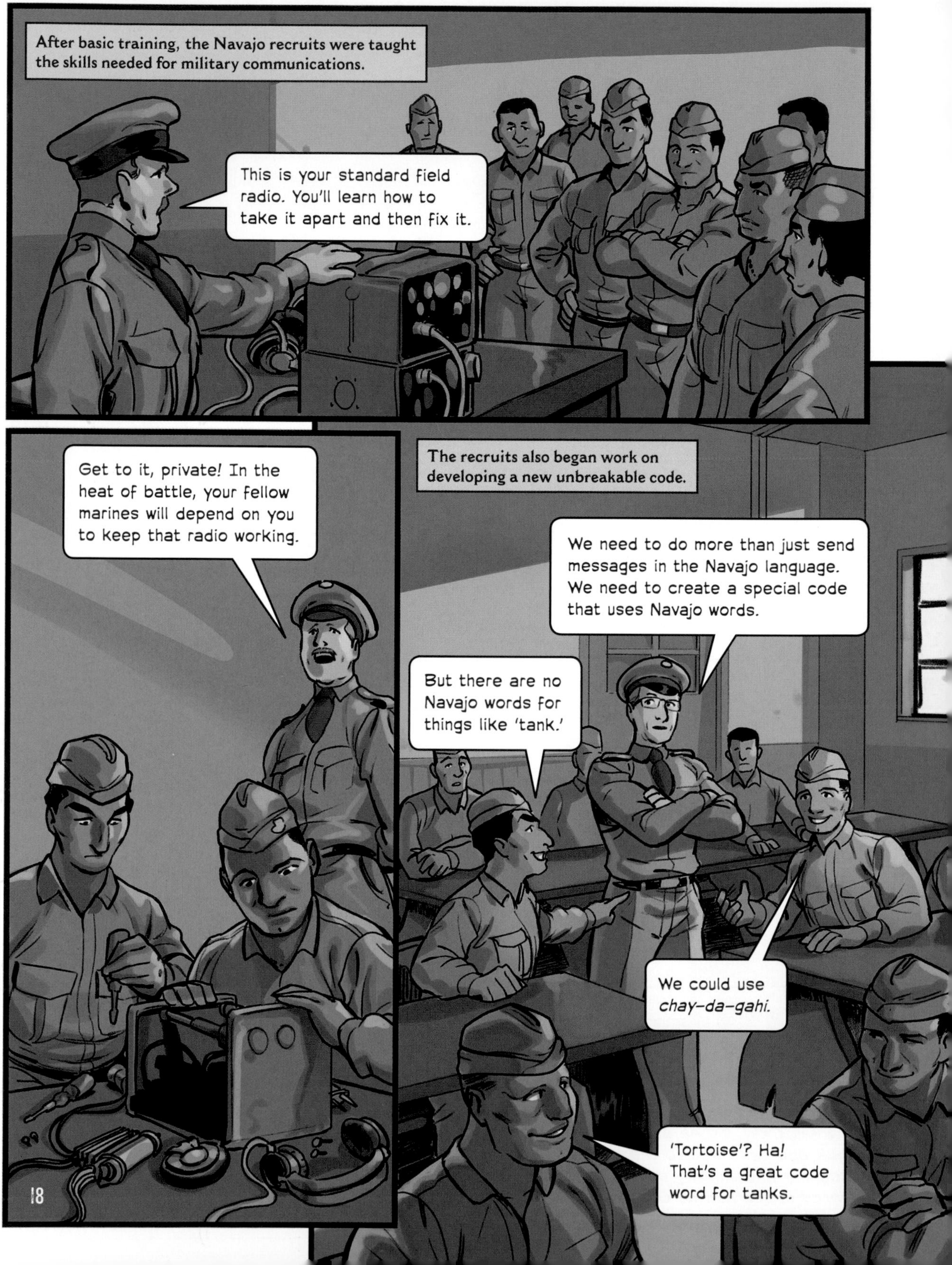
After basic training, the Navajo recruits were taught the skills needed for military communications.
This is your standard field radio. You'll learn how to take it apart and then fix it.
Get to it, private! In the heat of battle, your fellow marines will depend on you to keep that radio working.
The recruits also began work on developing a new unbreakable code.
We need to do more than just send messages in the Navajo language. We need to create a special code that uses Navajo words.
But there are no Navajo words for things like 'tank.'
We could use *chay-da-gahi.*
'Tortoise'? Ha! That's a great code word for tanks.

The Navajo started with a dictionary of more than 200 code words. All of the words had to be memorized during their training. They also created a coded alphabet to spell out other words. More words would be added later.

	MILITARY TERM	NAVAJO CODE WORD	ENGLISH TRANSLATION
SHIPS	BATTLESHIP	LO-TSO	WHALE
	CRUISER	LO-TSO-YAZZIE	SMALL WHALE
	DESTROYER	CA-LO	SHARK
PLANES	BOMBER PLANE	JAY-SHO	BUZZARD
	FIGHTER PLANE	DA-HE-TIH-HI	HUMMING BIRD
	TRANSPORT PLANE	ATSHA	EAGLE
OTHER WORDS	BOMB	A-YE-SHI	EGGS
	GRENADE	NI-MA-SI	POTATOES
	TANK	CHAY-DA-GAHI	TORTOISE

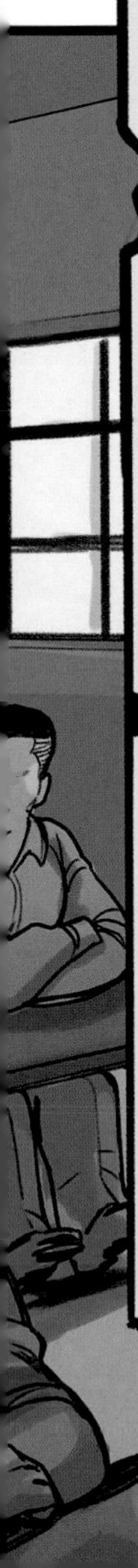

Of the first 30 recruits, 29 completed their training. A couple of them were ordered to return to the Navajo reservation to enlist and train more recruits. By the end of the war about 450 Navajo code talkers would be trained.

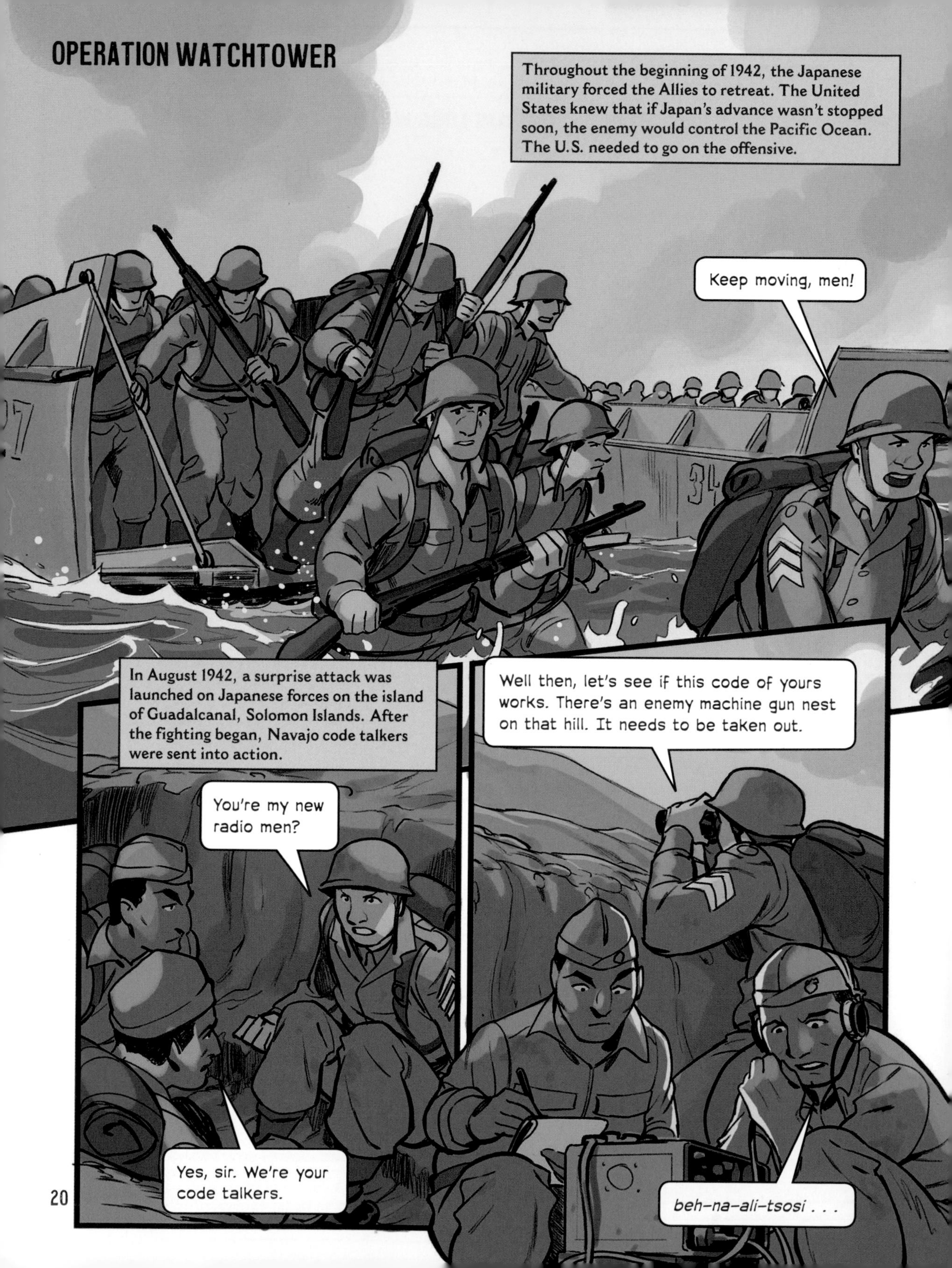

OPERATION WATCHTOWER
Throughout the beginning of 1942, the Japanese military forced the Allies to retreat. The United States knew that if Japan's advance wasn't stopped soon, the enemy would control the Pacific Ocean. The U.S. needed to go on the offensive.
Keep moving, men!
In August 1942, a surprise attack was launched on Japanese forces on the island of Guadalcanal, Solomon Islands. After the fighting began, Navajo code talkers were sent into action.
You're my new radio men?
Yes, sir. We're your code talkers.
Well then, let's see if this code of yours works. There's an enemy machine gun nest on that hill. It needs to be taken out.
beh-na-ali-tsosi . . .

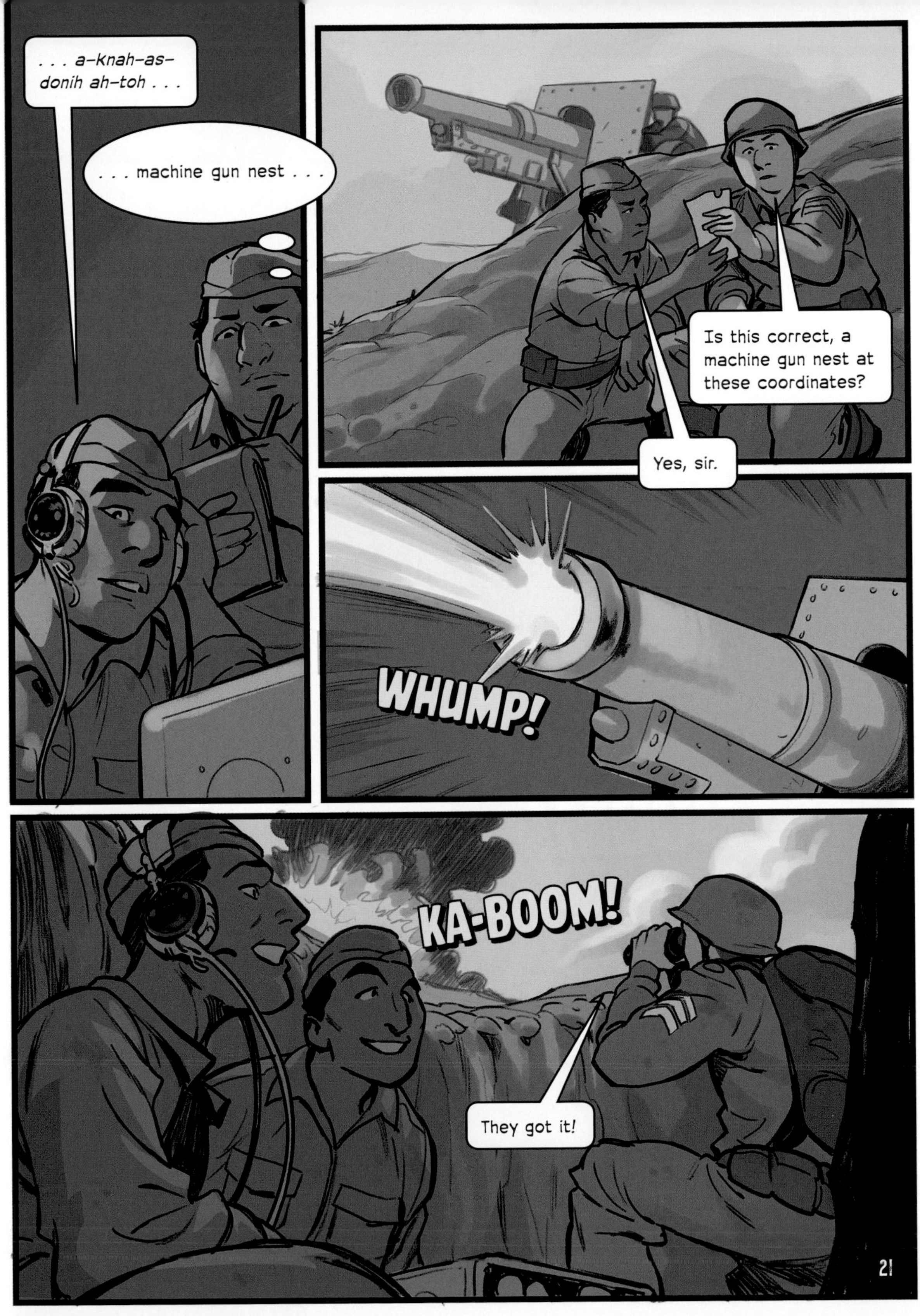

. . . a-knah-as-donih ah-toh . . .
. . . machine gun nest . . .
Is this correct, a machine gun nest at these coordinates?
Yes, sir.
WHUMP!
KA-BOOM!
They got it!

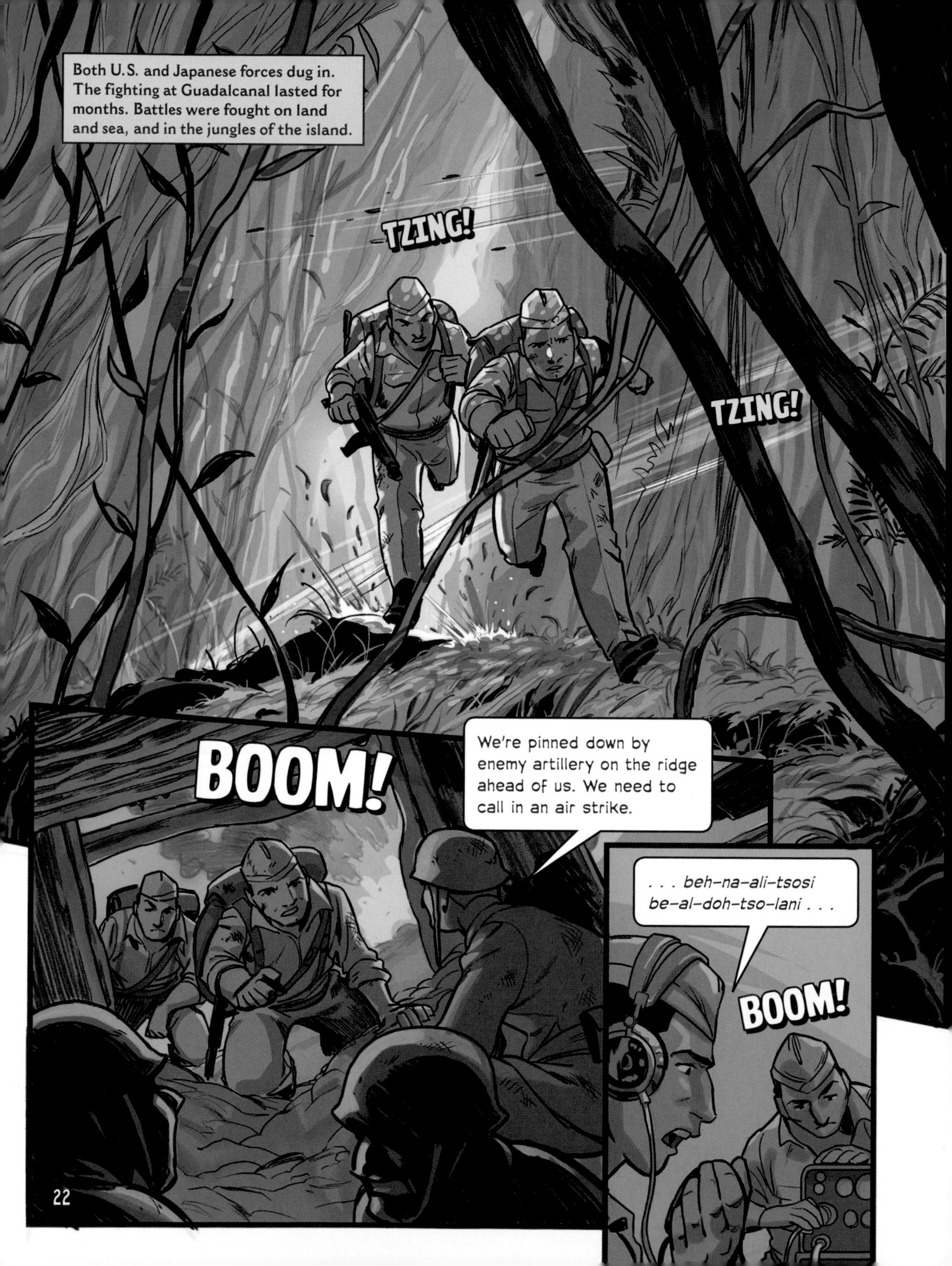

Both U.S. and Japanese forces dug in. The fighting at Guadalcanal lasted for months. Battles were fought on land and sea, and in the jungles of the island.
TZING!
TZING!
BOOM!
We're pinned down by enemy artillery on the ridge ahead of us. We need to call in an air strike.
. . . beh-na-ali-tsosi be-al-doh-tso-lani . . .
BOOM!

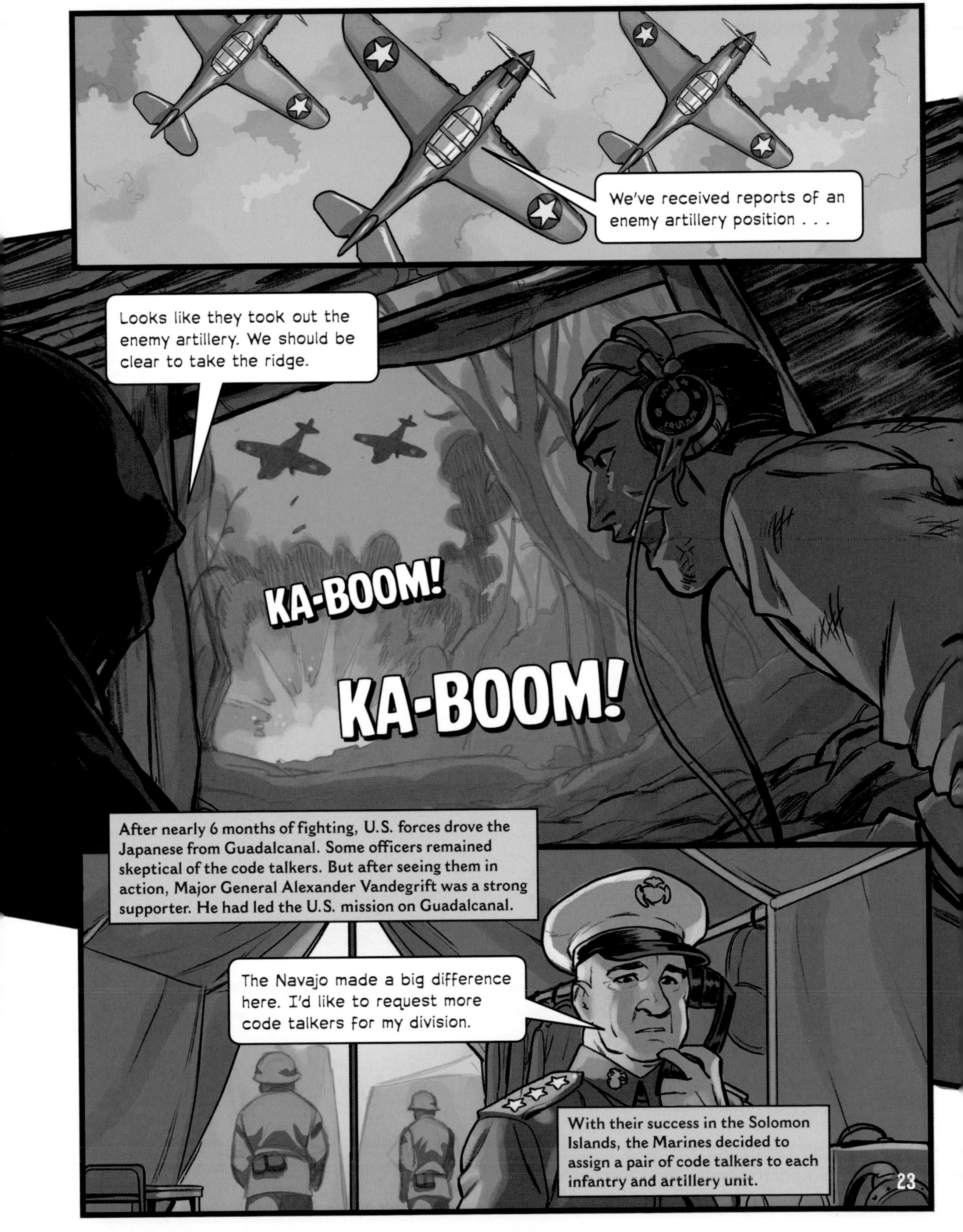
We've received reports of an enemy artillery position . . .
Looks like they took out the enemy artillery. We should be clear to take the ridge.
KA-BOOM!
KA-BOOM!
After nearly 6 months of fighting, U.S. forces drove the Japanese from Guadalcanal. Some officers remained skeptical of the code talkers. But after seeing them in action, Major General Alexander Vandegrift was a strong supporter. He had led the U.S. mission on Guadalcanal.
The Navajo made a big difference here. I'd like to request more code talkers for my division.
With their success in the Solomon Islands, the Marines decided to assign a pair of code talkers to each infantry and artillery unit.

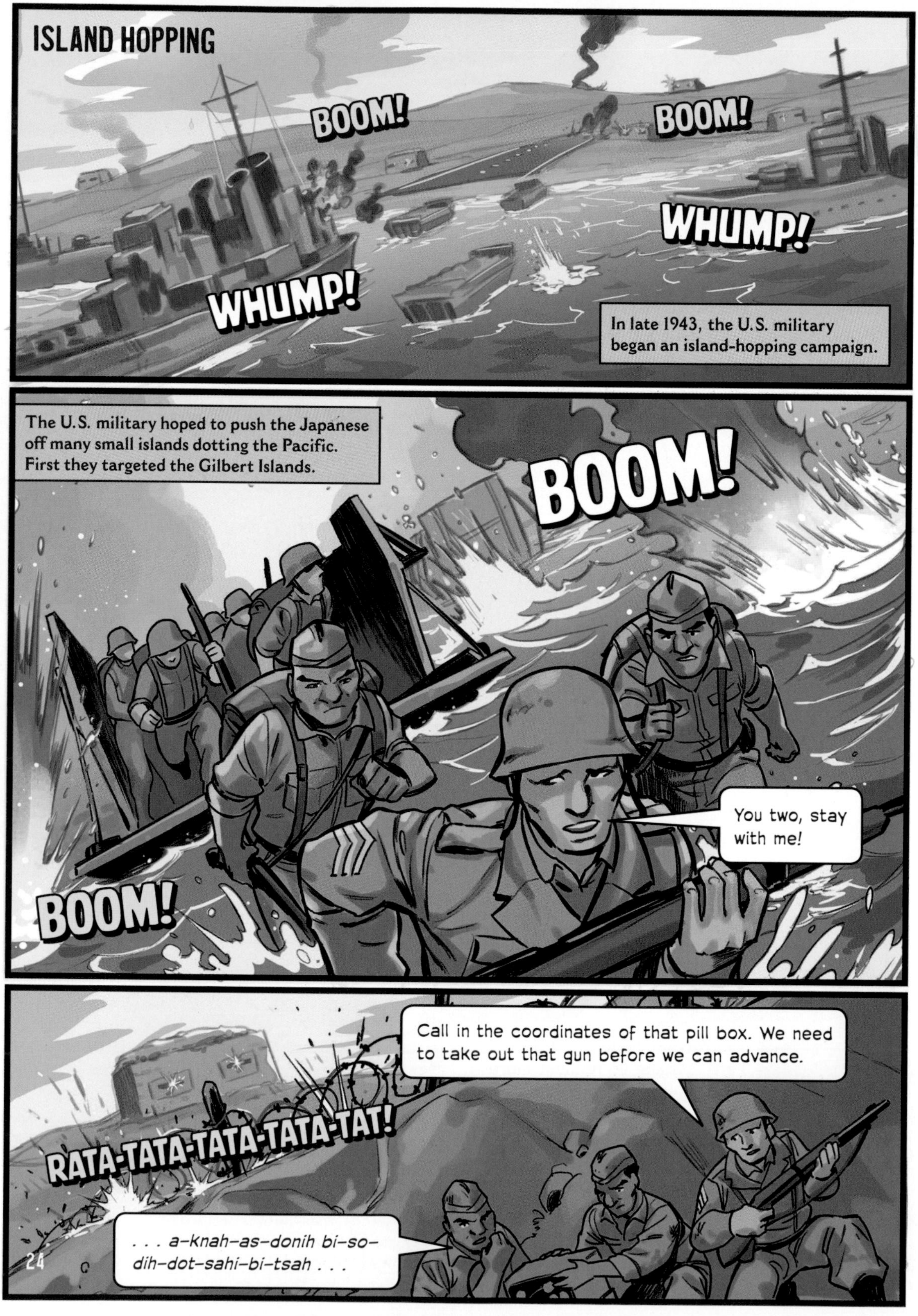
ISLAND HOPPING
BOOM!
BOOM!
WHUMP!
WHUMP!
In late 1943, the U.S. military began an island-hopping campaign.
The U.S. military hoped to push the Japanese off many small islands dotting the Pacific. First they targeted the Gilbert Islands.
BOOM!
You two, stay with me!
BOOM!
Call in the coordinates of that pill box. We need to take out that gun before we can advance.
RATA-TATA-TATA-TATA-TAT!
. . . a-knah-as-donih bi-so-dih-dot-sahi-bi-tsah . . .

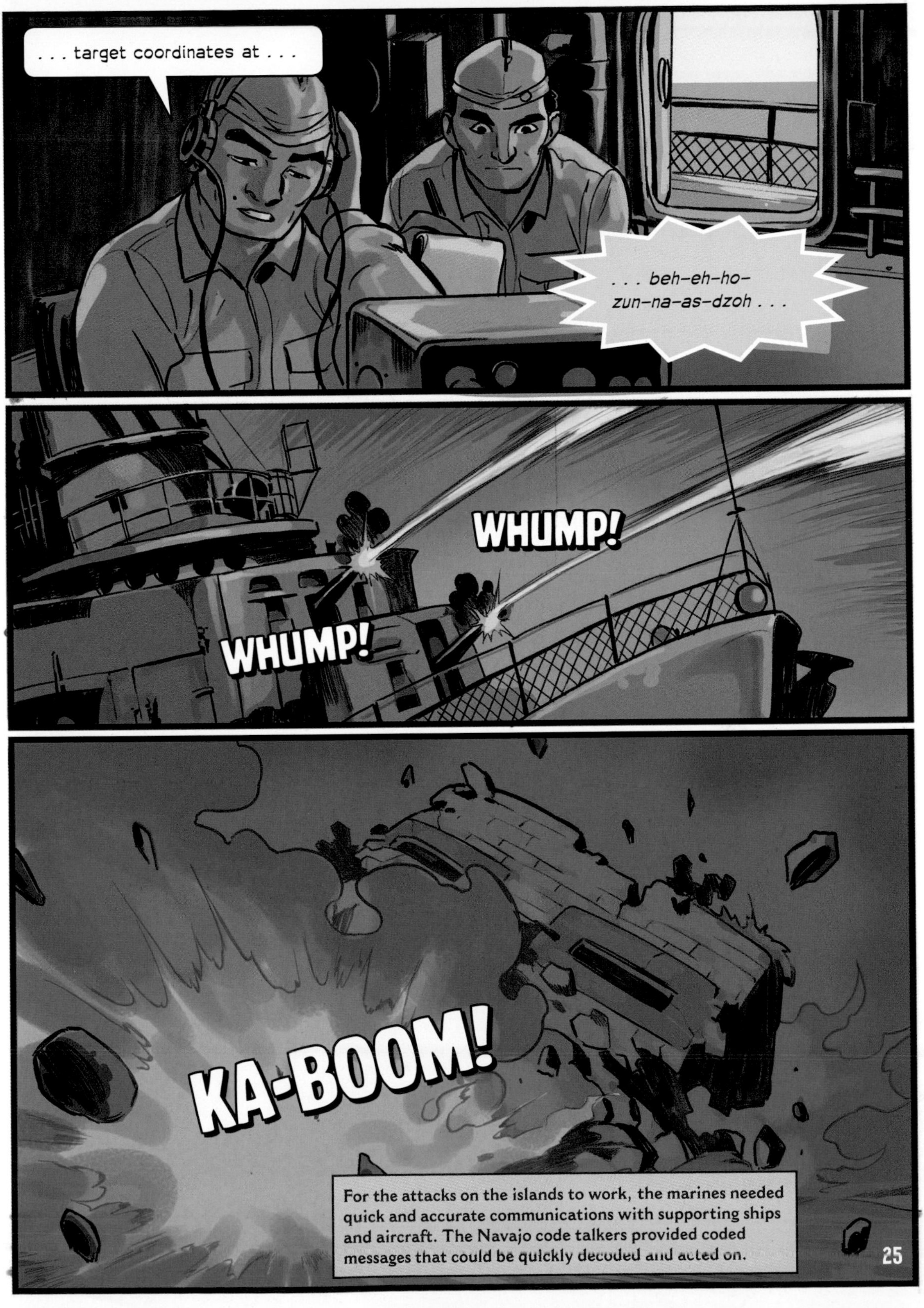
. . . target coordinates at . . .
. . . beh-eh-ho-zun-na-as-dzoh . . .
WHUMP!
WHUMP!
KA-BOOM!
For the attacks on the islands to work, the marines needed quick and accurate communications with supporting ships and aircraft. The Navajo code talkers provided coded messages that could be quickly decoded and acted on.

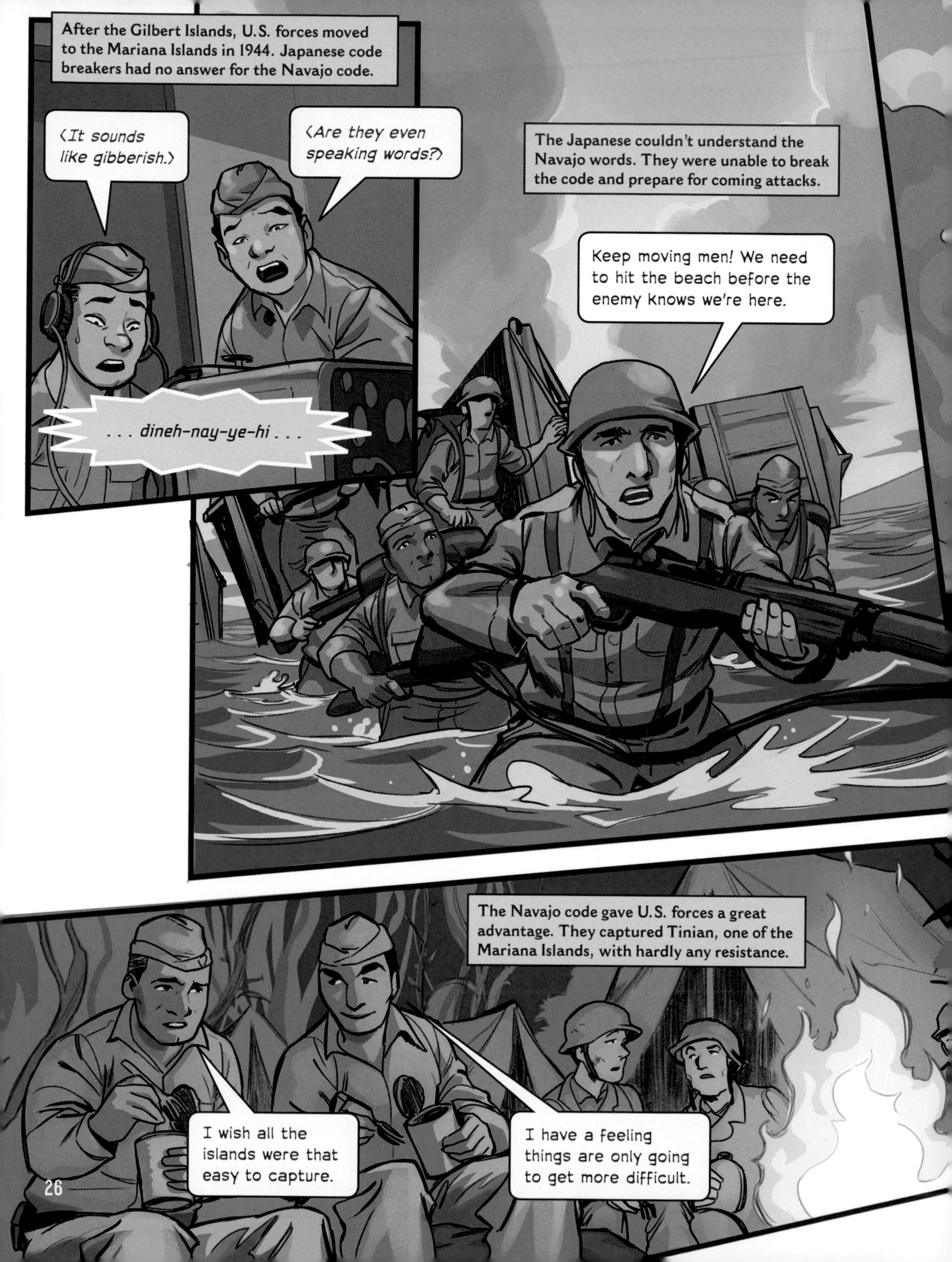

After the Gilbert Islands, U.S. forces moved to the Mariana Islands in 1944. Japanese code breakers had no answer for the Navajo code.
‹It sounds like gibberish.›
‹Are they even speaking words?›
. . . dineh-nay-ye-hi . . .
The Japanese couldn't understand the Navajo words. They were unable to break the code and prepare for coming attacks.
Keep moving men! We need to hit the beach before the enemy knows we're here.
The Navajo code gave U.S. forces a great advantage. They captured Tinian, one of the Mariana Islands, with hardly any resistance.
I wish all the islands were that easy to capture.
I have a feeling things are only going to get more difficult.

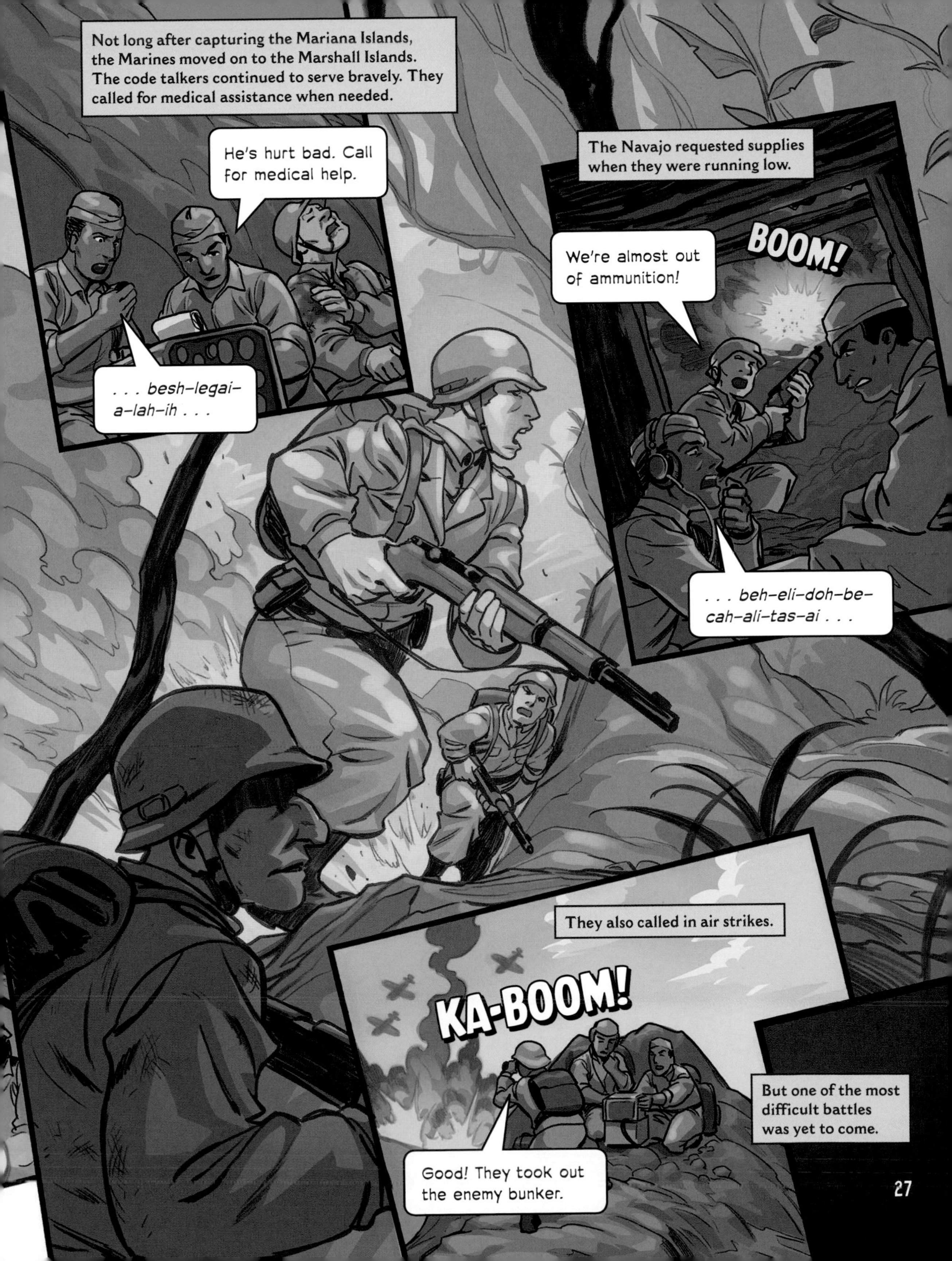

Not long after capturing the Mariana Islands, the Marines moved on to the Marshall Islands. The code talkers continued to serve bravely. They called for medical assistance when needed.
He's hurt bad. Call for medical help.
. . . besh-legai-a-lah-ih . . .
The Navajo requested supplies when they were running low.
BOOM!
We're almost out of ammunition!
. . . beh-eli-doh-be-cah-ali-tas-ai . . .
They also called in air strikes.
KA-BOOM!
Good! They took out the enemy bunker.
But one of the most difficult battles was yet to come.

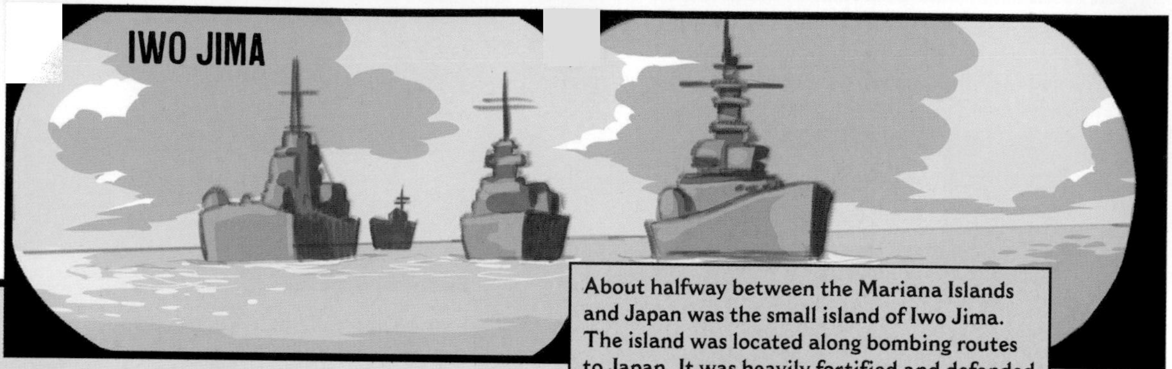
IWO JIMA
About halfway between the Mariana Islands and Japan was the small island of Iwo Jima. The island was located along bombing routes to Japan. It was heavily fortified and defended by more than 20,000 Japanese soldiers.

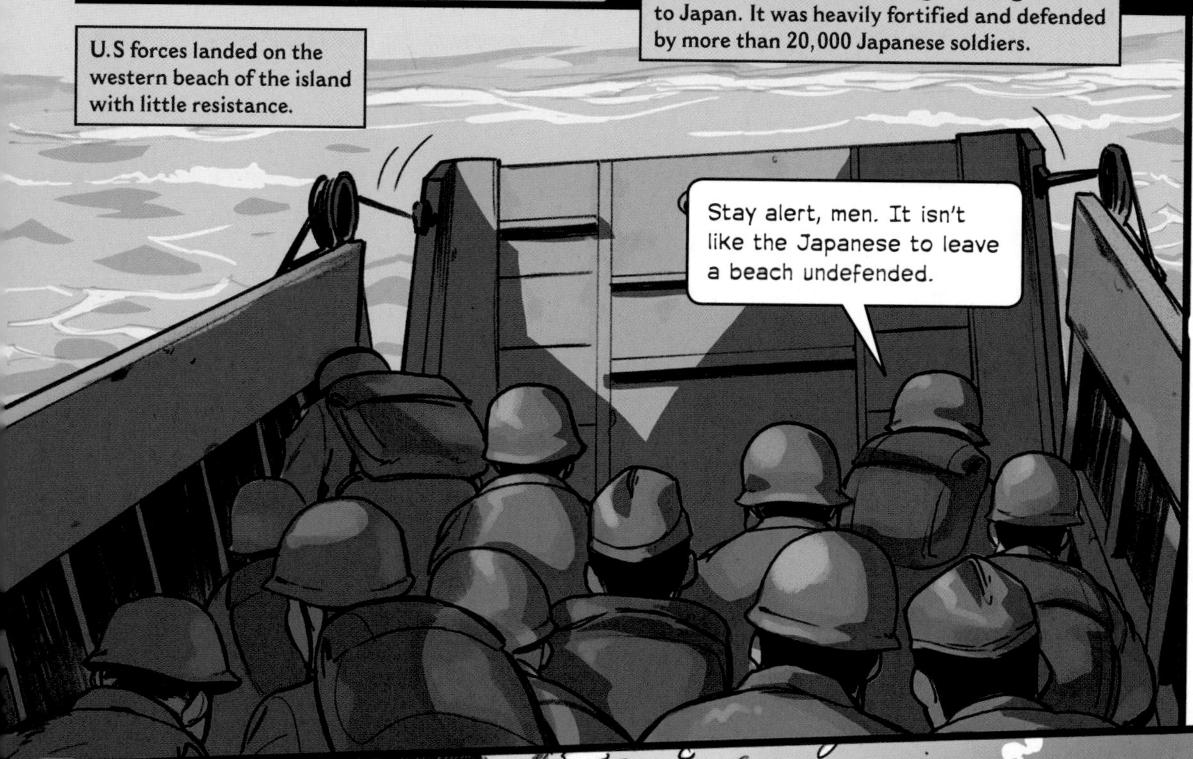
U.S forces landed on the western beach of the island with little resistance.
Stay alert, men. It isn't like the Japanese to leave a beach undefended.

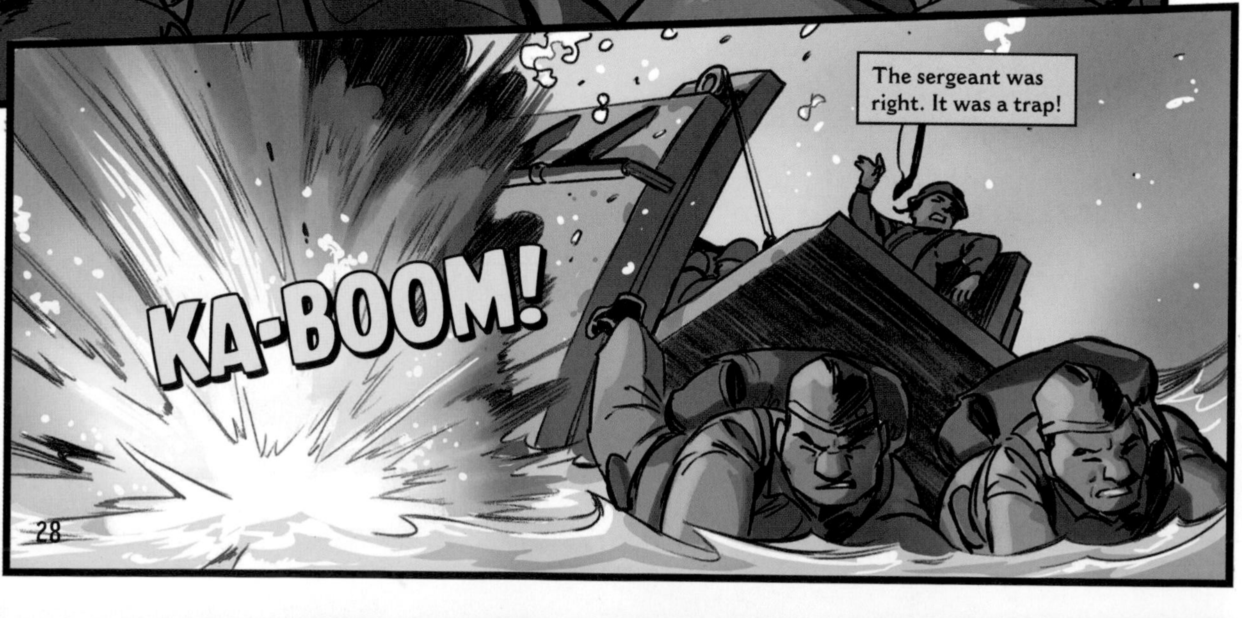
The sergeant was right. It was a trap!
KA-BOOM!

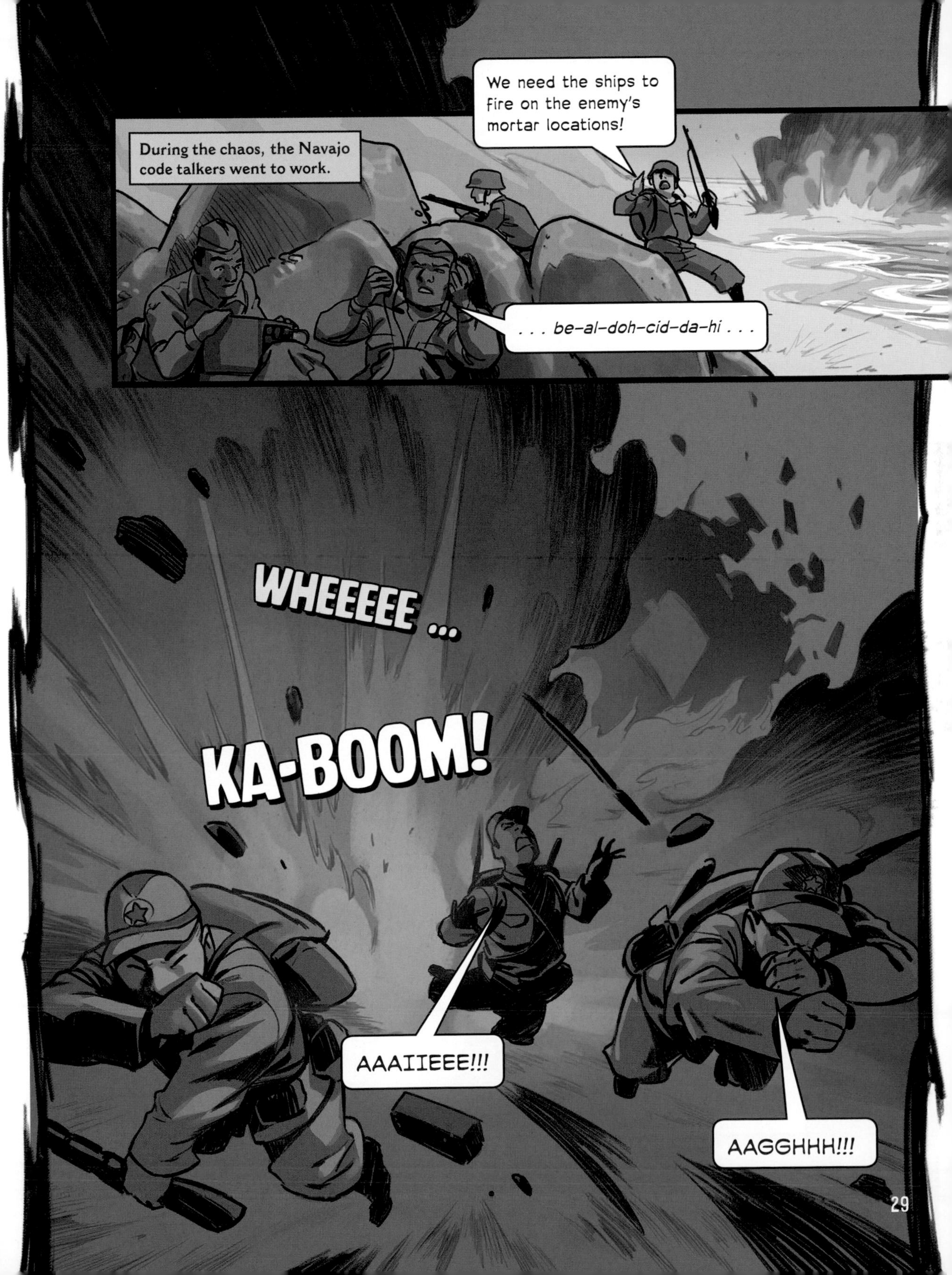
During the chaos, the Navajo code talkers went to work.
We need the ships to fire on the enemy's mortar locations!
. . . be-al-doh-cid-da-hi . . .
WHEEEEE ...
KA-BOOM!
AAAIIEEE!!!
AAGGHHH!!!

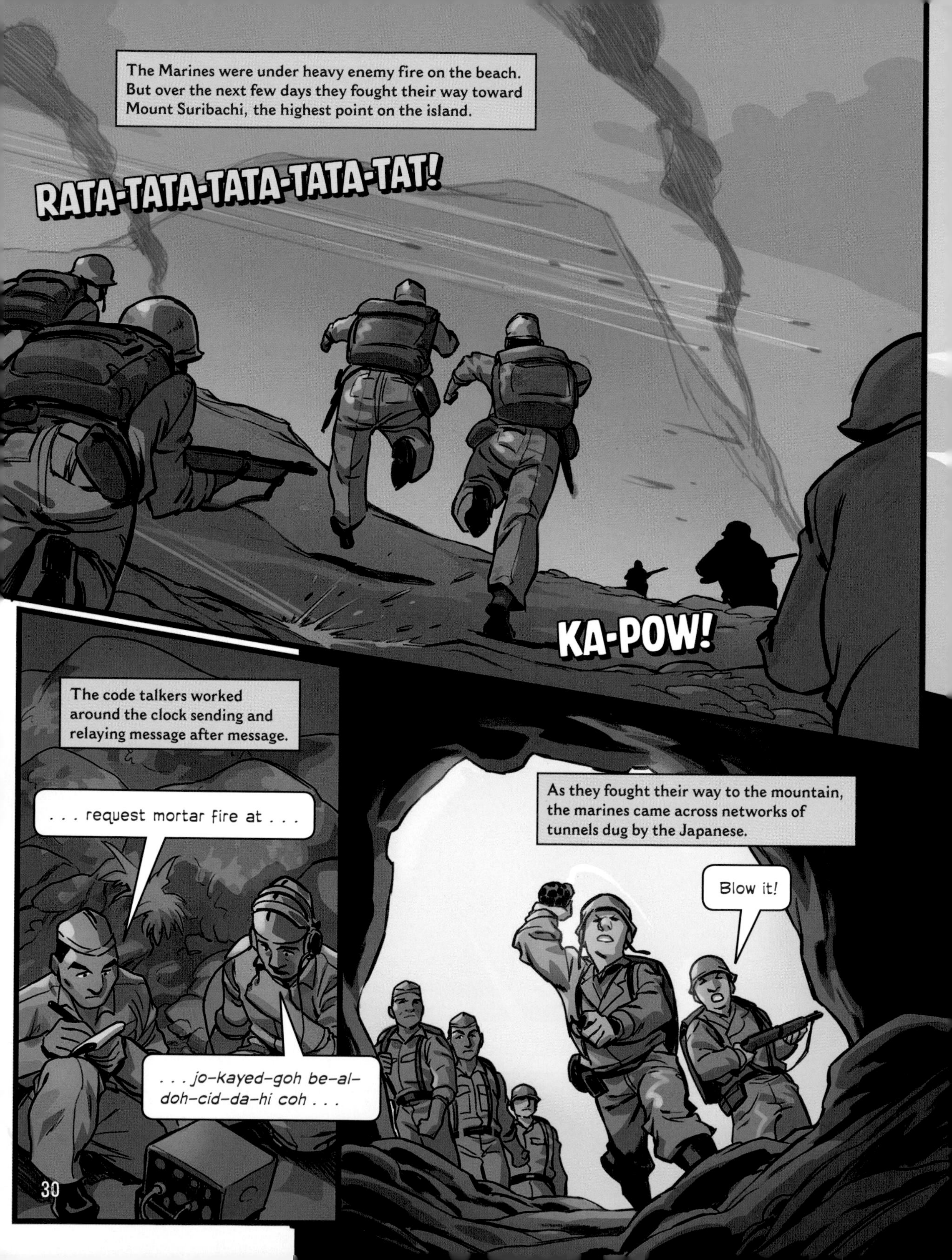

The Marines were under heavy enemy fire on the beach. But over the next few days they fought their way toward Mount Suribachi, the highest point on the island.
RATA-TATA-TATA-TATA-TAT!
KA-POW!
The code talkers worked around the clock sending and relaying message after message.
. . . request mortar fire at . . .
. . . jo-kayed-goh be-al-doh-cid-da-hi coh . . .
As they fought their way to the mountain, the marines came across networks of tunnels dug by the Japanese.
Blow it!

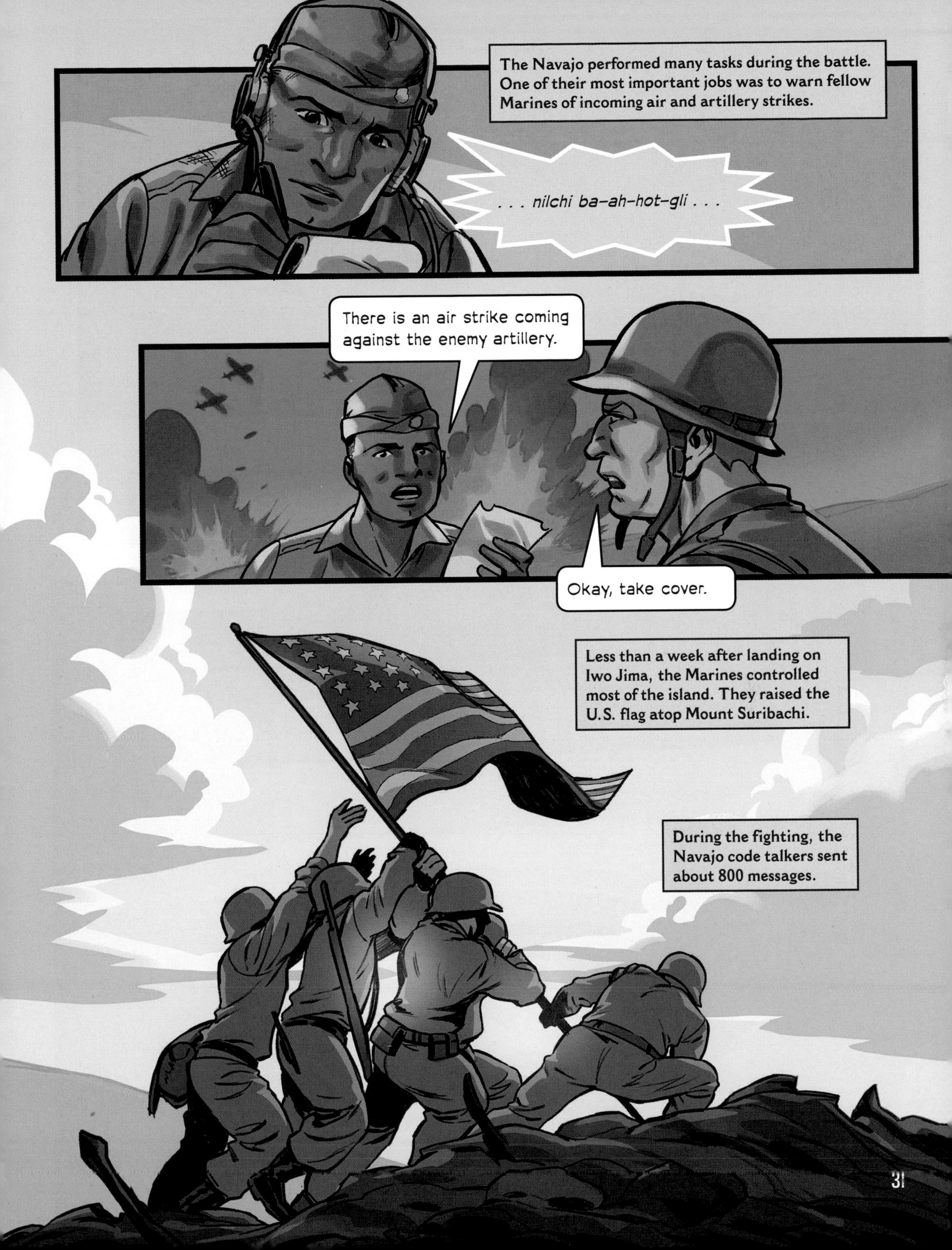
The Navajo performed many tasks during the battle. One of their most important jobs was to warn fellow Marines of incoming air and artillery strikes.
. . . nilchi ba-ah-hot-gli . . .
There is an air strike coming against the enemy artillery.
Okay, take cover.
Less than a week after landing on Iwo Jima, the Marines controlled most of the island. They raised the U.S. flag atop Mount Suribachi.
During the fighting, the Navajo code talkers sent about 800 messages.

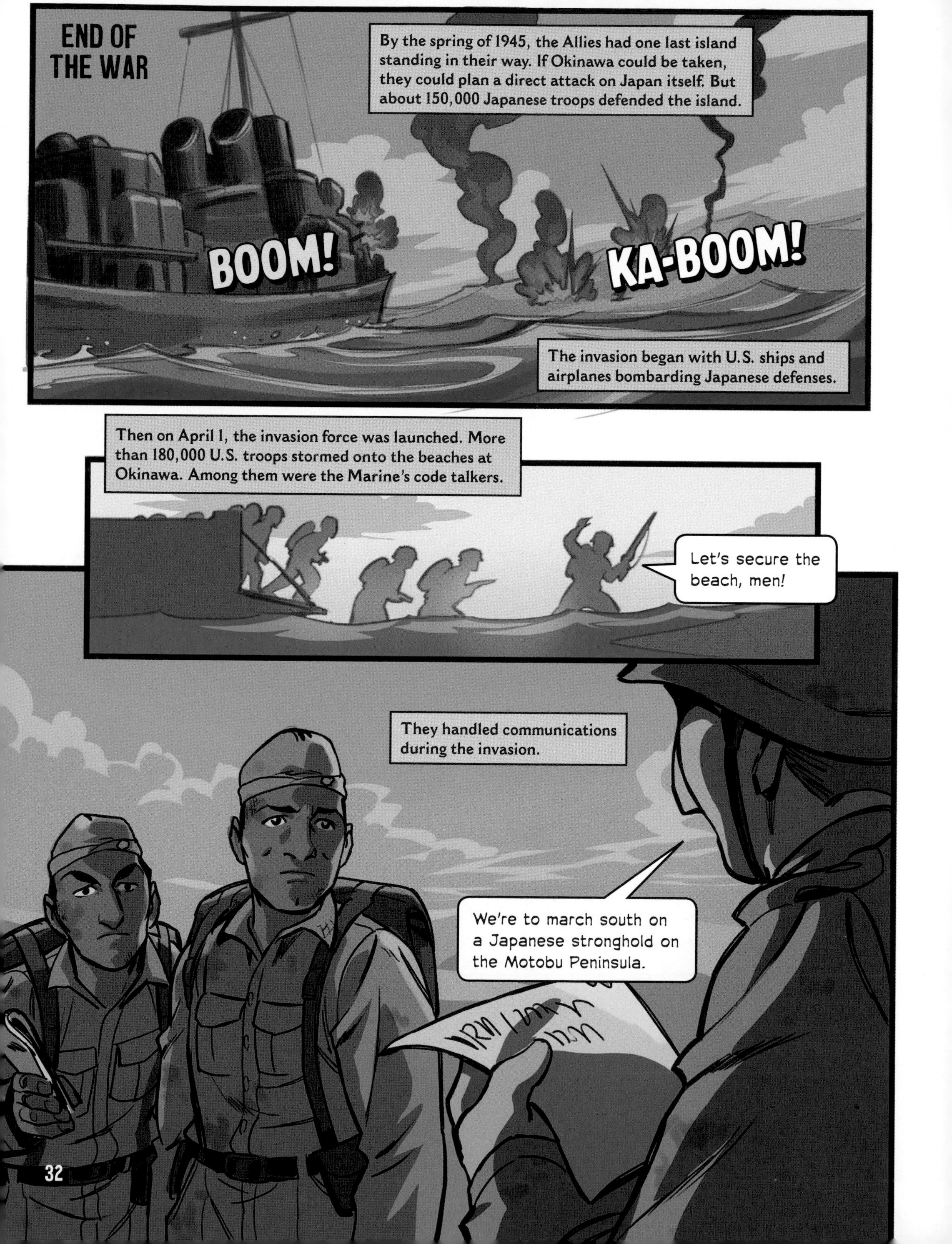
END OF THE WAR
By the spring of 1945, the Allies had one last island standing in their way. If Okinawa could be taken, they could plan a direct attack on Japan itself. But about 150,000 Japanese troops defended the island.
BOOM!
KA-BOOM!
The invasion began with U.S. ships and airplanes bombarding Japanese defenses.
Then on April 1, the invasion force was launched. More than 180,000 U.S. troops stormed onto the beaches at Okinawa. Among them were the Marine's code talkers.
Let's secure the beach, men!
They handled communications during the invasion.
We're to march south on a Japanese stronghold on the Motobu Peninsula.

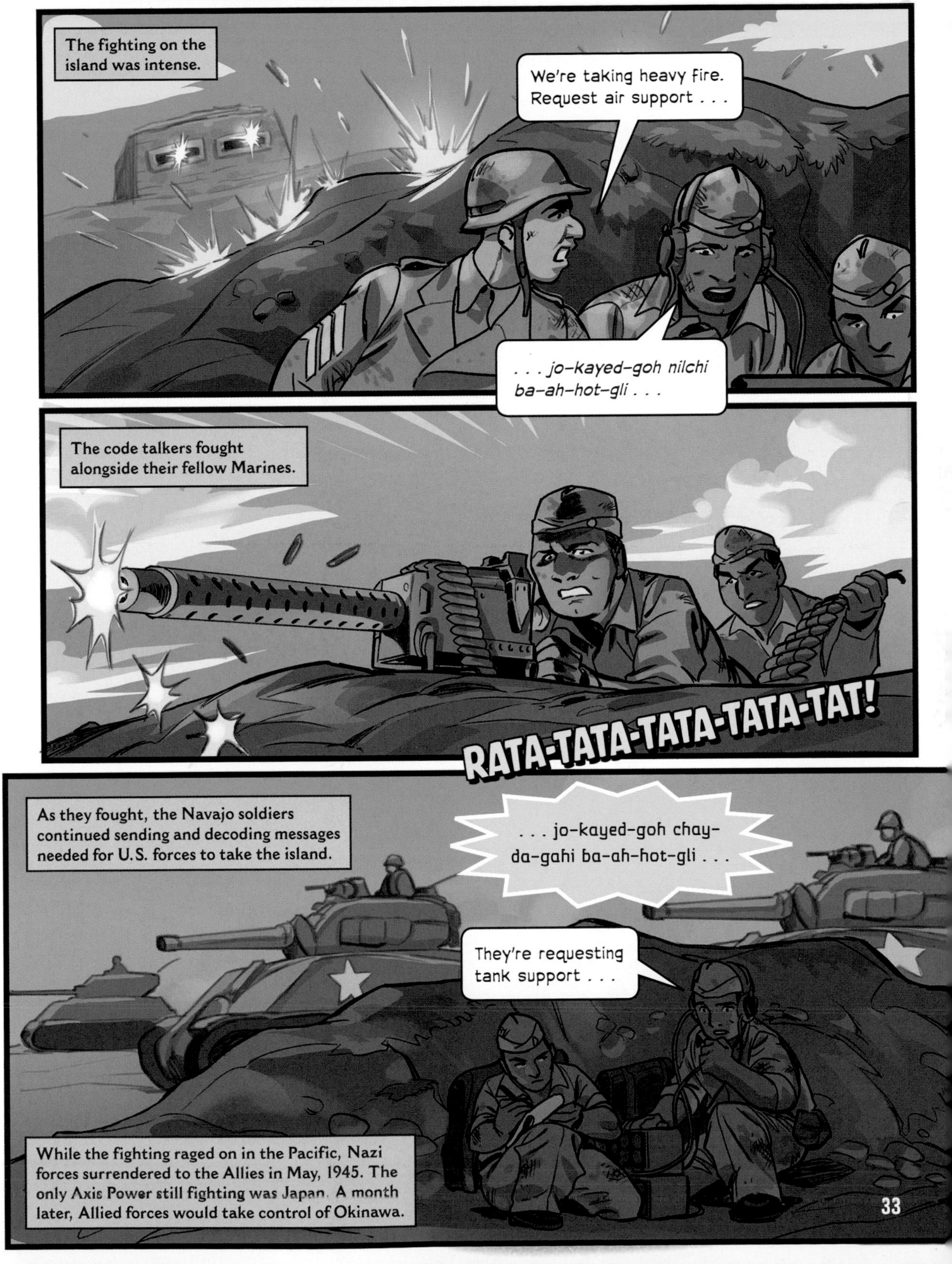
The fighting on the island was intense.
We're taking heavy fire. Request air support . . .
. . . jo-kayed-goh nilchi ba-ah-hot-gli . . .
The code talkers fought alongside their fellow Marines.
RATA-TATA-TATA-TATA-TAT!
As they fought, the Navajo soldiers continued sending and decoding messages needed for U.S. forces to take the island.
. . . jo-kayed-goh chay-da-gahi ba-ah-hot-gli . . .
They're requesting tank support . . .
While the fighting raged on in the Pacific, Nazi forces surrendered to the Allies in May, 1945. The only Axis Power still fighting was Japan. A month later, Allied forces would take control of Okinawa.

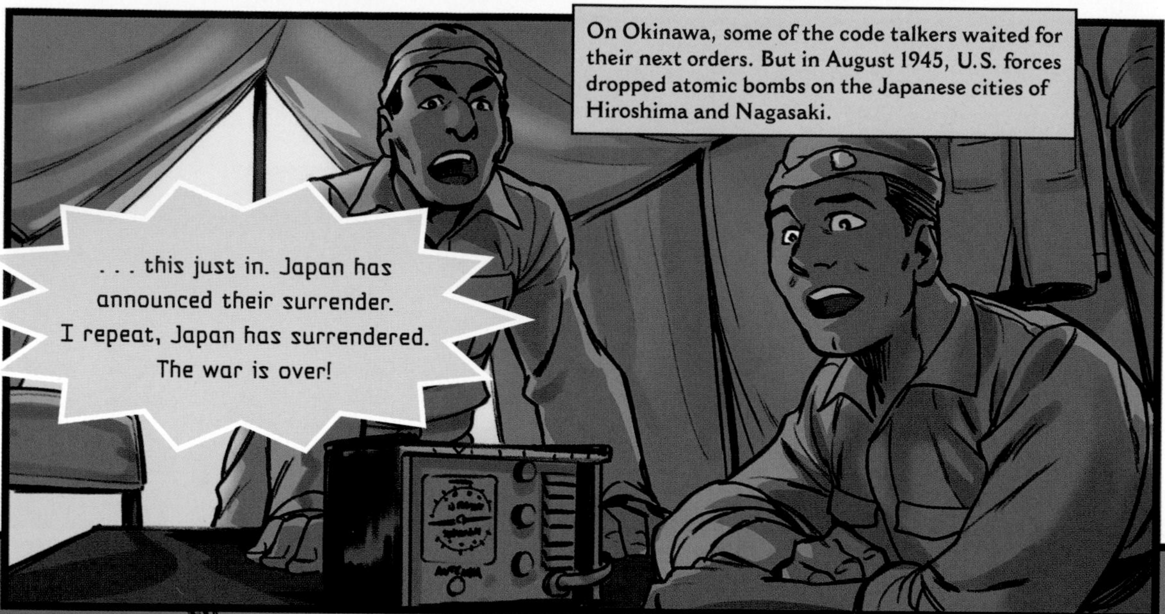
On Okinawa, some of the code talkers waited for their next orders. But in August 1945, U.S. forces dropped atomic bombs on the Japanese cities of Hiroshima and Nagasaki.
. . . this just in. Japan has announced their surrender. I repeat, Japan has surrendered. The war is over!

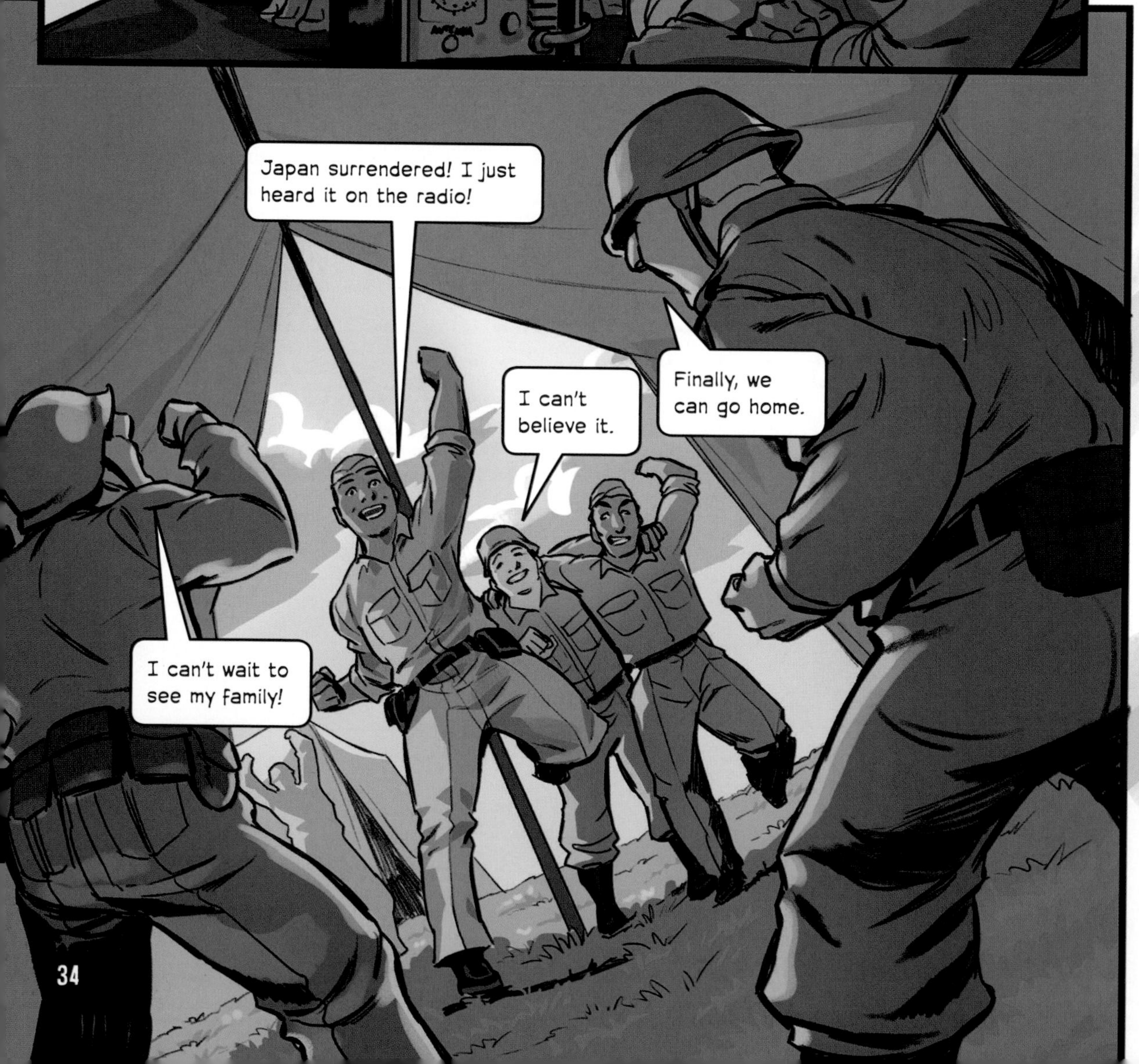
Japan surrendered! I just heard it on the radio!
I can't believe it.
Finally, we can go home.
I can't wait to see my family!

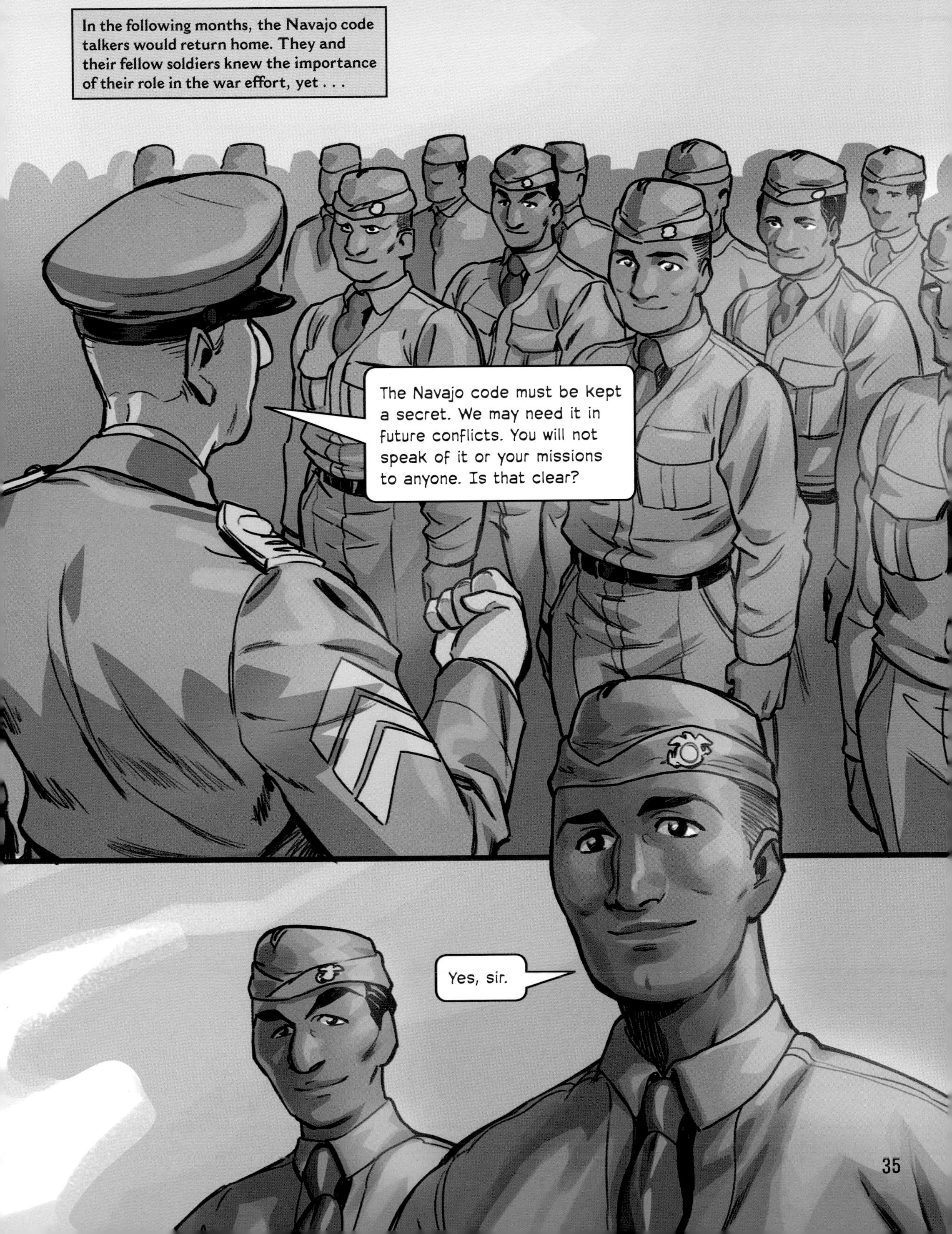
In the following months, the Navajo code talkers would return home. They and their fellow soldiers knew the importance of their role in the war effort, yet . . .
The Navajo code must be kept a secret. We may need it in future conflicts. You will not speak of it or your missions to anyone. Is that clear?
Yes, sir.

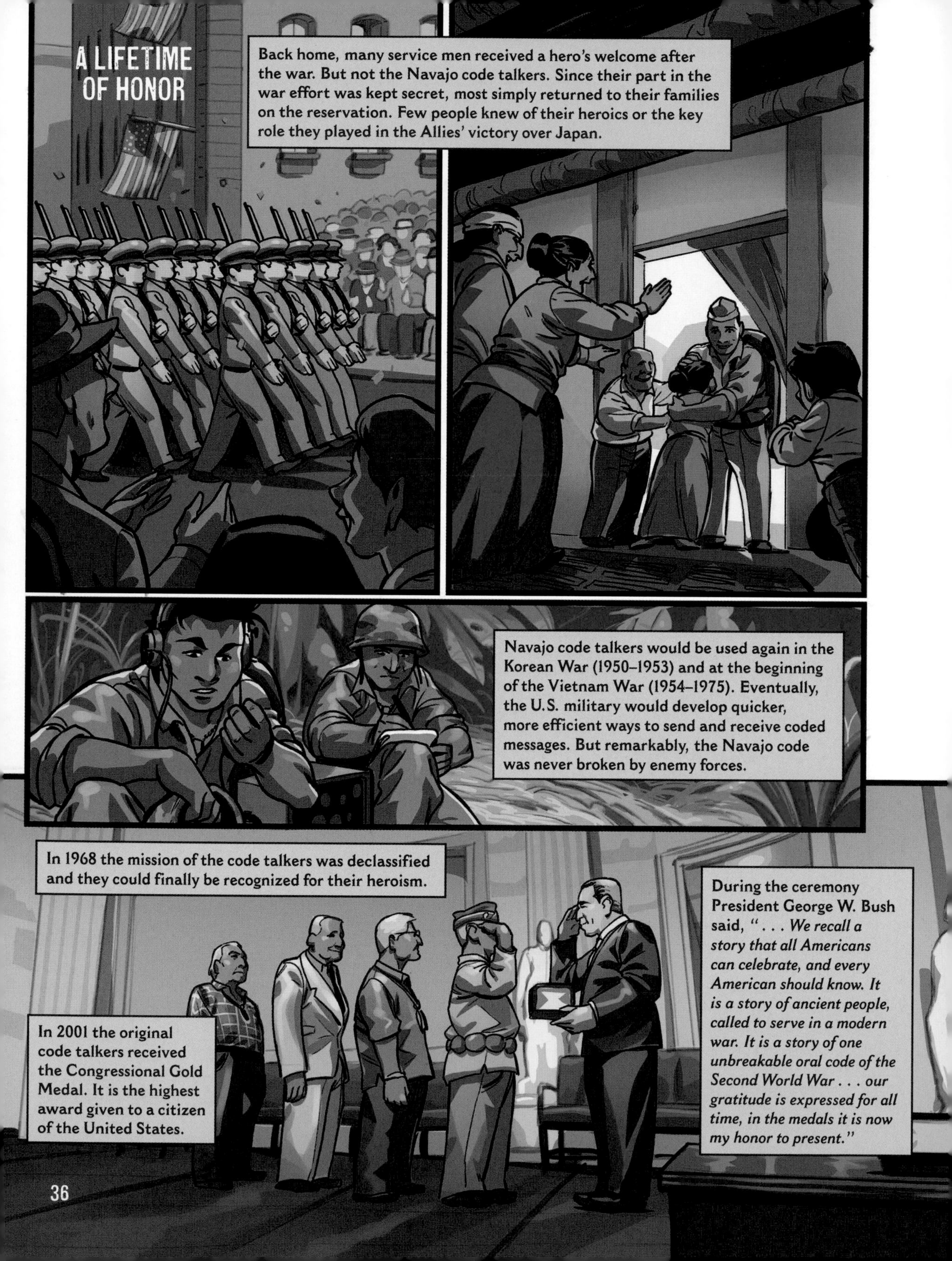
A LIFETIME OF HONOR
Back home, many service men received a hero's welcome after the war. But not the Navajo code talkers. Since their part in the war effort was kept secret, most simply returned to their families on the reservation. Few people knew of their heroics or the key role they played in the Allies' victory over Japan.
Navajo code talkers would be used again in the Korean War (1950–1953) and at the beginning of the Vietnam War (1954–1975). Eventually, the U.S. military would develop quicker, more efficient ways to send and receive coded messages. But remarkably, the Navajo code was never broken by enemy forces.
In 1968 the mission of the code talkers was declassified and they could finally be recognized for their heroism.
In 2001 the original code talkers received the Congressional Gold Medal. It is the highest award given to a citizen of the United States.
During the ceremony President George W. Bush said, "*. . . We recall a story that all Americans can celebrate, and every American should know. It is a story of ancient people, called to serve in a modern war. It is a story of one unbreakable oral code of the Second World War . . . our gratitude is expressed for all time, in the medals it is now my honor to present.*"

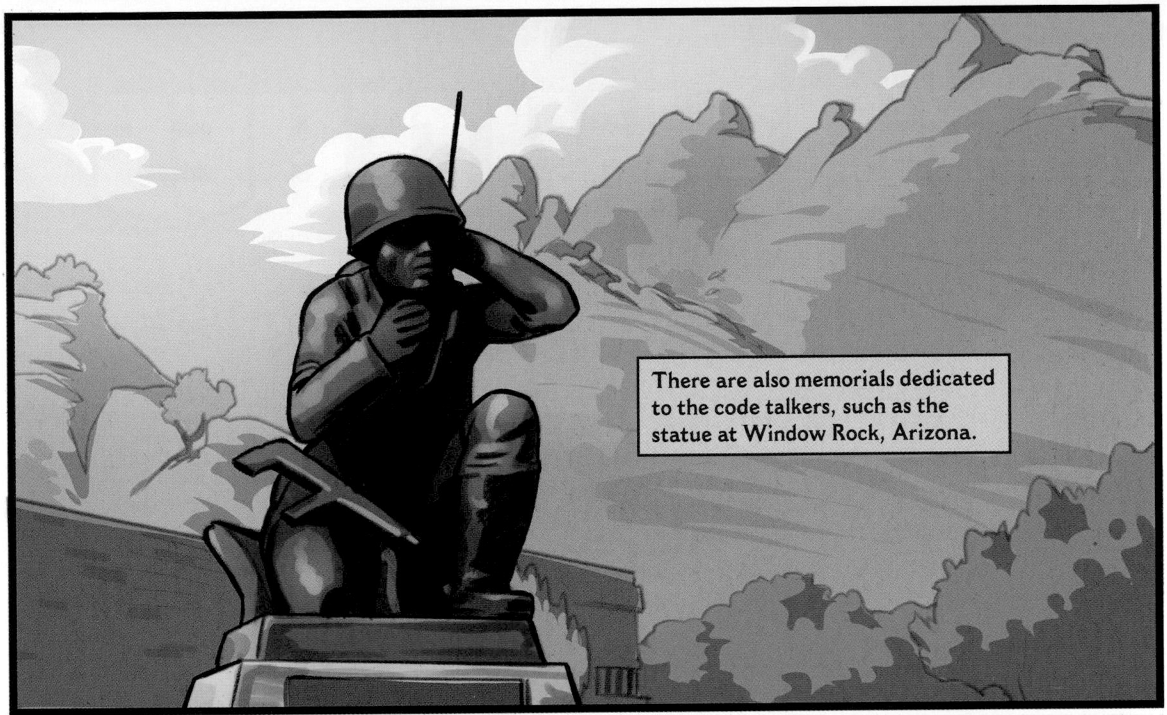
There are also memorials dedicated to the code talkers, such as the statue at Window Rock, Arizona.

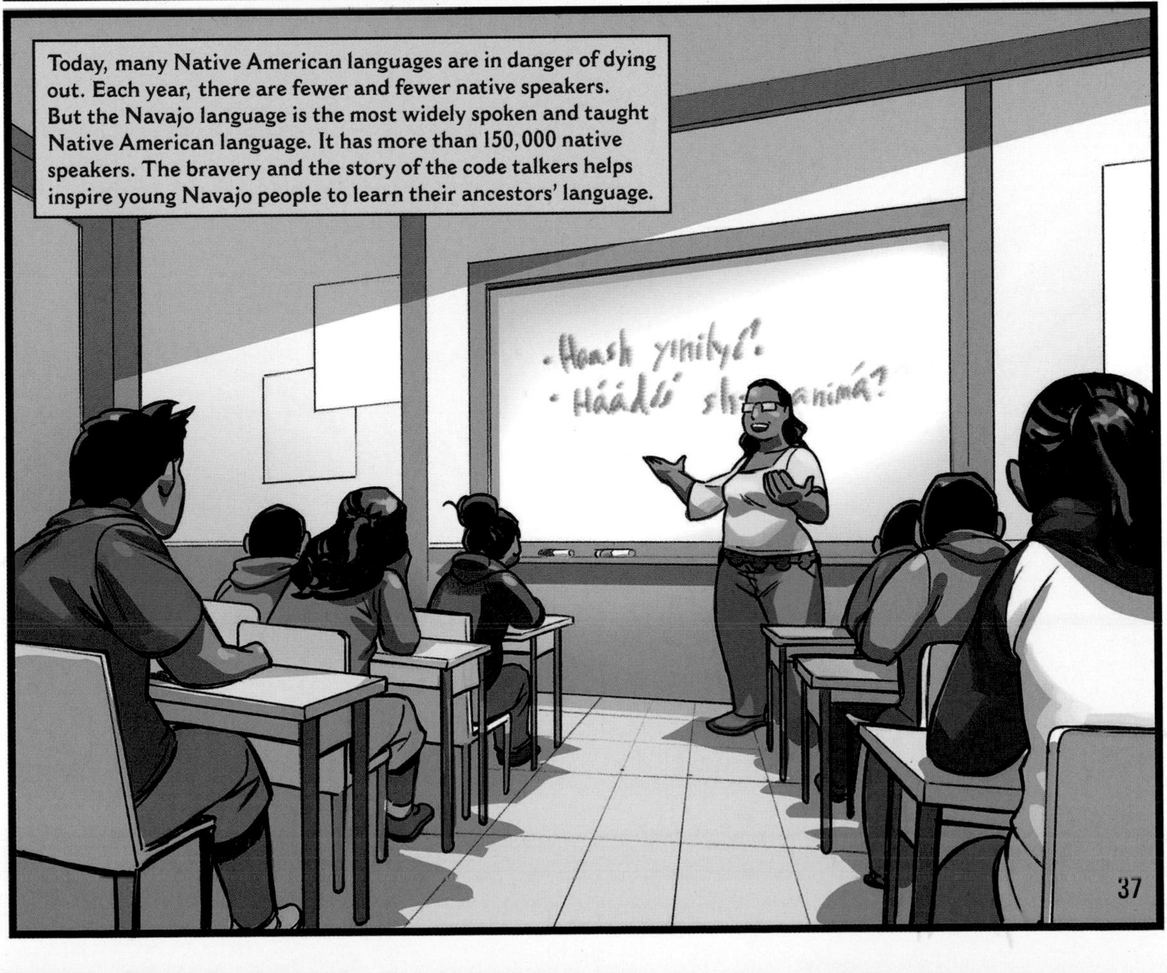
Today, many Native American languages are in danger of dying out. Each year, there are fewer and fewer native speakers. But the Navajo language is the most widely spoken and taught Native American language. It has more than 150,000 native speakers. The bravery and the story of the code talkers helps inspire young Navajo people to learn their ancestors' language.

NIGHT WITCHES AT WAR

THE SOVIET WOMEN PILOTS OF WORLD WAR II

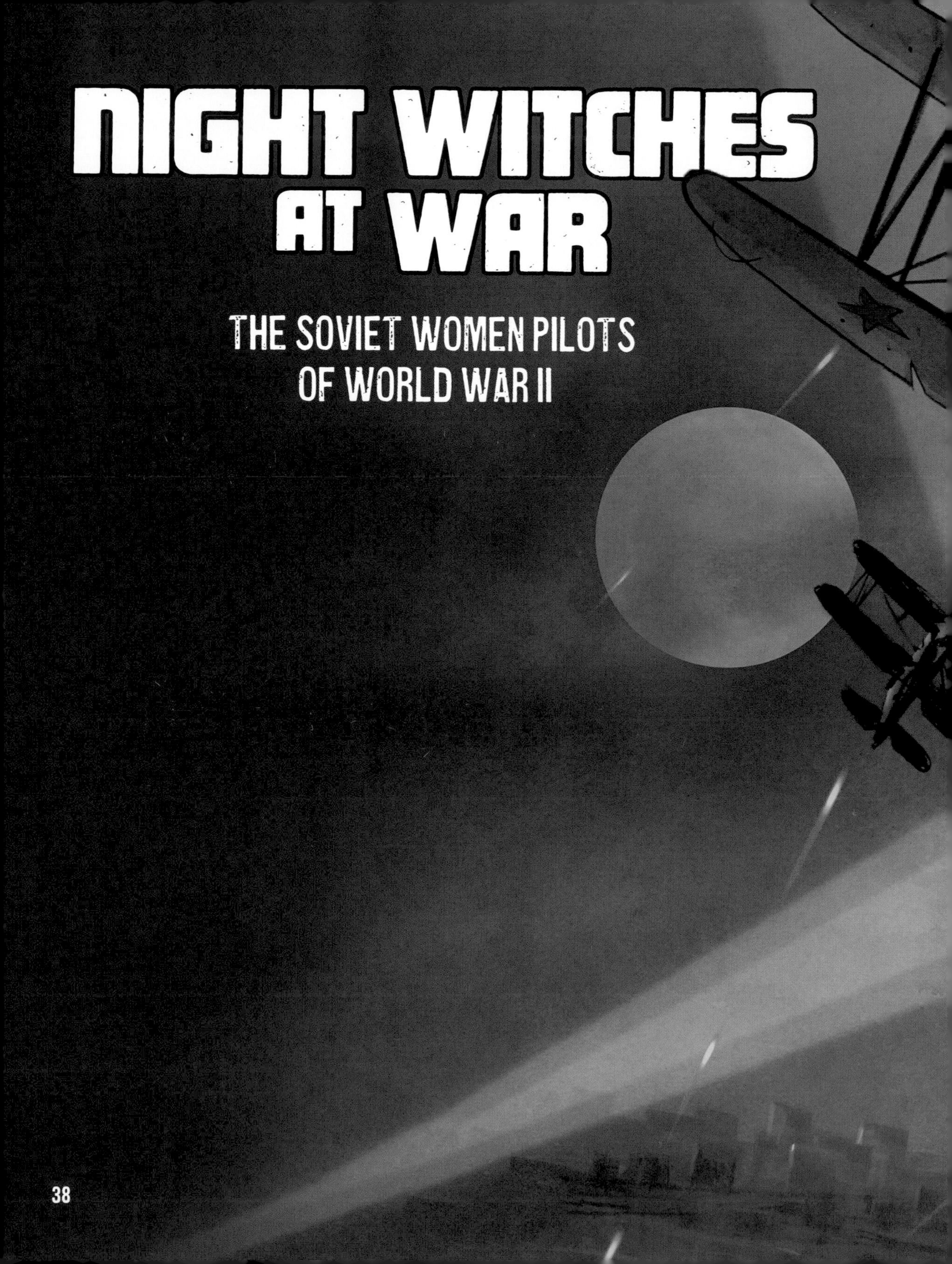

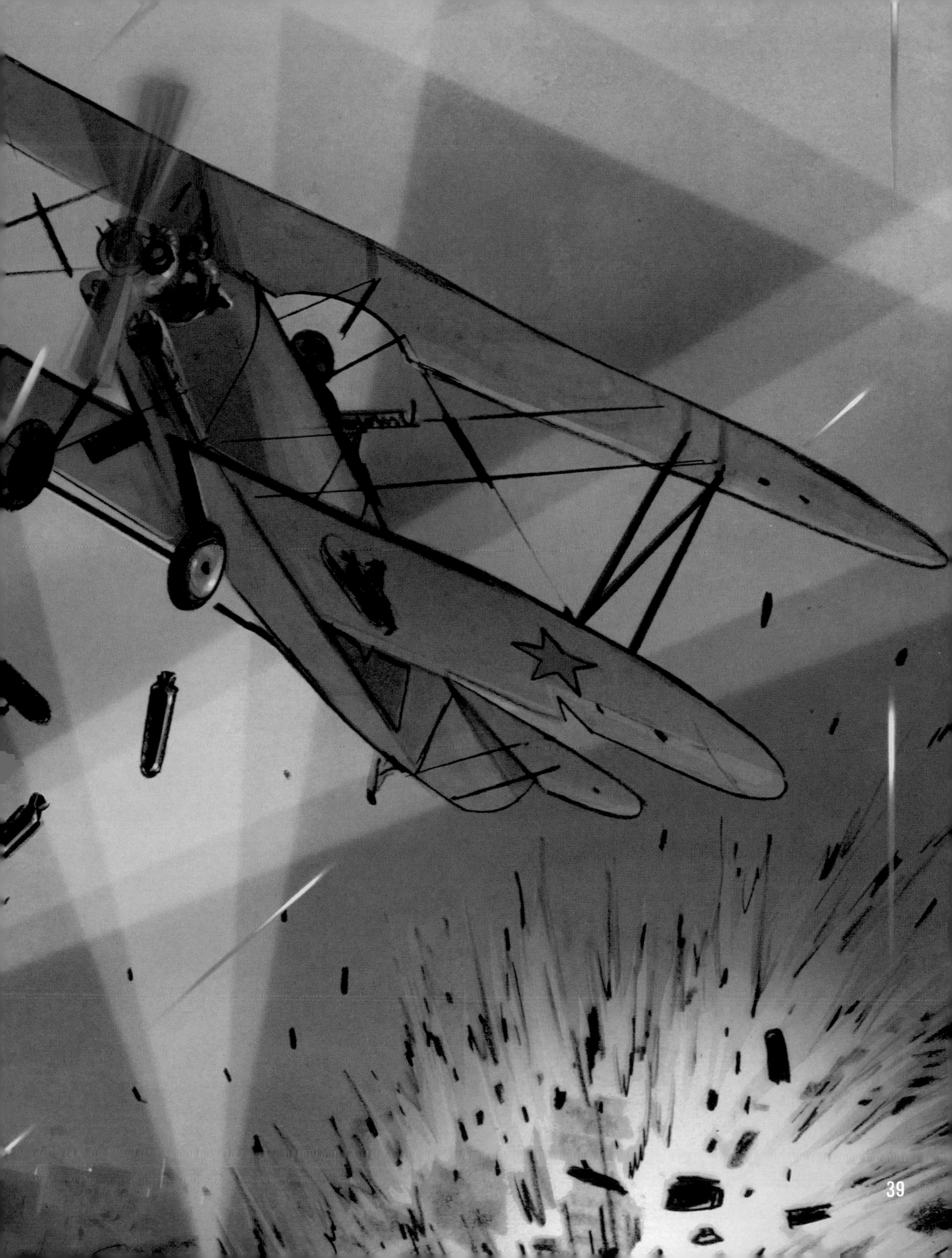

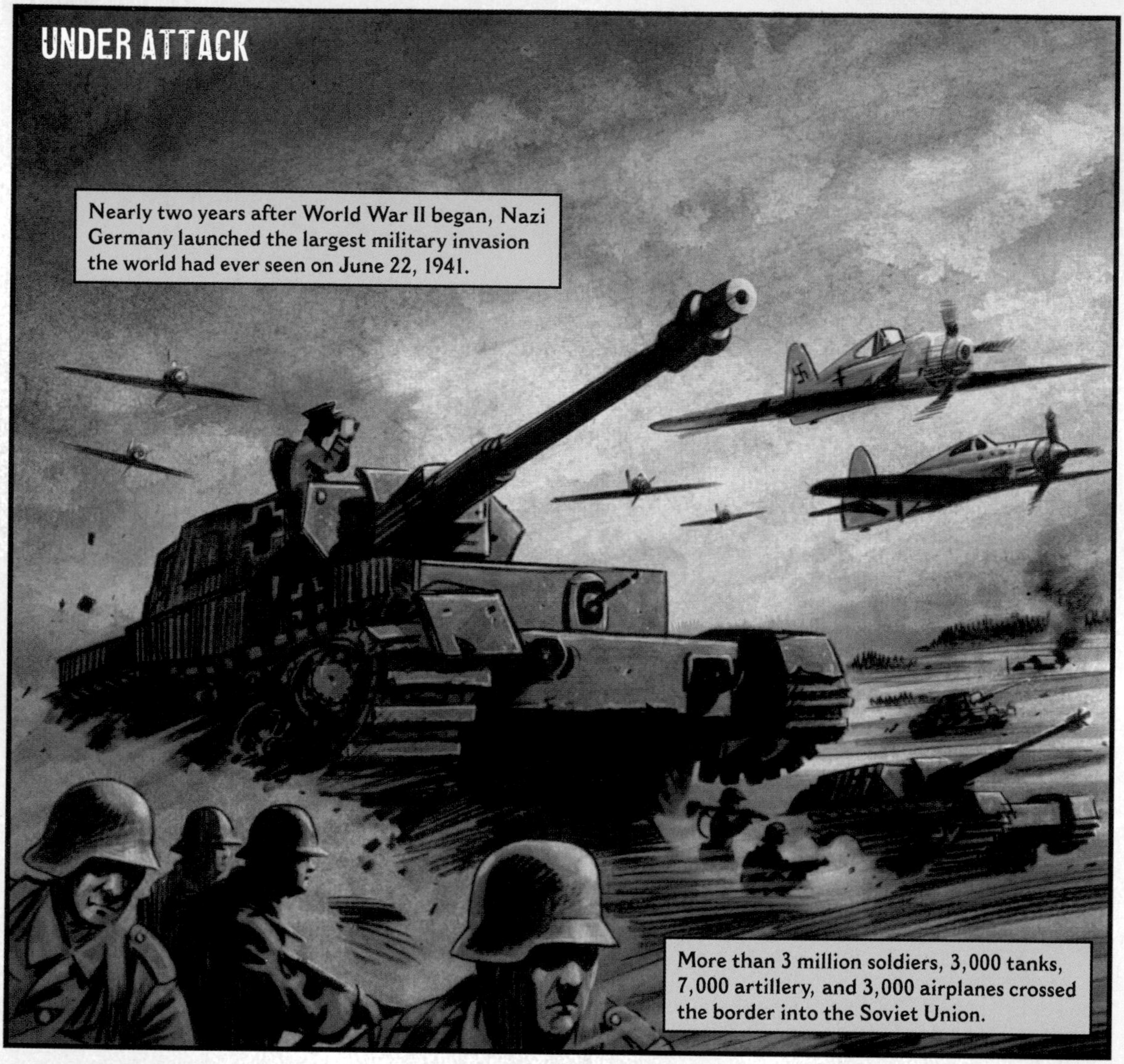
UNDER ATTACK
Nearly two years after World War II began, Nazi Germany launched the largest military invasion the world had ever seen on June 22, 1941.
More than 3 million soldiers, 3,000 tanks, 7,000 artillery, and 3,000 airplanes crossed the border into the Soviet Union.

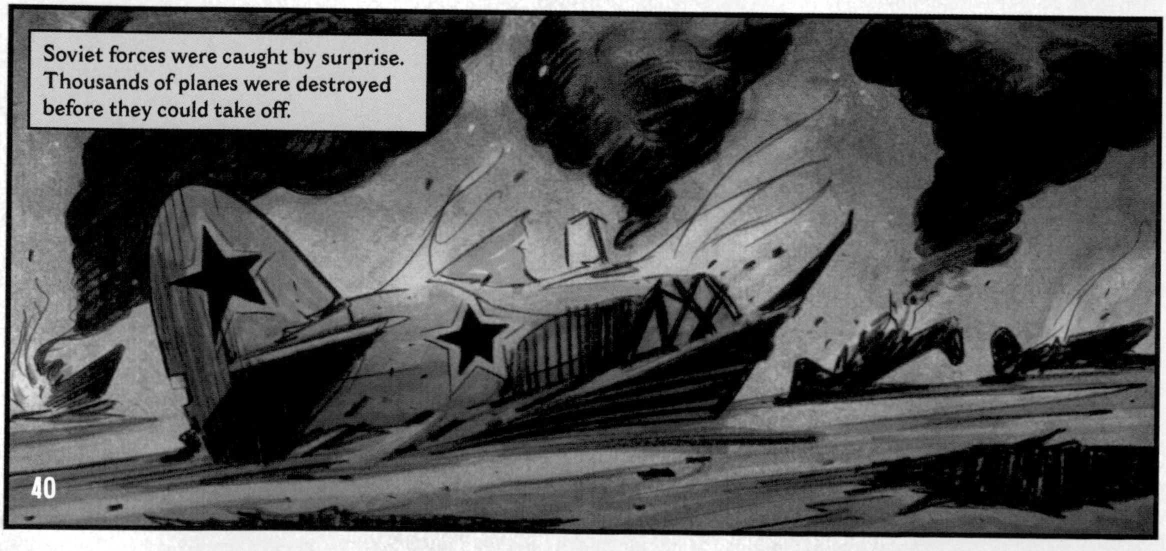
Soviet forces were caught by surprise. Thousands of planes were destroyed before they could take off.

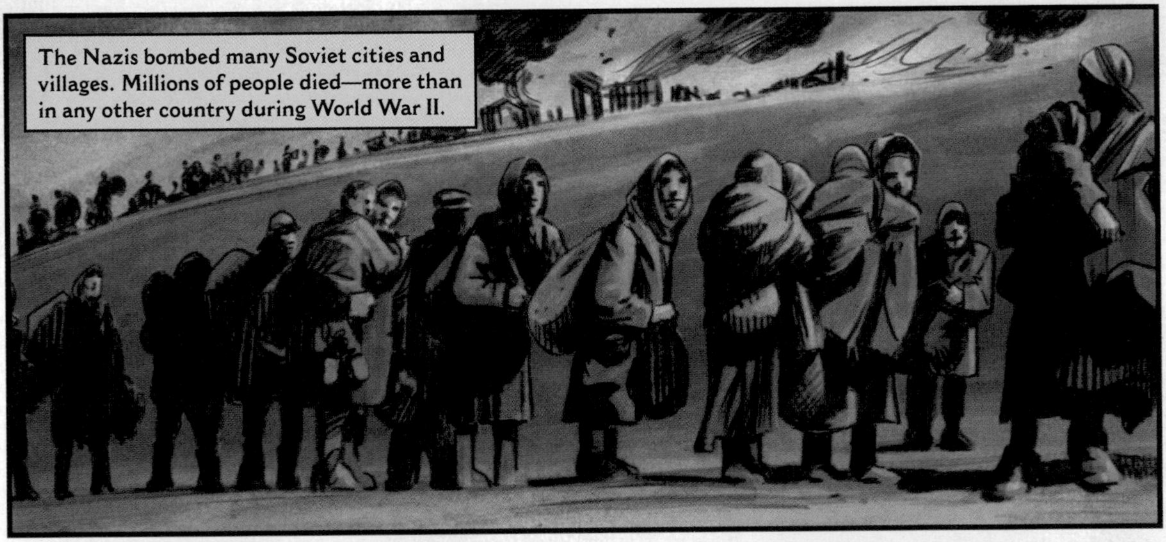
The Nazis bombed many Soviet cities and villages. Millions of people died—more than in any other country during World War II.

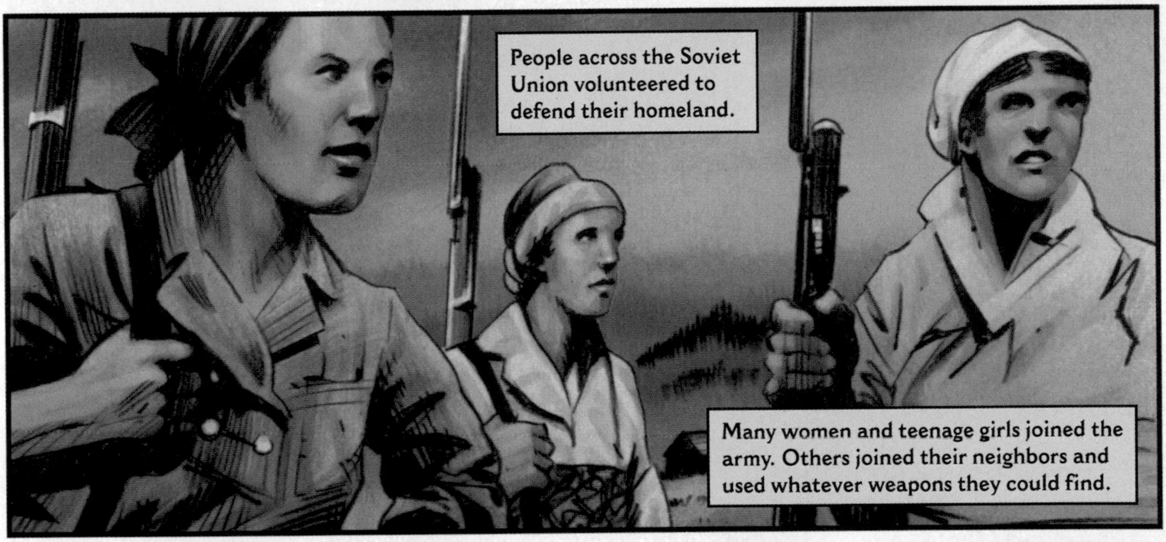
People across the Soviet Union volunteered to defend their homeland.
Many women and teenage girls joined the army. Others joined their neighbors and used whatever weapons they could find.

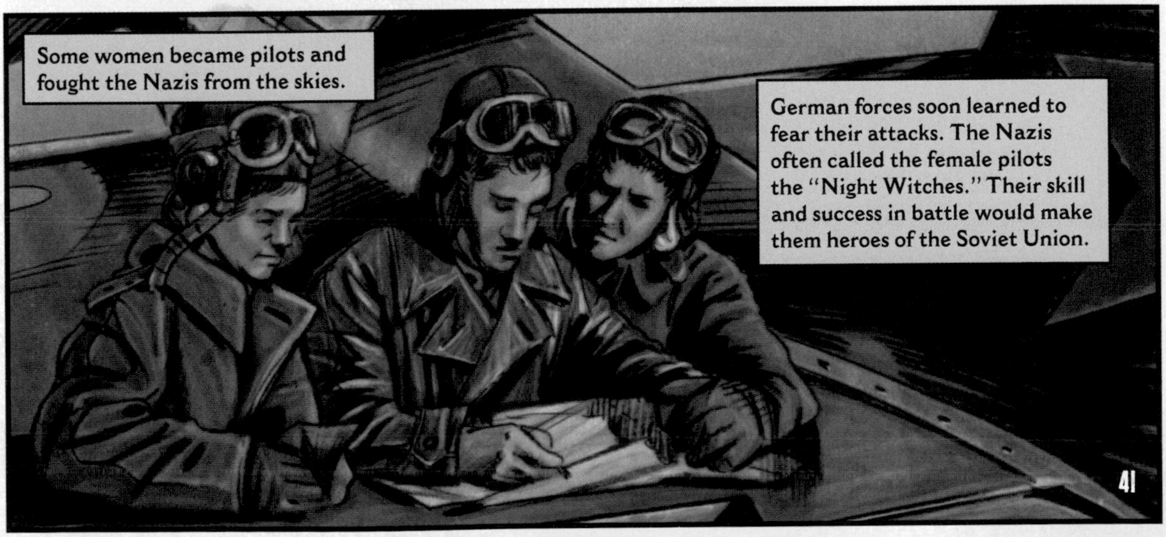
Some women became pilots and fought the Nazis from the skies.
German forces soon learned to fear their attacks. The Nazis often called the female pilots the "Night Witches." Their skill and success in battle would make them heroes of the Soviet Union.

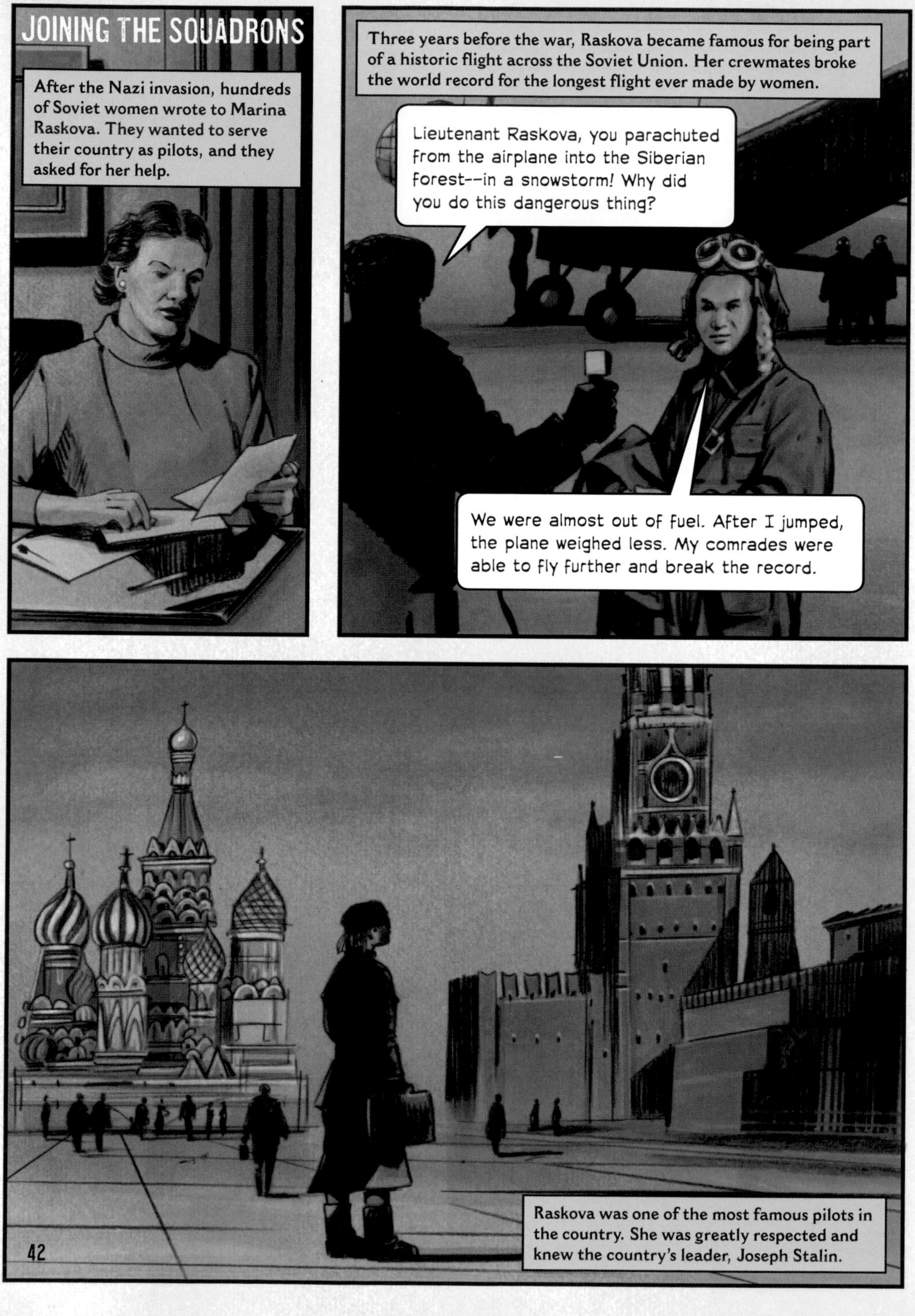
JOINING THE SQUADRONS
After the Nazi invasion, hundreds of Soviet women wrote to Marina Raskova. They wanted to serve their country as pilots, and they asked for her help.
Three years before the war, Raskova became famous for being part of a historic flight across the Soviet Union. Her crewmates broke the world record for the longest flight ever made by women.
Lieutenant Raskova, you parachuted from the airplane into the Siberian forest--in a snowstorm! Why did you do this dangerous thing?
We were almost out of fuel. After I jumped, the plane weighed less. My comrades were able to fly further and break the record.
Raskova was one of the most famous pilots in the country. She was greatly respected and knew the country's leader, Joseph Stalin.

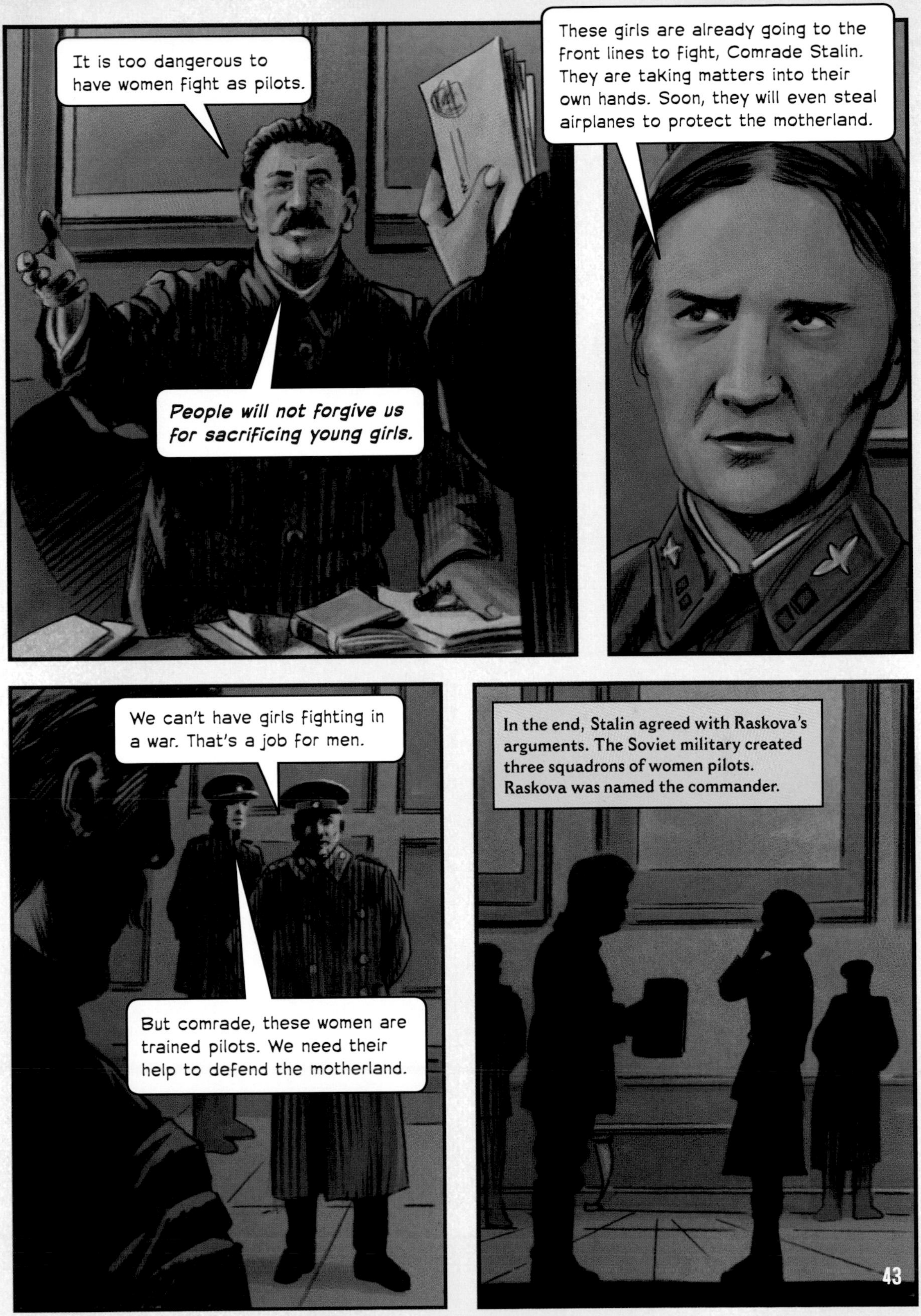
It is too dangerous to have women fight as pilots.
People will not forgive us for sacrificing young girls.
These girls are already going to the front lines to fight, Comrade Stalin. They are taking matters into their own hands. Soon, they will even steal airplanes to protect the motherland.
We can't have girls fighting in a war. That's a job for men.
But comrade, these women are trained pilots. We need their help to defend the motherland.
In the end, Stalin agreed with Raskova's arguments. The Soviet military created three squadrons of women pilots. Raskova was named the commander.

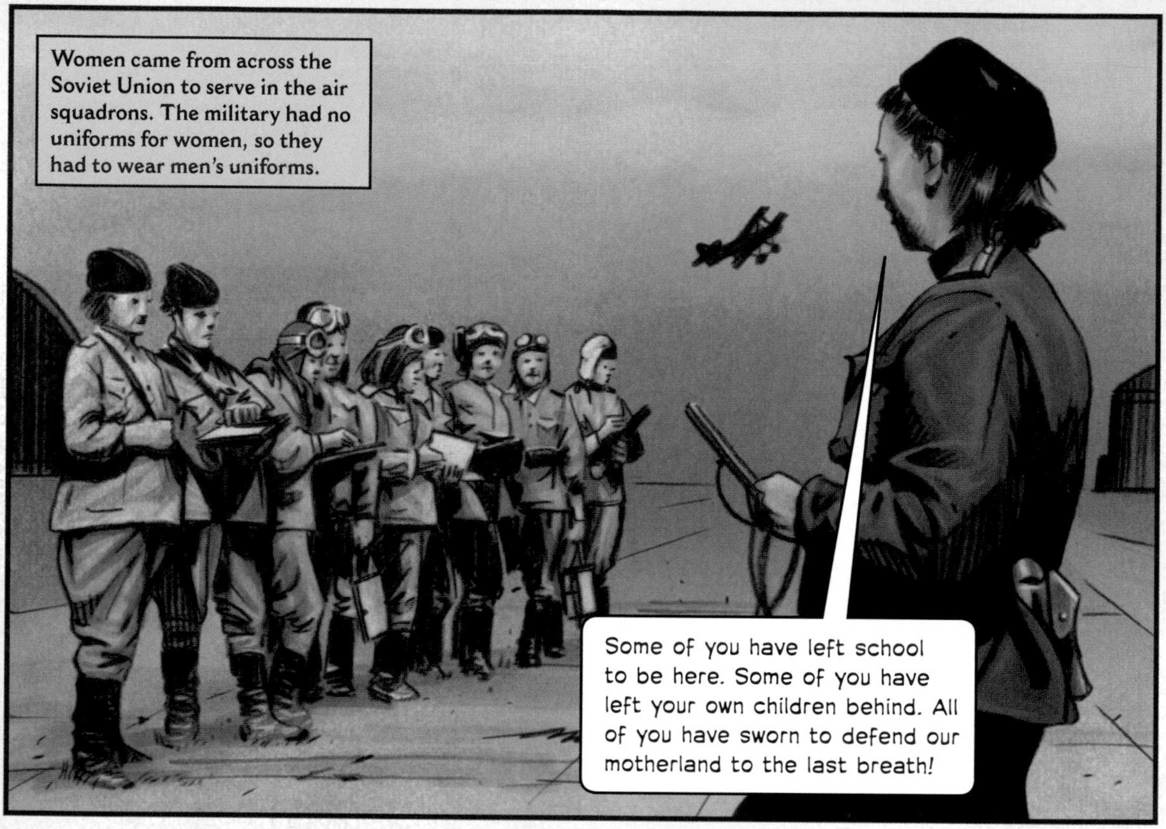
Women came from across the Soviet Union to serve in the air squadrons. The military had no uniforms for women, so they had to wear men's uniforms.
Some of you have left school to be here. Some of you have left your own children behind. All of you have sworn to defend our motherland to the last breath!

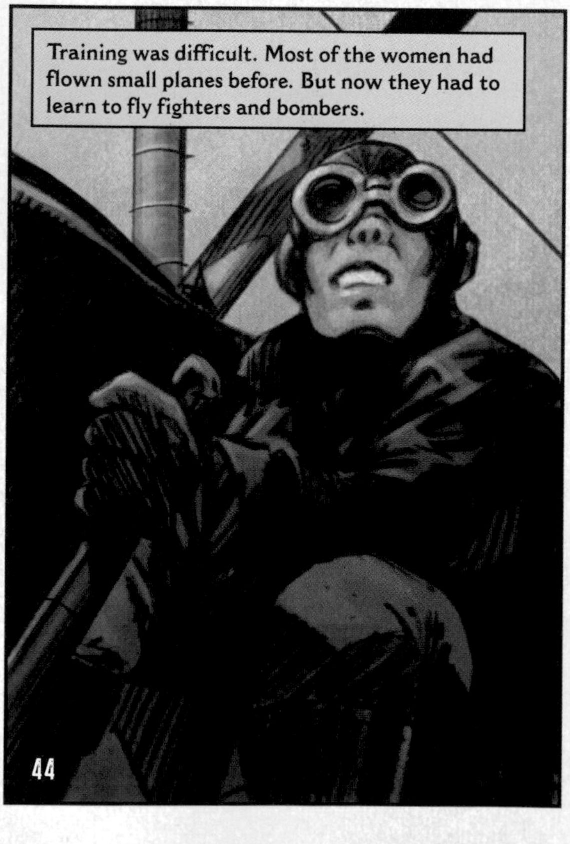
Training was difficult. Most of the women had flown small planes before. But now they had to learn to fly fighters and bombers.

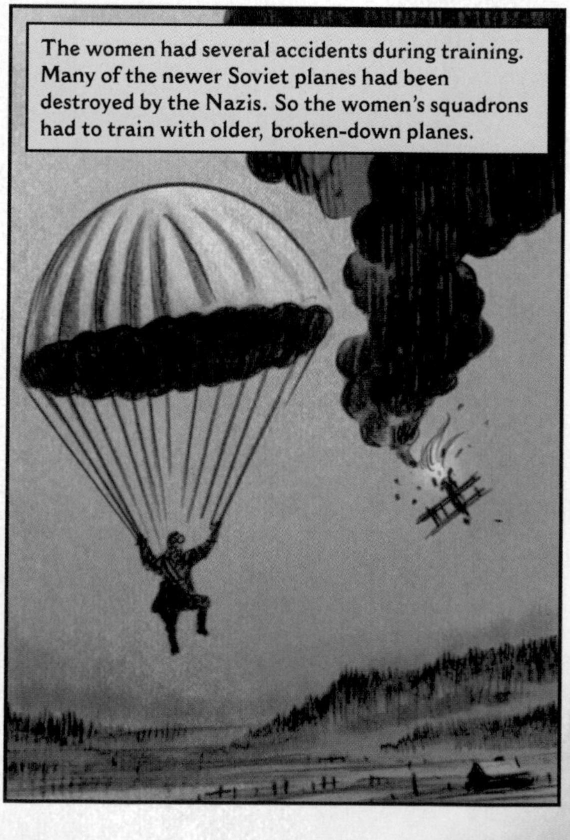
The women had several accidents during training. Many of the newer Soviet planes had been destroyed by the Nazis. So the women's squadrons had to train with older, broken-down planes.

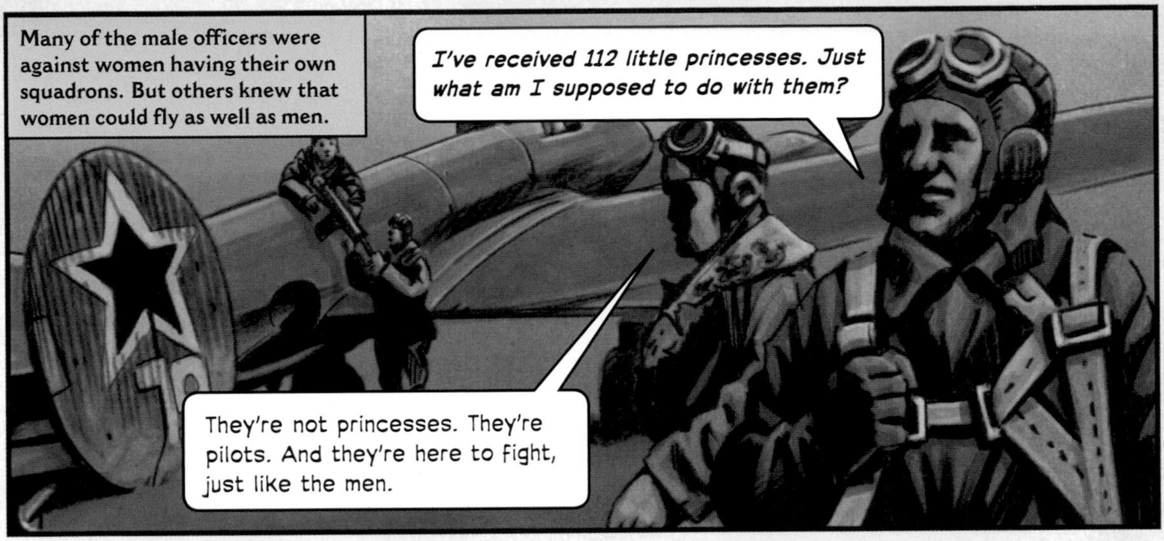
Many of the male officers were against women having their own squadrons. But others knew that women could fly as well as men.
I've received 112 little princesses. Just what am I supposed to do with them?
They're not princesses. They're pilots. And they're here to fight, just like the men.

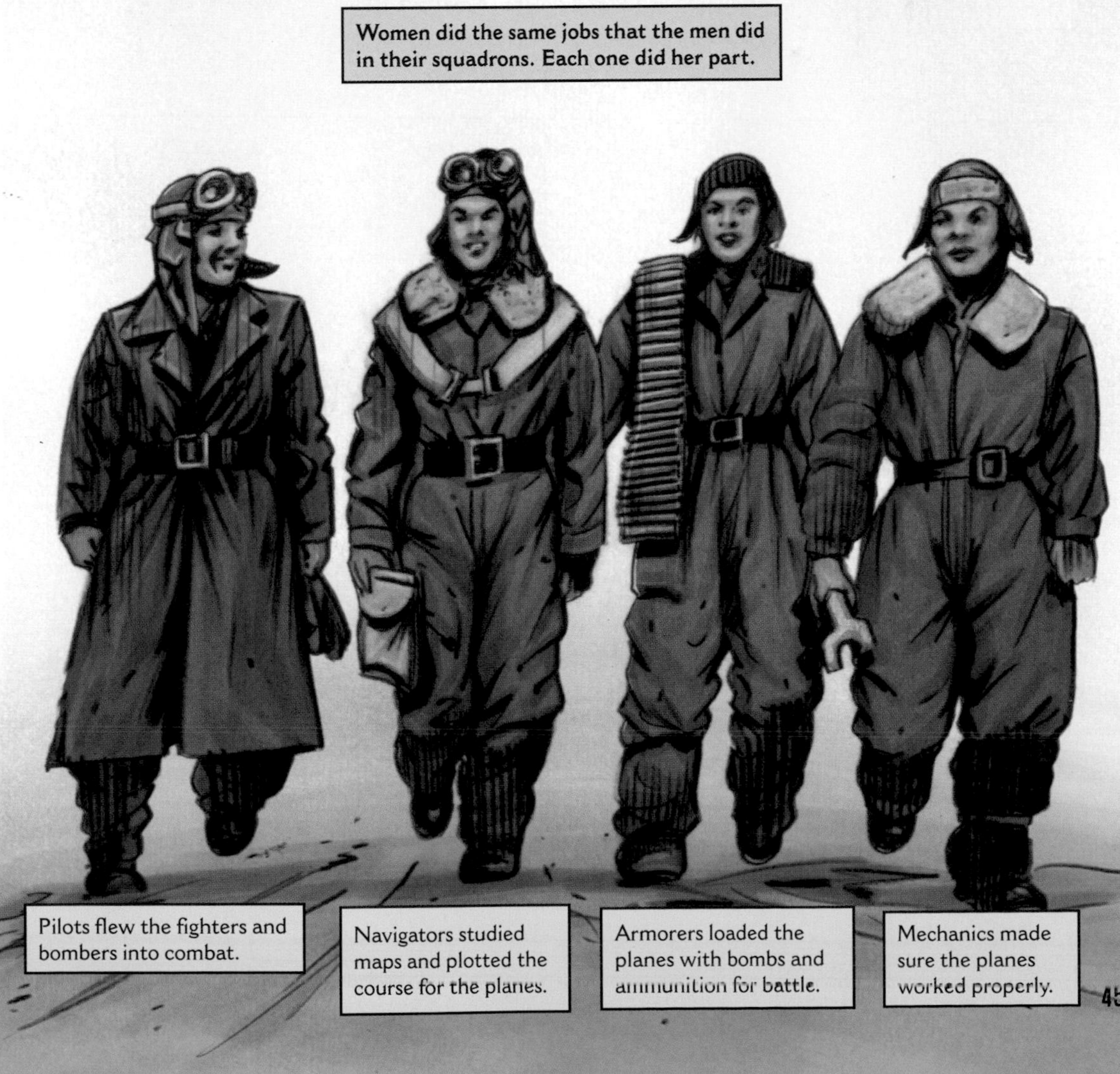
Women did the same jobs that the men did in their squadrons. Each one did her part.
Pilots flew the fighters and bombers into combat.
Navigators studied maps and plotted the course for the planes.
Armorers loaded the planes with bombs and ammunition for battle.
Mechanics made sure the planes worked properly.

In 1942 the Nazis were at the height of their power. Their empire stretched across Europe.

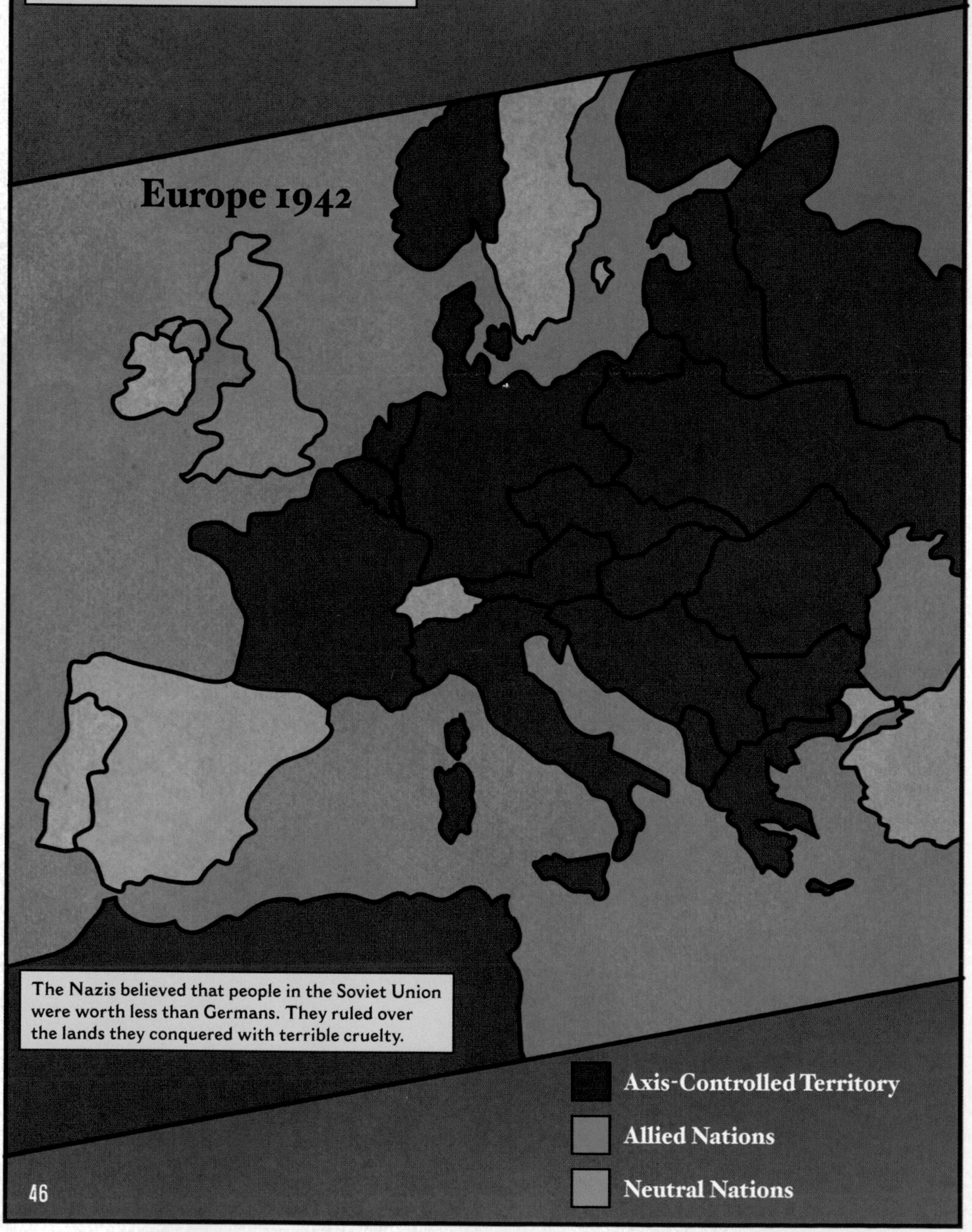
Europe 1942
Axis-Controlled Territory
Allied Nations
Neutral Nations

The Nazis believed that people in the Soviet Union were worth less than Germans. They ruled over the lands they conquered with terrible cruelty.

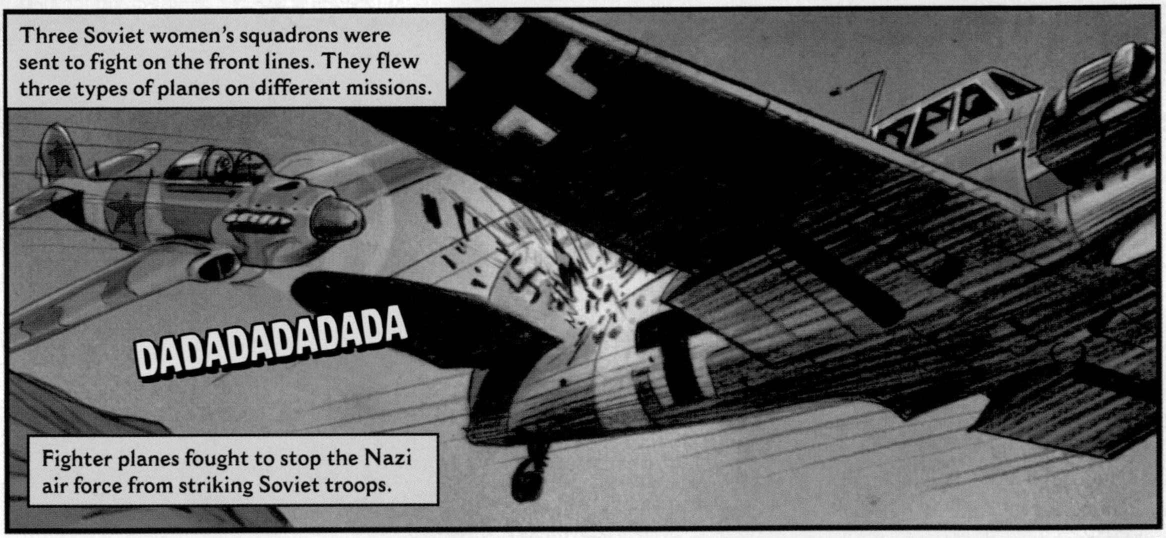
Three Soviet women's squadrons were sent to fight on the front lines. They flew three types of planes on different missions.
DADADADADADA
Fighter planes fought to stop the Nazi air force from striking Soviet troops.

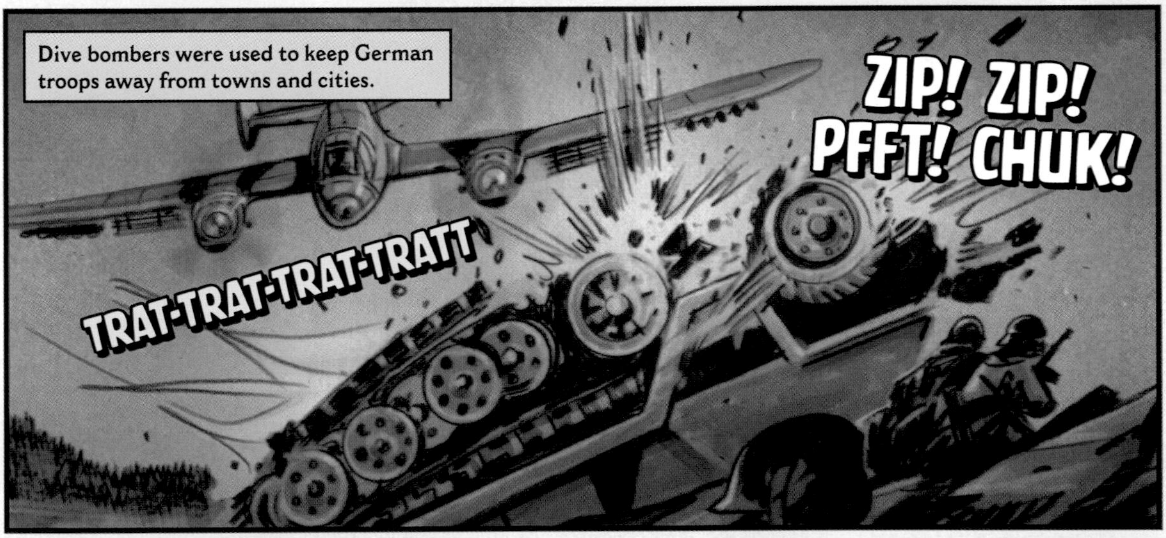
Dive bombers were used to keep German troops away from towns and cities.
ZIP! ZIP! PFFT! CHUK!
TRAT-TRAT-TRAT-TRATT

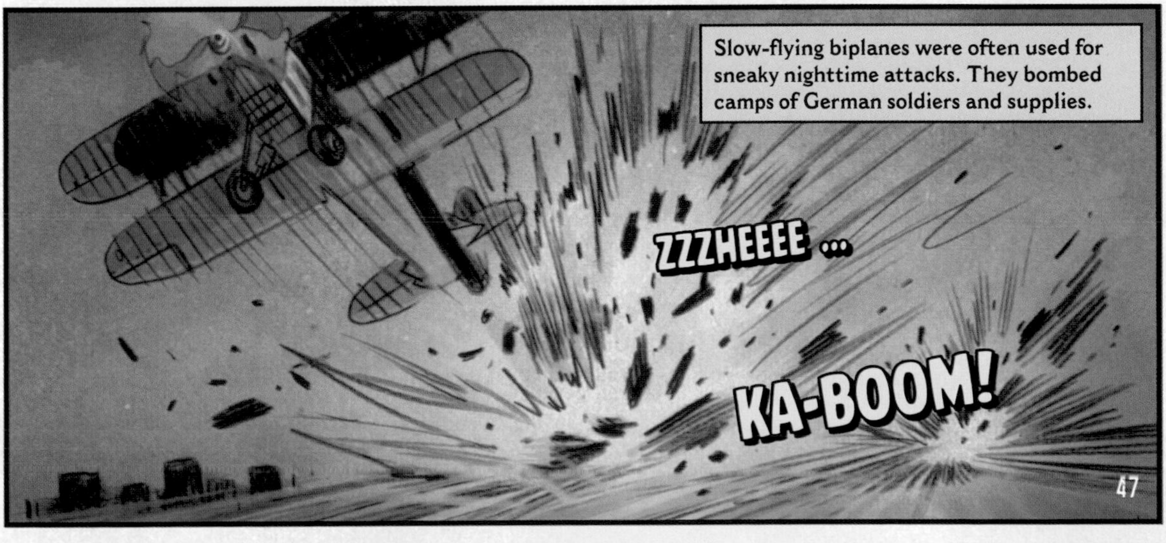
Slow-flying biplanes were often used for sneaky nighttime attacks. They bombed camps of German soldiers and supplies.
ZZZHEEEE ...
KA-BOOM!

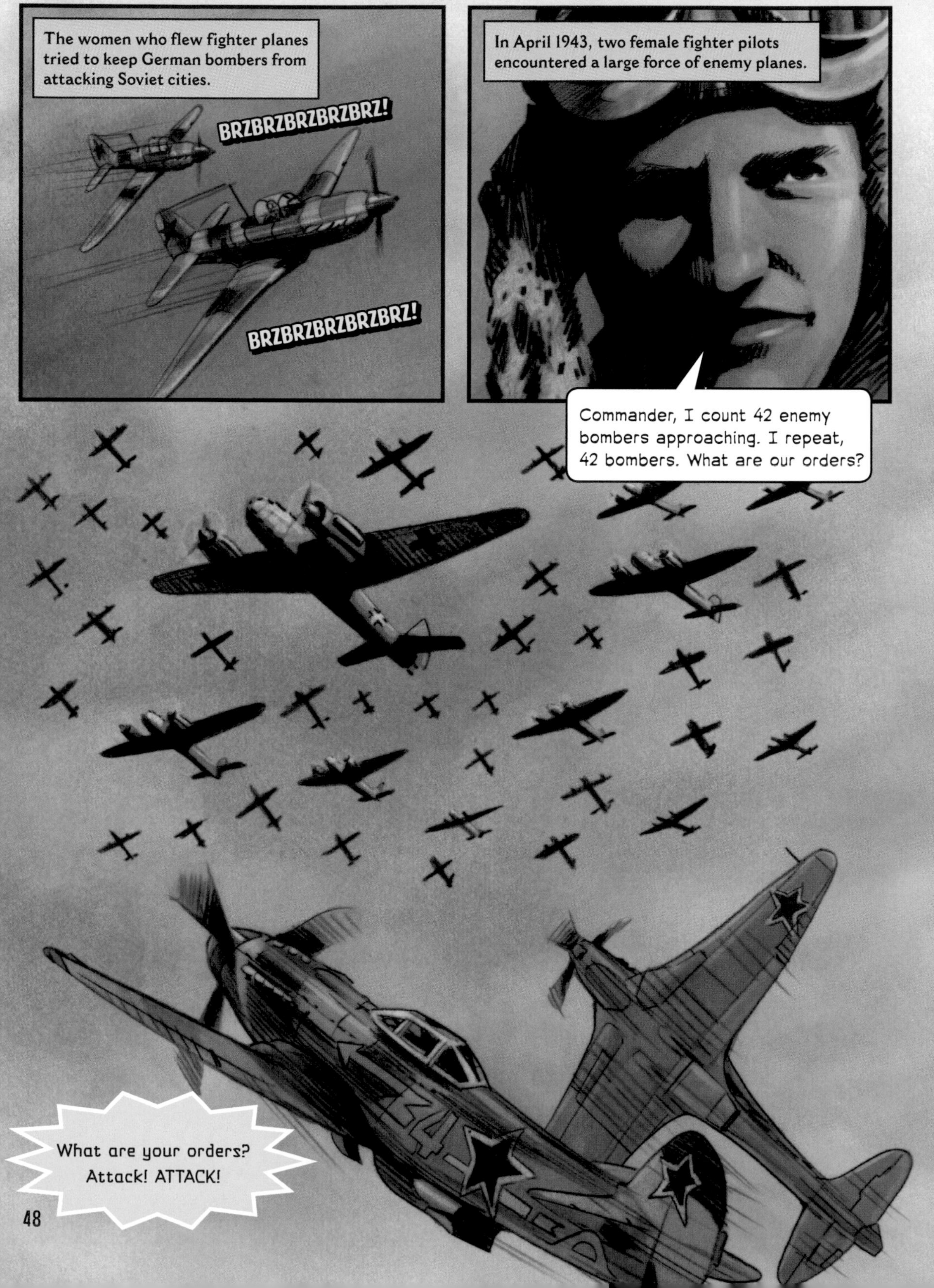

The women who flew fighter planes tried to keep German bombers from attacking Soviet cities.
BRZBRZBRZBRZBRZ!
BRZBRZBRZBRZBRZ!
In April 1943, two female fighter pilots encountered a large force of enemy planes.
Commander, I count 42 enemy bombers approaching. I repeat, 42 bombers. What are our orders?
What are your orders? Attack! ATTACK!

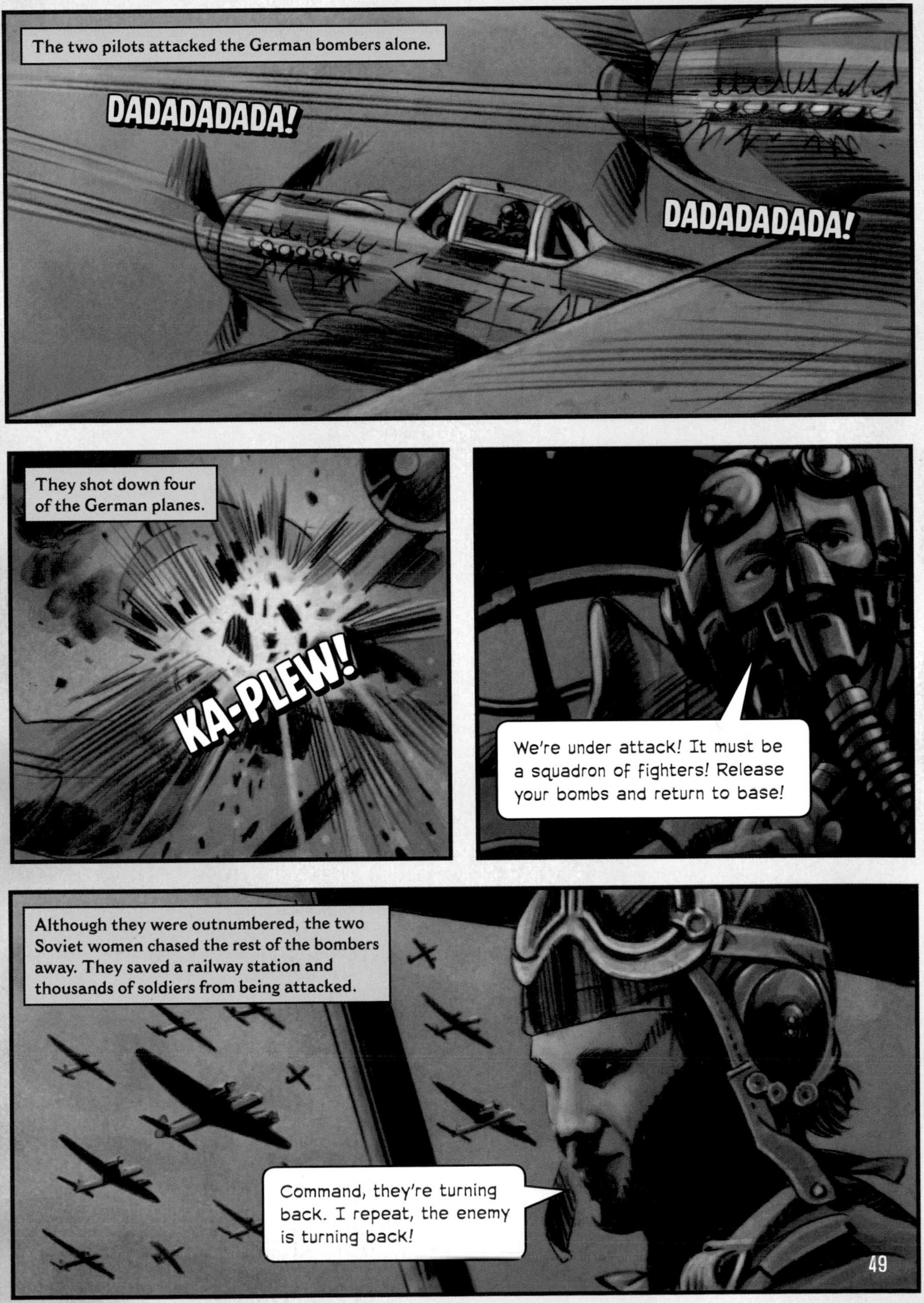
The two pilots attacked the German bombers alone.
DADADADADA!
DADADADADA!
They shot down four of the German planes.
KA-PLEW!
We're under attack! It must be a squadron of fighters! Release your bombs and return to base!
Although they were outnumbered, the two Soviet women chased the rest of the bombers away. They saved a railway station and thousands of soldiers from being attacked.
Command, they're turning back. I repeat, the enemy is turning back!

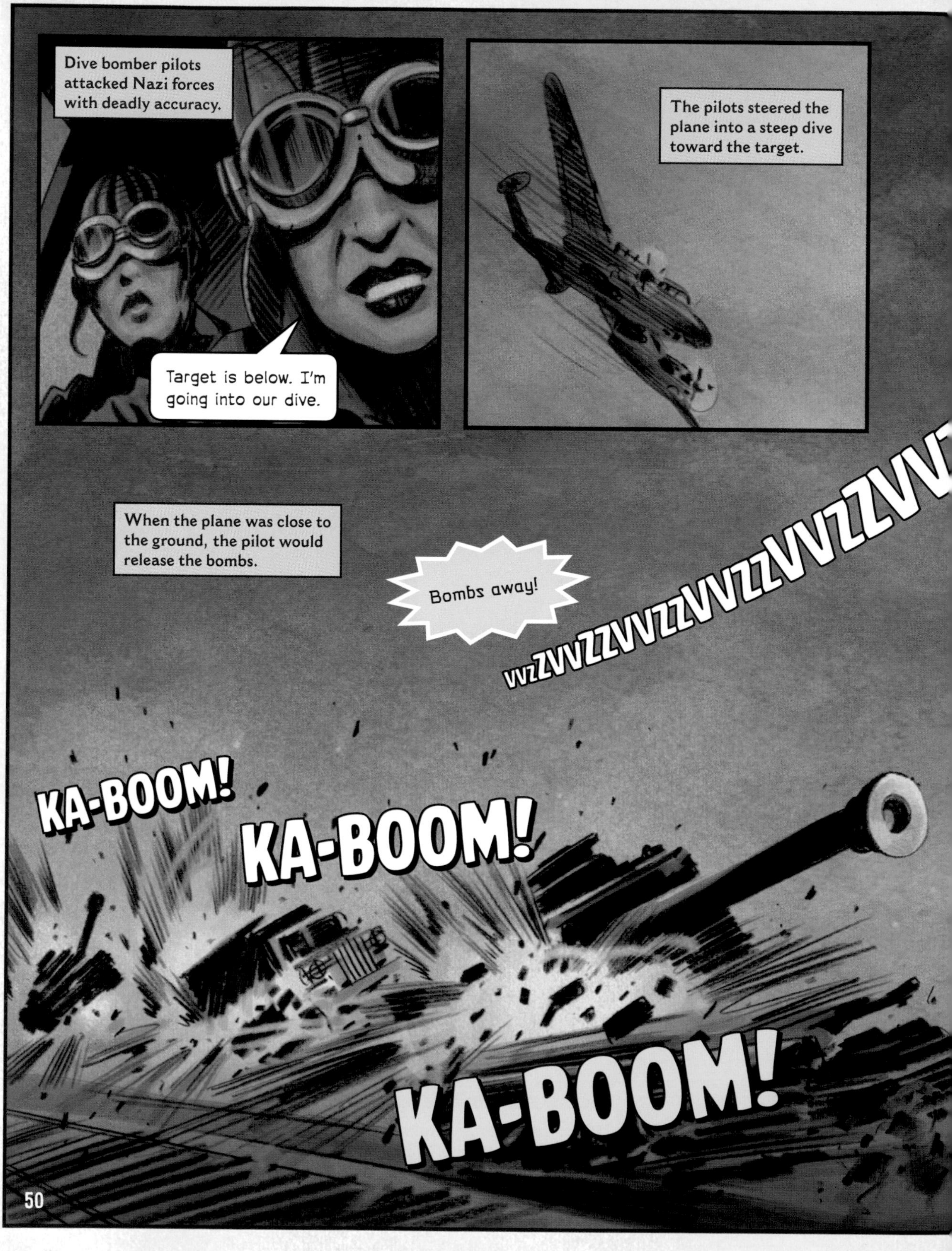
Dive bomber pilots attacked Nazi forces with deadly accuracy.
Target is below. I'm going into our dive.
The pilots steered the plane into a steep dive toward the target.
When the plane was close to the ground, the pilot would release the bombs.
Bombs away!
VVZZVVZZVVZZVVZZVVZZVV
KA-BOOM!
KA-BOOM!
KA-BOOM!

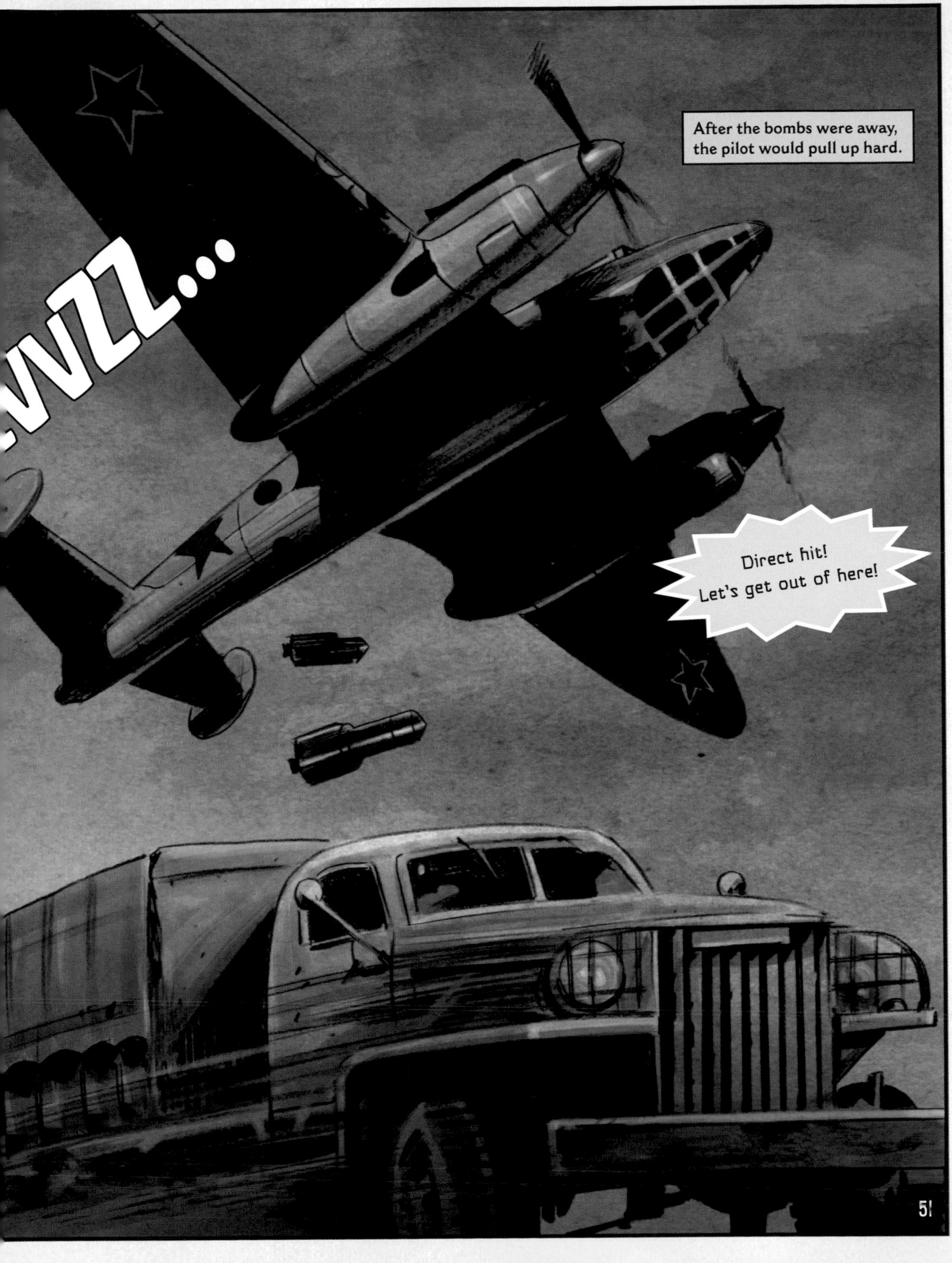

After the bombs were away, the pilot would pull up hard.
VVZZ...
Direct hit!
Let's get out of here!

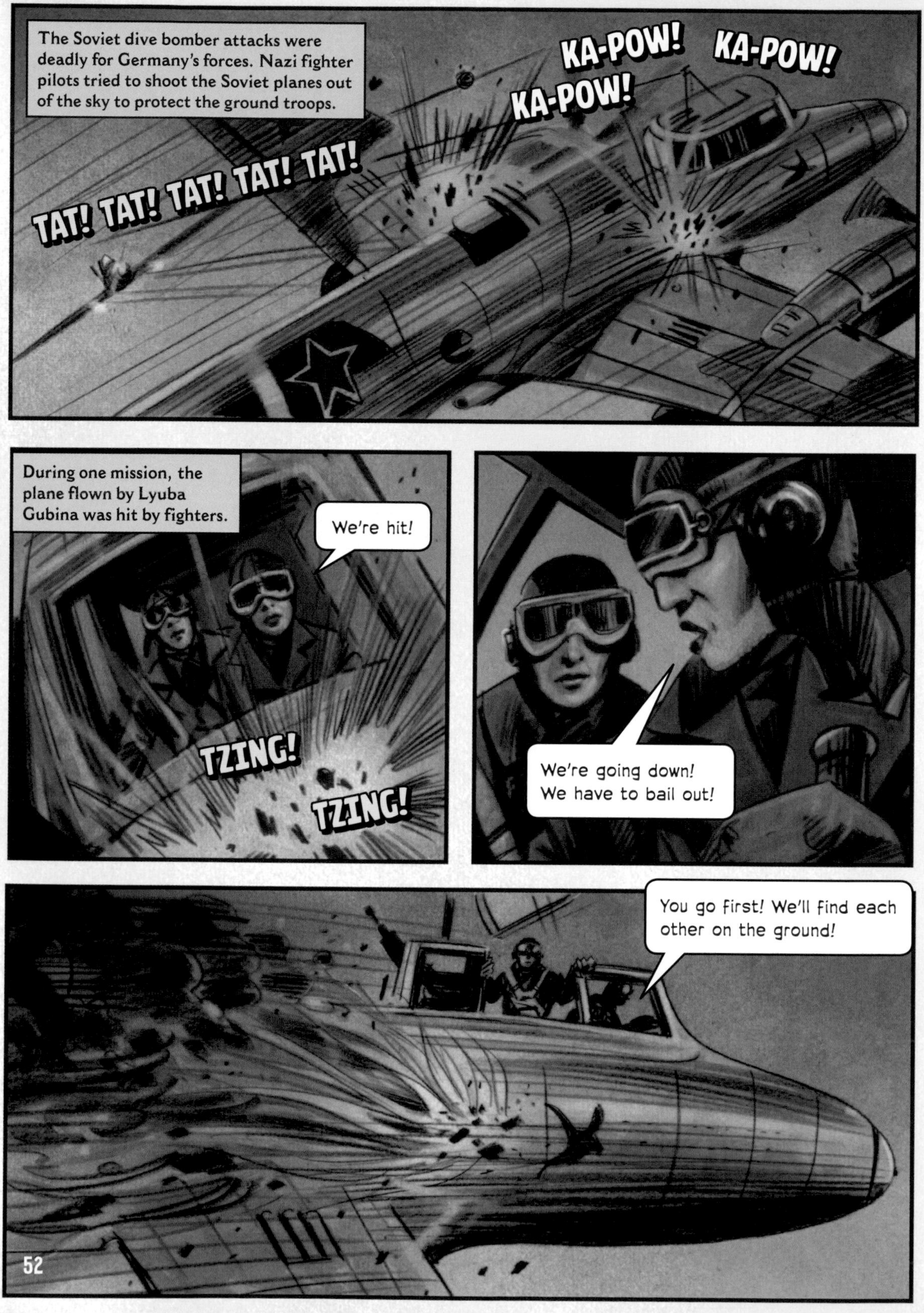
The Soviet dive bomber attacks were deadly for Germany's forces. Nazi fighter pilots tried to shoot the Soviet planes out of the sky to protect the ground troops.
KA-POW! KA-POW!
KA-POW!
TAT! TAT! TAT! TAT! TAT!
During one mission, the plane flown by Lyuba Gubina was hit by fighters.
We're hit!
TZING!
TZING!
We're going down! We have to bail out!
You go first! We'll find each other on the ground!

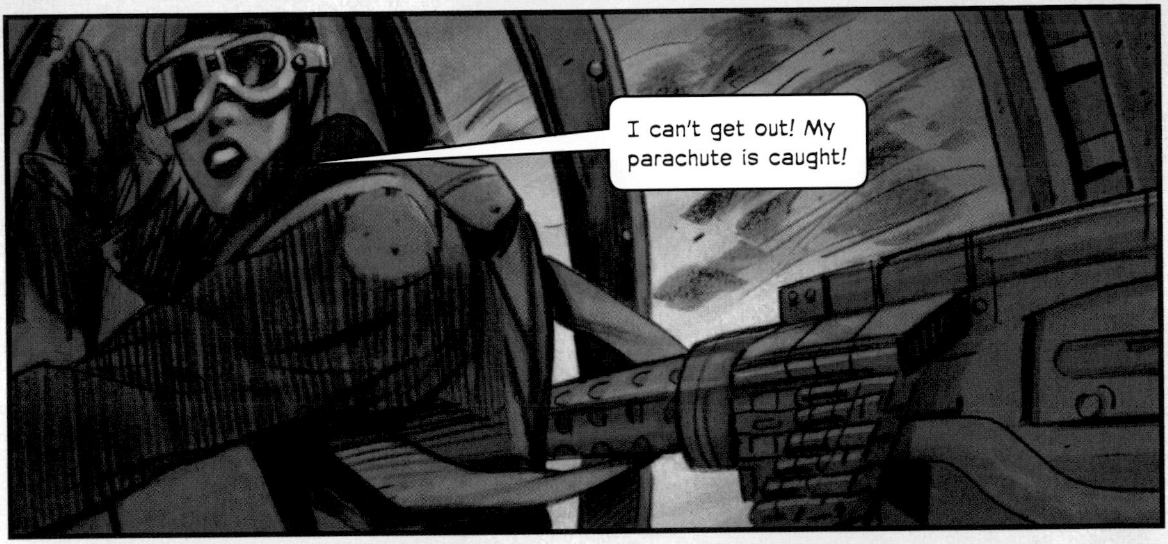
I can't get out! My parachute is caught!

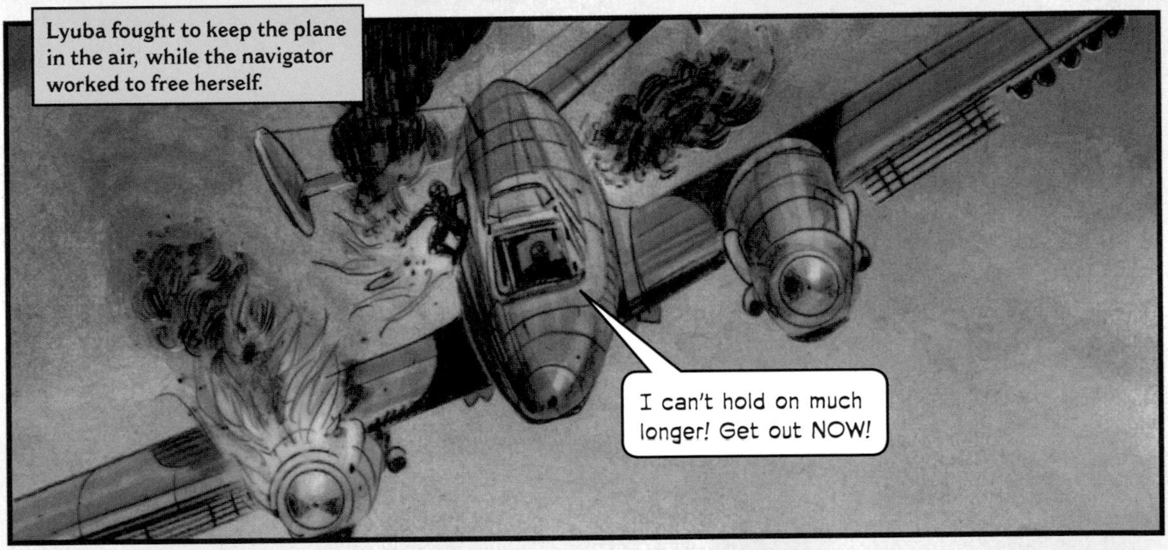
Lyuba fought to keep the plane in the air, while the navigator worked to free herself.
I can't hold on much longer! Get out NOW!

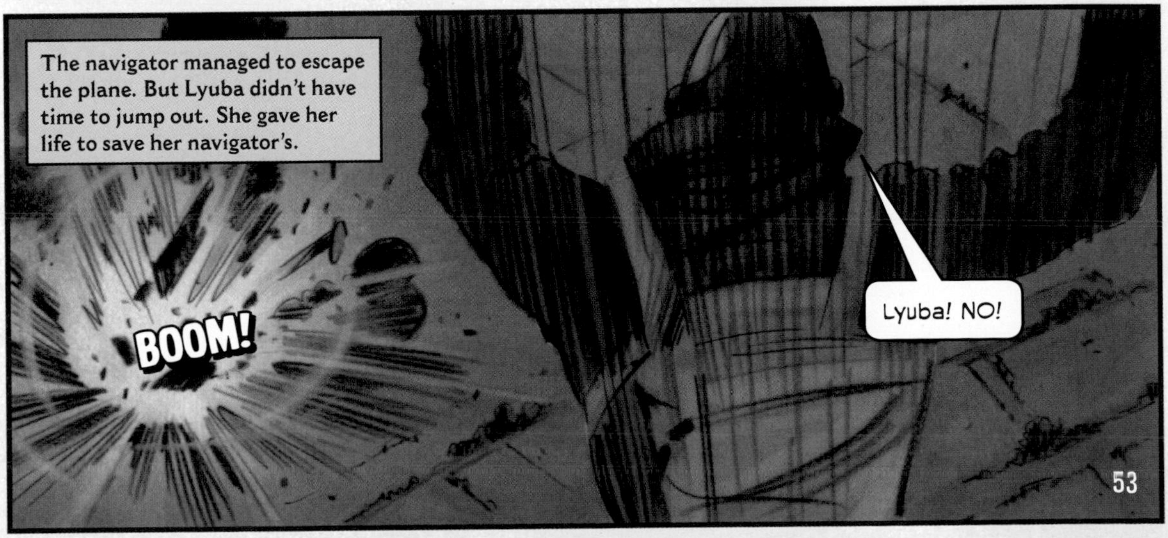
The navigator managed to escape the plane. But Lyuba didn't have time to jump out. She gave her life to save her navigator's.
BOOM!
Lyuba! NO!

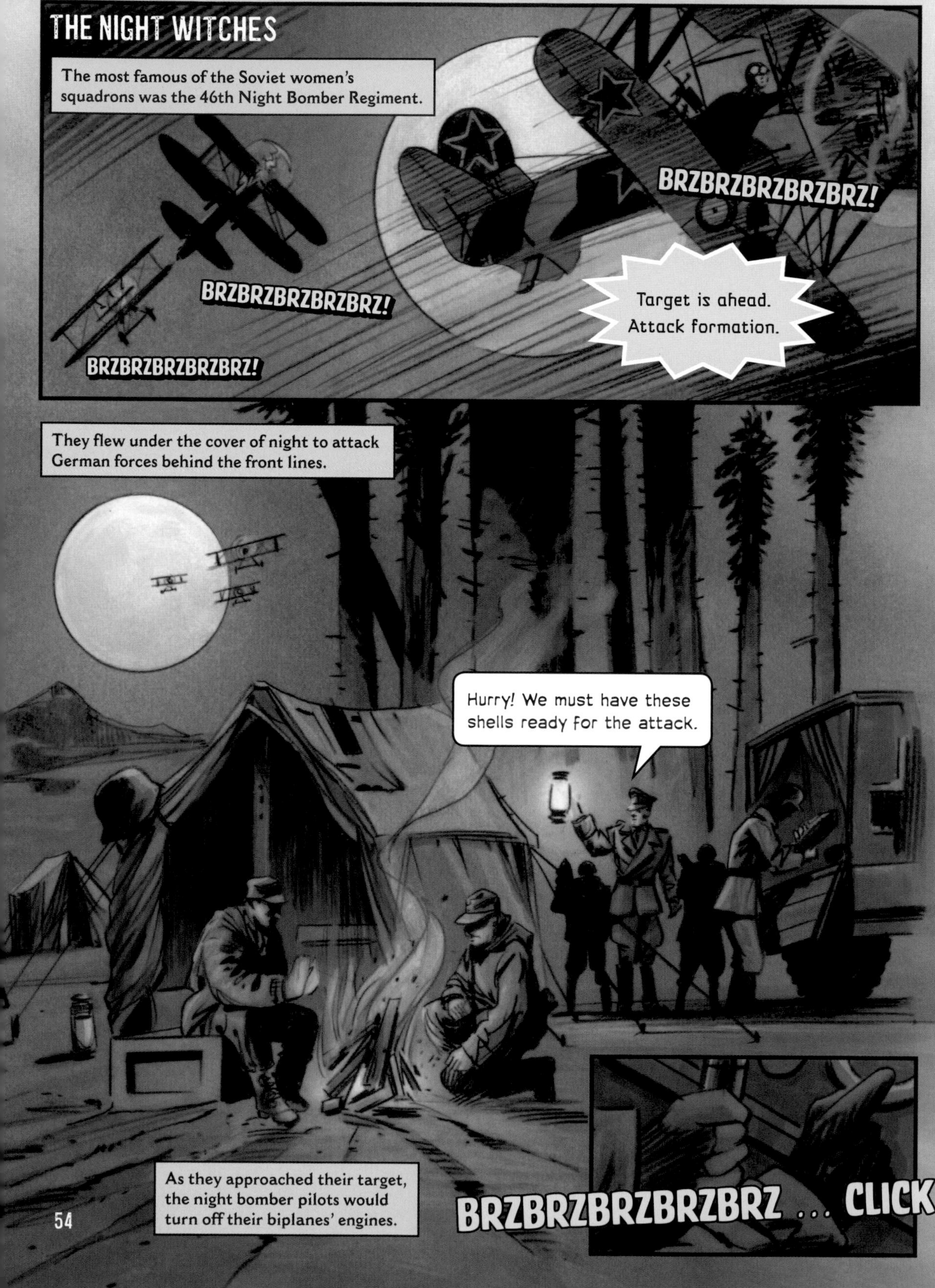
THE NIGHT WITCHES
The most famous of the Soviet women's squadrons was the 46th Night Bomber Regiment.
BRZBRZBRZBRZBRZ!
BRZBRZBRZBRZBRZ!
BRZBRZBRZBRZBRZ!
Target is ahead. Attack formation.
They flew under the cover of night to attack German forces behind the front lines.
Hurry! We must have these shells ready for the attack.
As they approached their target, the night bomber pilots would turn off their biplanes' engines.
BRZBRZBRZBRZBRZ . . . CLICK

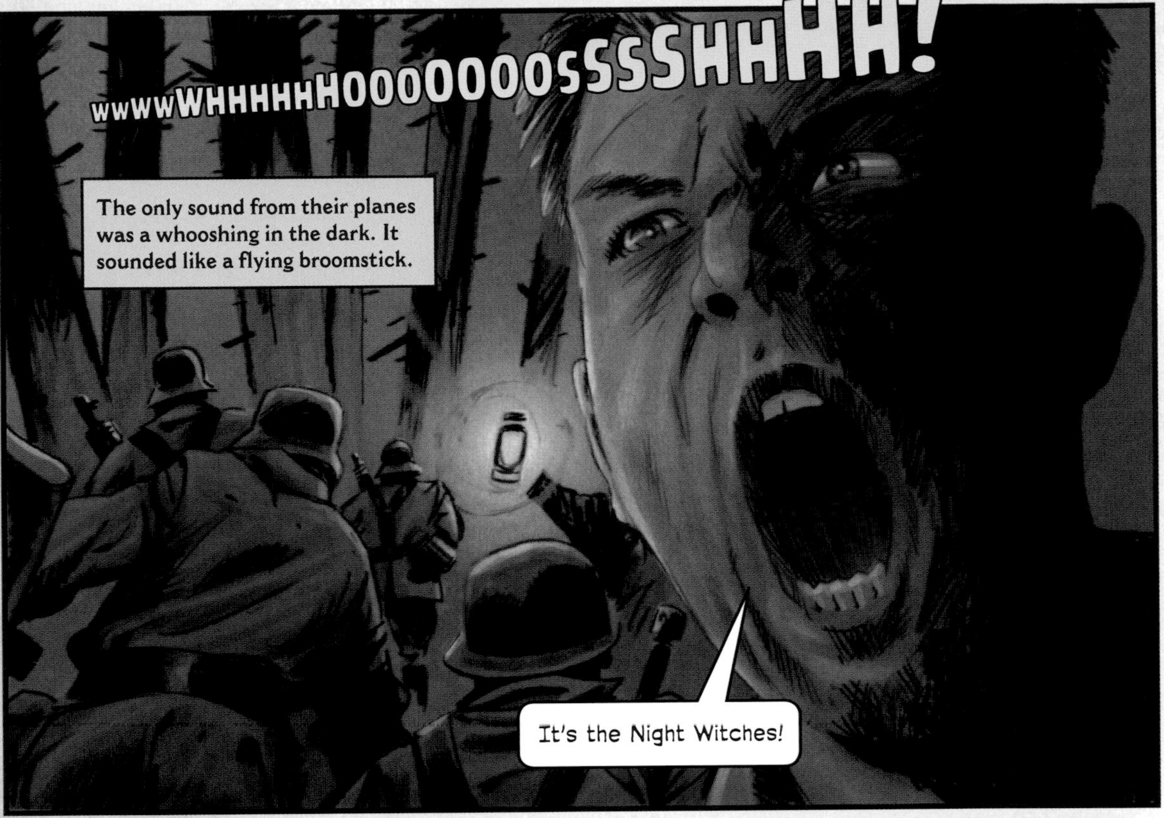
wwwwWHHHHHHOOOOOOOOsSSSHHHH!
The only sound from their planes was a whooshing in the dark. It sounded like a flying broomstick.
It's the Night Witches!

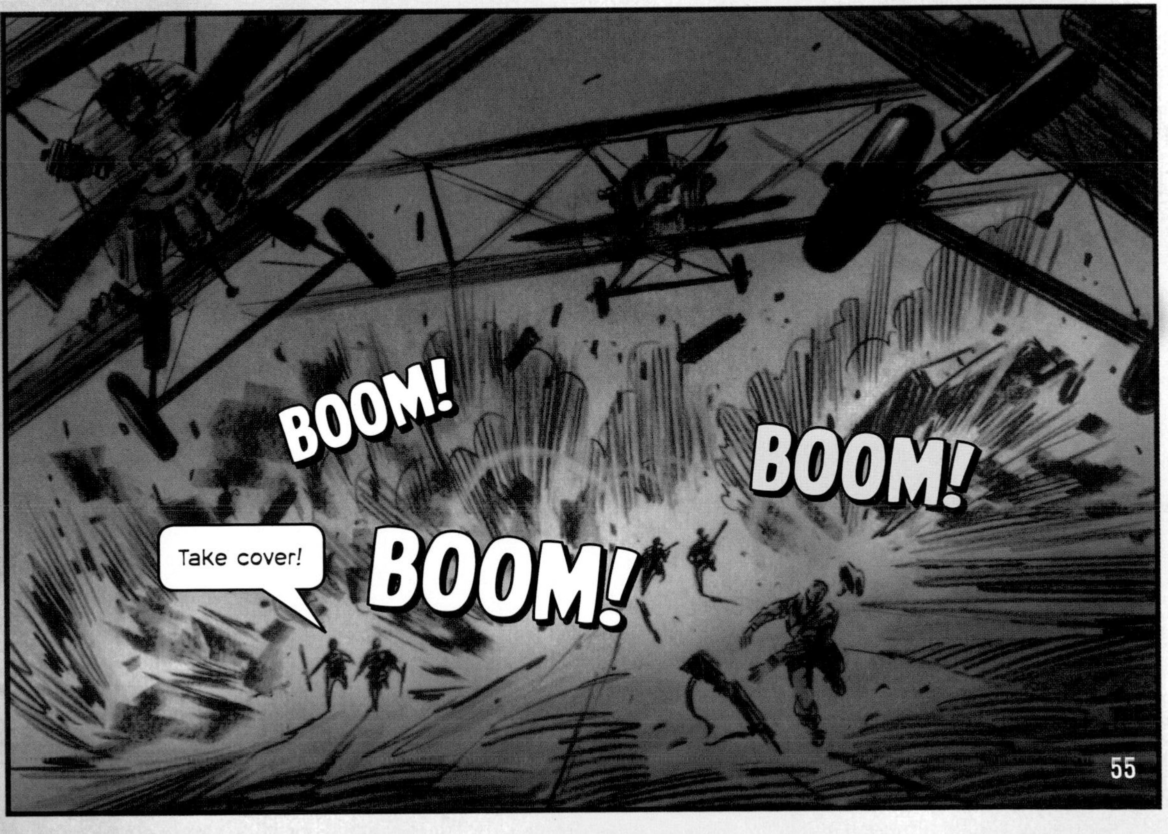
BOOM!
BOOM!
Take cover!
BOOM!

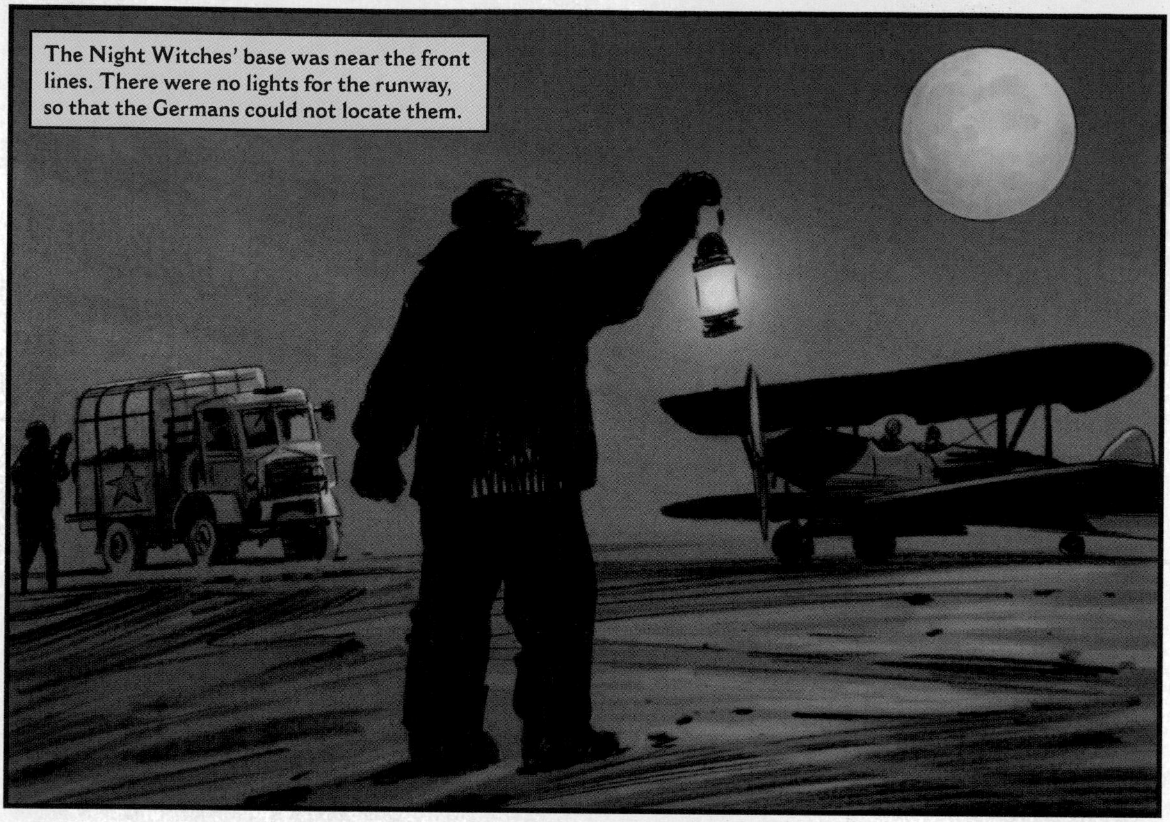
The Night Witches' base was near the front lines. There were no lights for the runway, so that the Germans could not locate them.

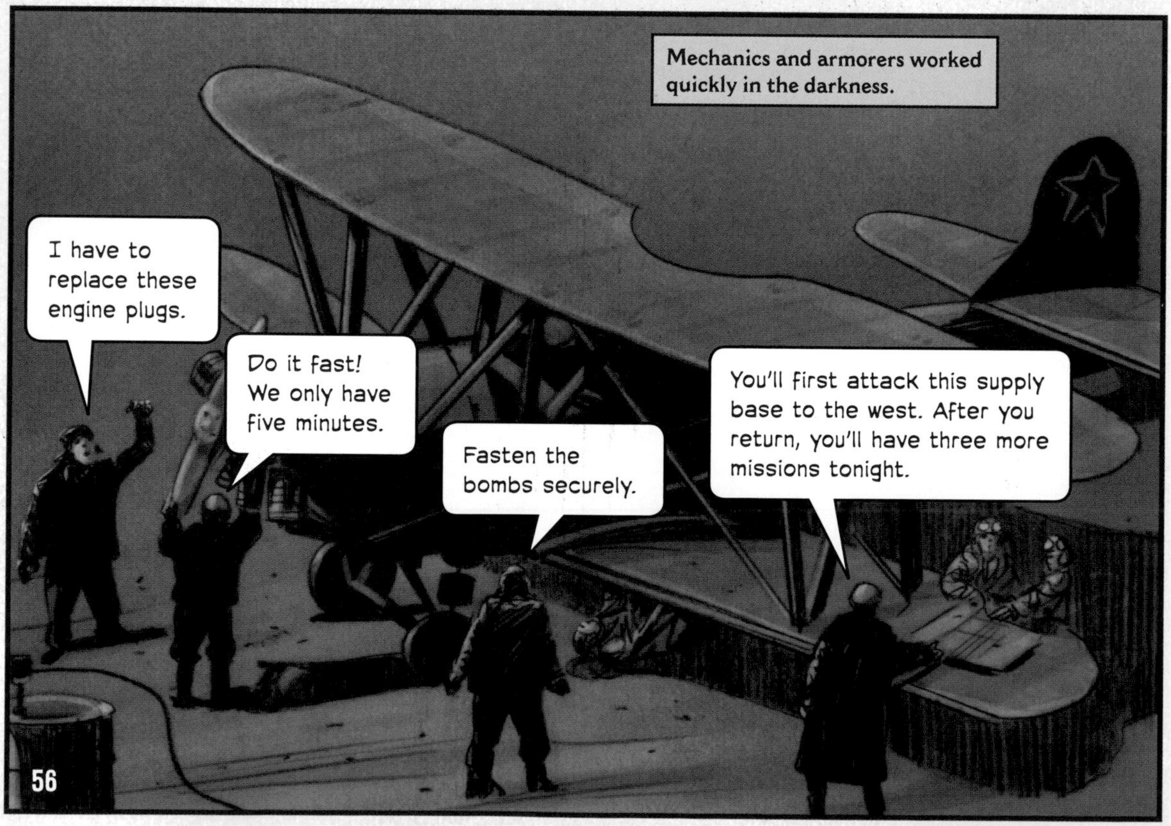
Mechanics and armorers worked quickly in the darkness.
I have to replace these engine plugs.
Do it fast! We only have five minutes.
Fasten the bombs securely.
You'll first attack this supply base to the west. After you return, you'll have three more missions tonight.

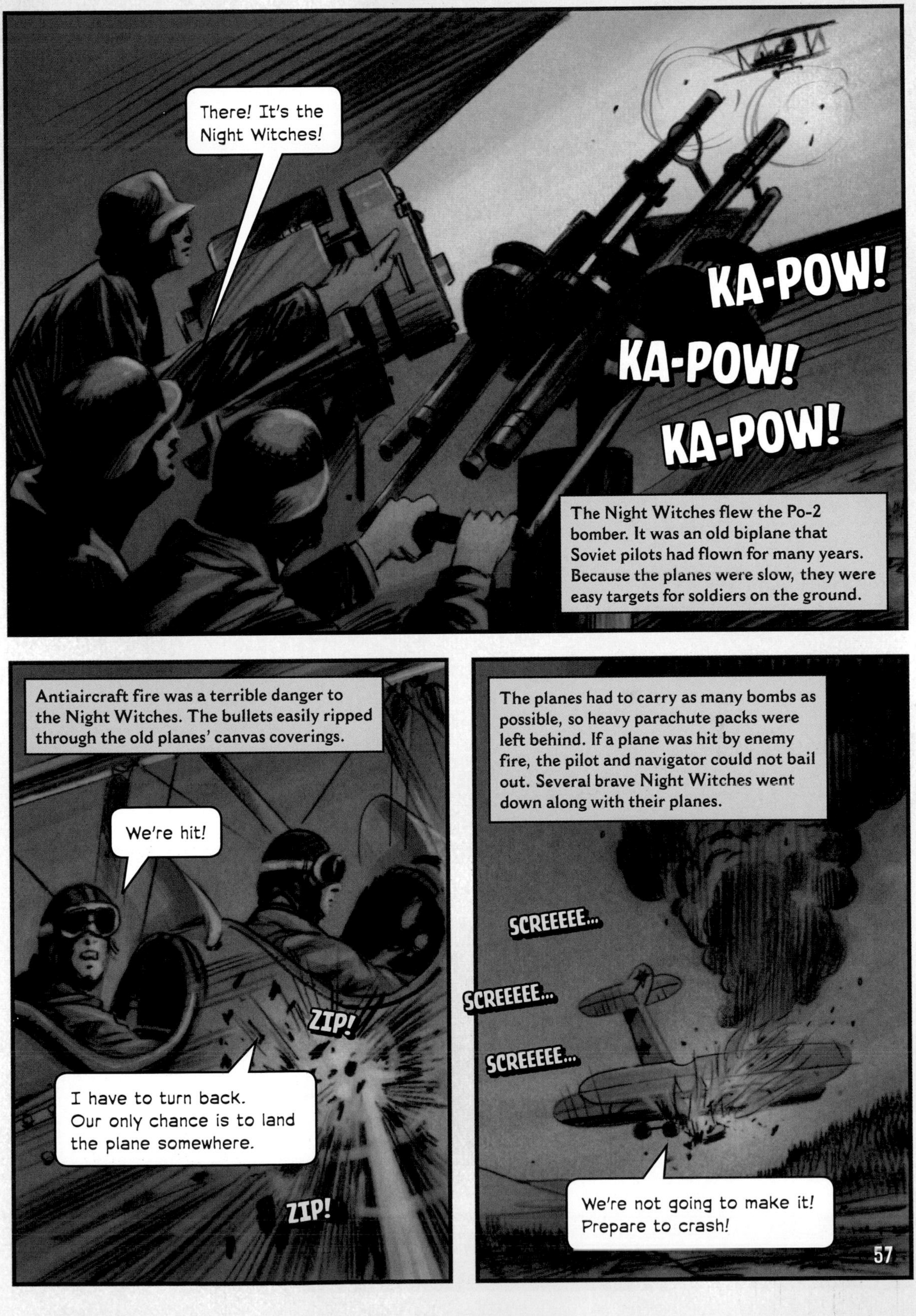

There! It's the Night Witches!
KA-POW!
KA-POW!
KA-POW!
The Night Witches flew the Po-2 bomber. It was an old biplane that Soviet pilots had flown for many years. Because the planes were slow, they were easy targets for soldiers on the ground.
Antiaircraft fire was a terrible danger to the Night Witches. The bullets easily ripped through the old planes' canvas coverings.
We're hit!
ZIP!
I have to turn back. Our only chance is to land the plane somewhere.
ZIP!
The planes had to carry as many bombs as possible, so heavy parachute packs were left behind. If a plane was hit by enemy fire, the pilot and navigator could not bail out. Several brave Night Witches went down along with their planes.
SCREEEEE...
SCREEEEE...
SCREEEEE...
We're not going to make it! Prepare to crash!

DANGEROUS MISSIONS

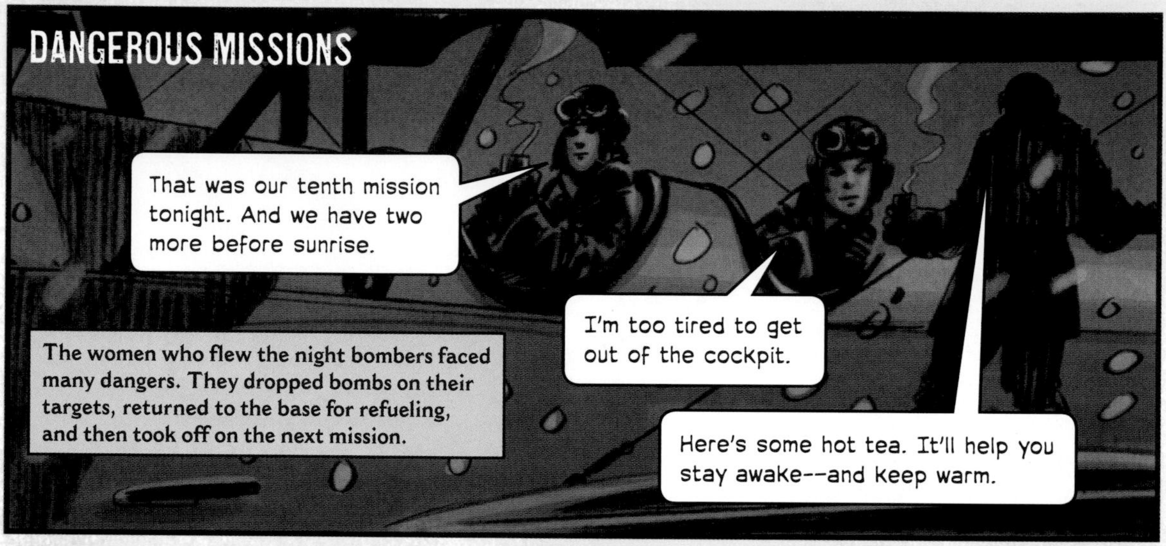

That was our tenth mission tonight. And we have two more before sunrise.
The women who flew the night bombers faced many dangers. They dropped bombs on their targets, returned to the base for refueling, and then took off on the next mission.
I'm too tired to get out of the cockpit.
Here's some hot tea. It'll help you stay awake--and keep warm.

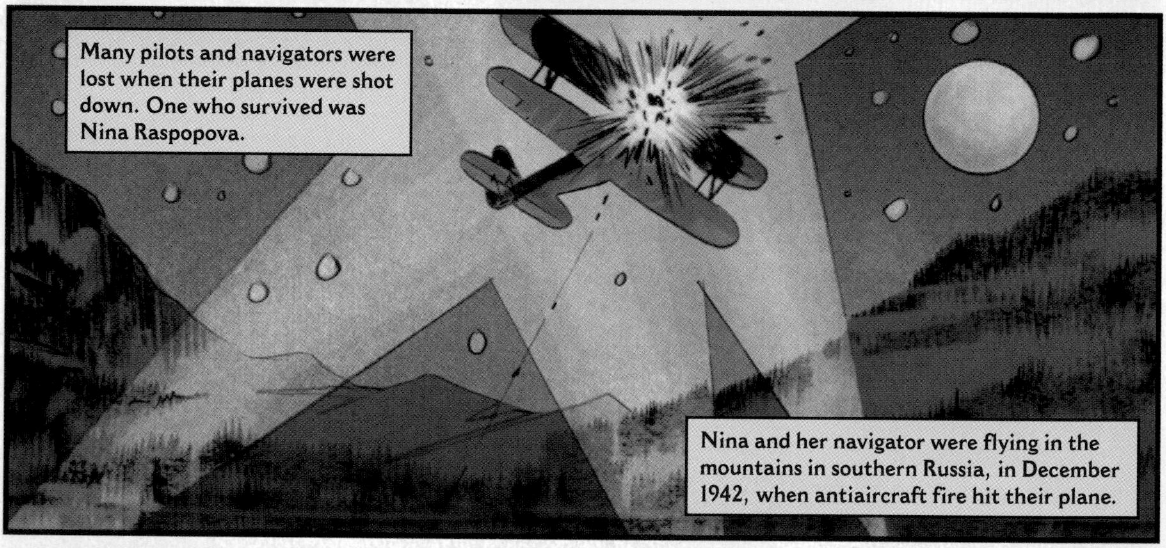

Many pilots and navigators were lost when their planes were shot down. One who survived was Nina Raspopova.
Nina and her navigator were flying in the mountains in southern Russia, in December 1942, when antiaircraft fire hit their plane.

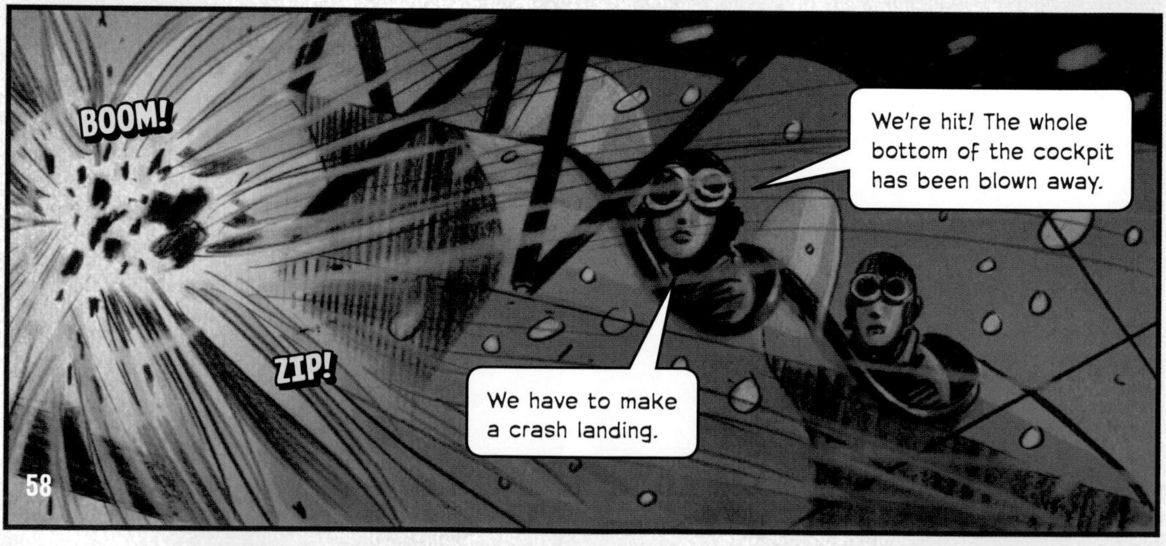

BOOM!
We're hit! The whole bottom of the cockpit has been blown away.
ZIP!
We have to make a crash landing.

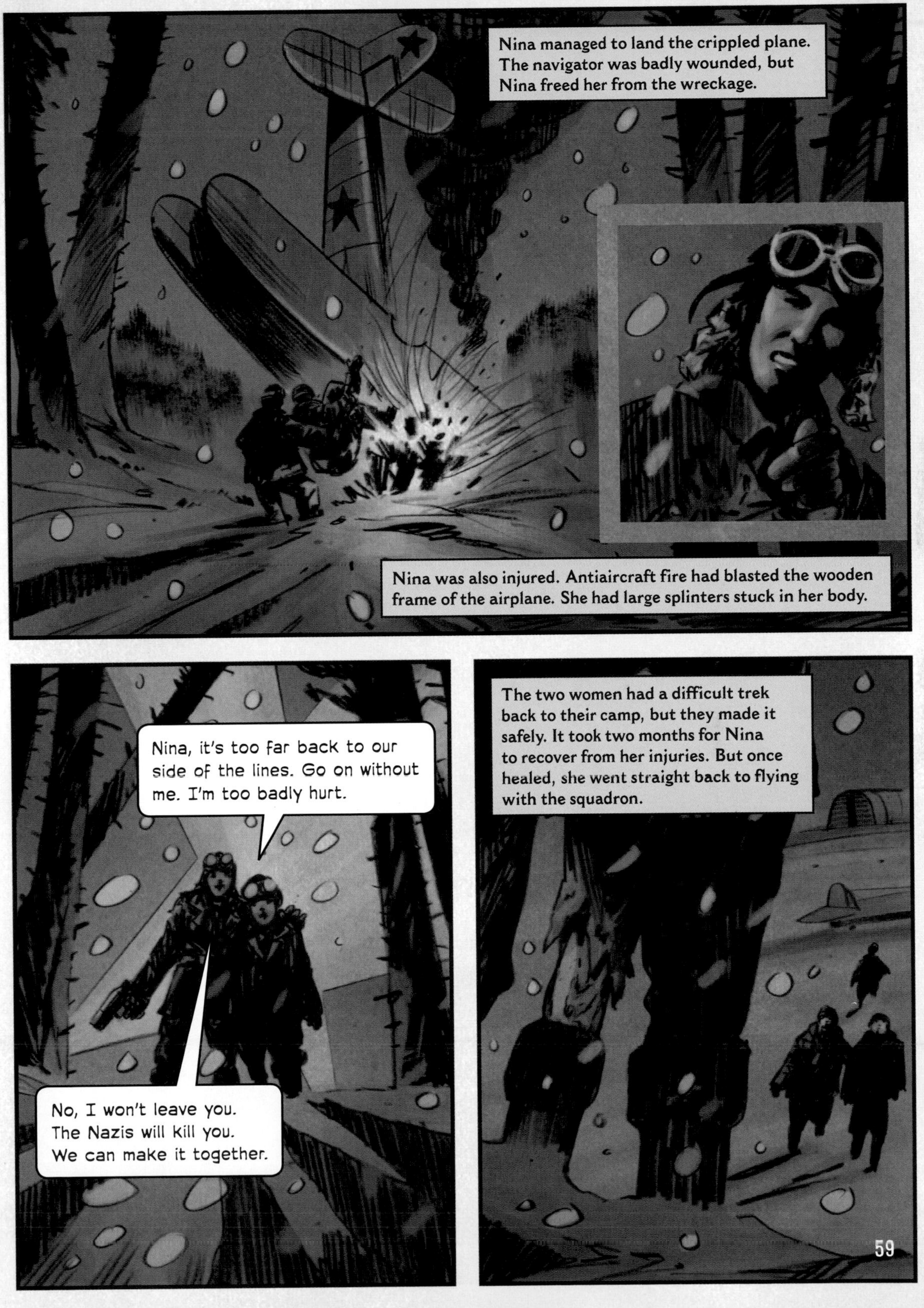
Nina managed to land the crippled plane. The navigator was badly wounded, but Nina freed her from the wreckage.
Nina was also injured. Antiaircraft fire had blasted the wooden frame of the airplane. She had large splinters stuck in her body.
Nina, it's too far back to our side of the lines. Go on without me. I'm too badly hurt.
No, I won't leave you. The Nazis will kill you. We can make it together.
The two women had a difficult trek back to their camp, but they made it safely. It took two months for Nina to recover from her injuries. But once healed, she went straight back to flying with the squadron.

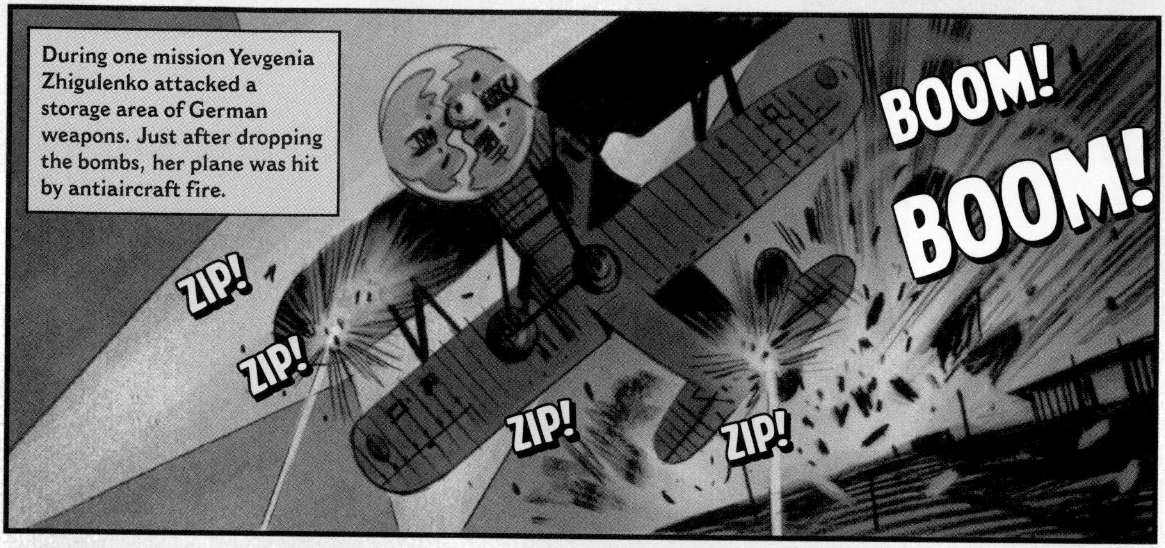
During one mission Yevgenia Zhigulenko attacked a storage area of German weapons. Just after dropping the bombs, her plane was hit by antiaircraft fire.
BOOM!
BOOM!
ZIP!
ZIP!
ZIP!
ZIP!

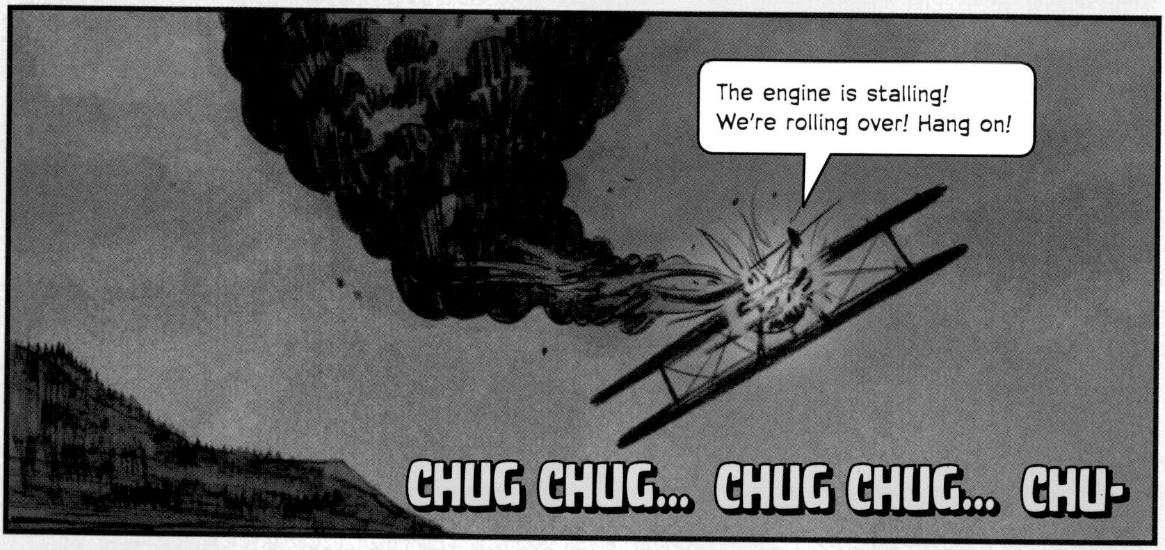
The engine is stalling! We're rolling over! Hang on!
CHUG CHUG... CHUG CHUG... CHU-

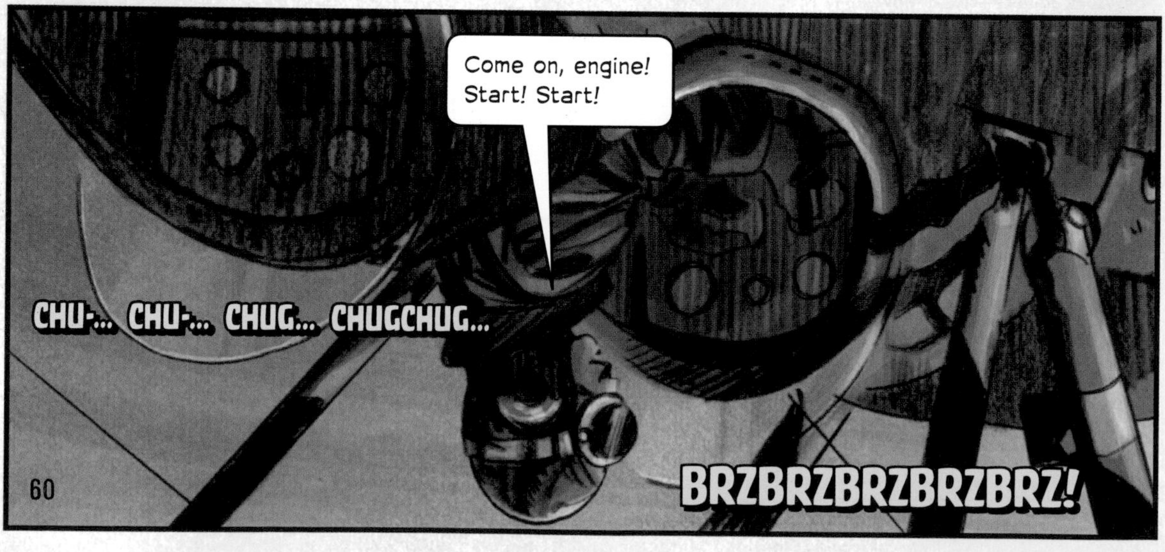
Come on, engine! Start! Start!
CHU-... CHU-... CHUG... CHUGCHUG...
BRZBRZBRZBRZBRZ!

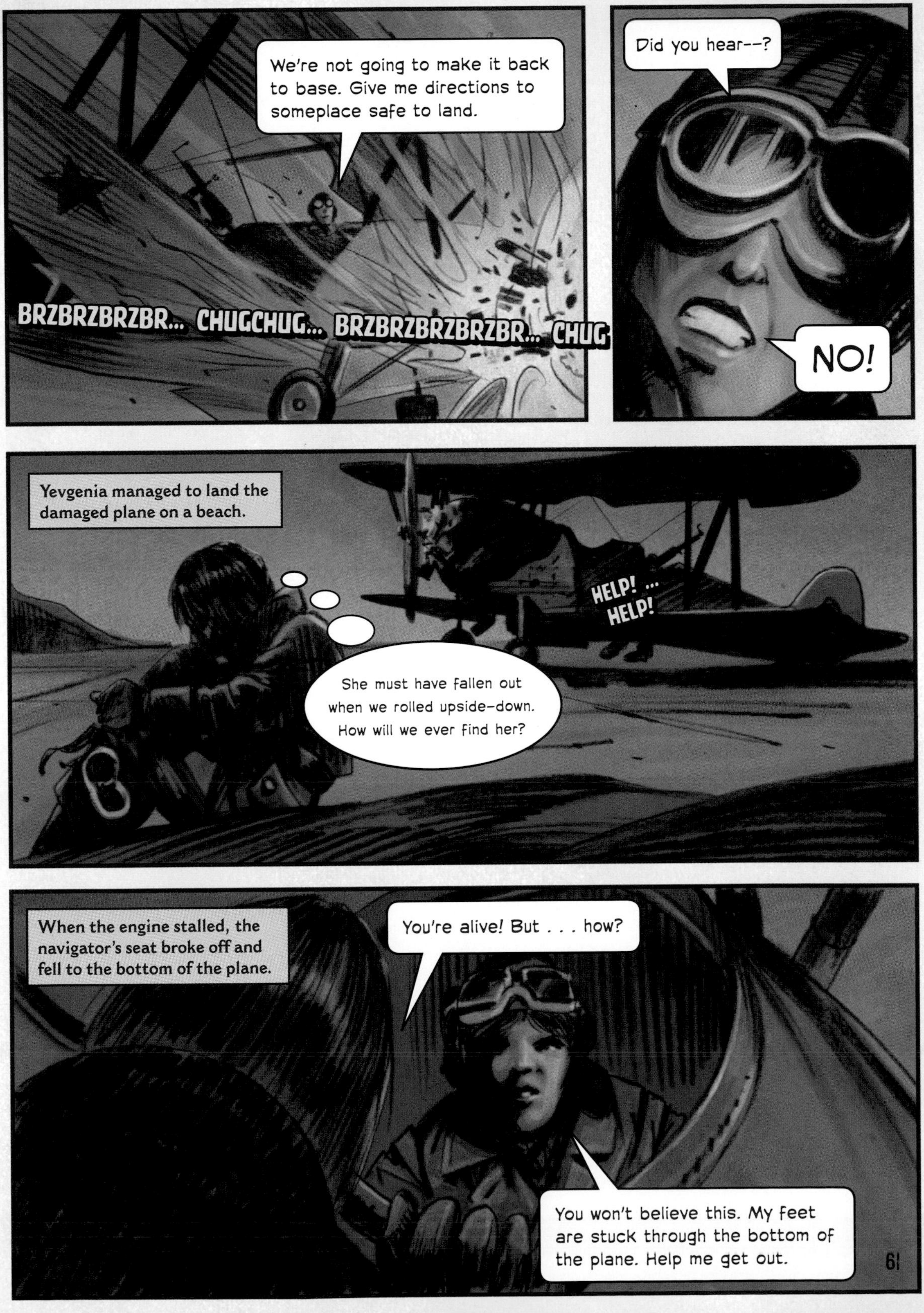
We're not going to make it back to base. Give me directions to someplace safe to land.
BRZBRZBRZBR... CHUGCHUG... BRZBRZBRZBRZBR... CHUG
Did you hear--?
NO!
Yevgenia managed to land the damaged plane on a beach.
HELP! ... HELP!
She must have fallen out when we rolled upside-down. How will we ever find her?
When the engine stalled, the navigator's seat broke off and fell to the bottom of the plane.
You're alive! But . . . how?
You won't believe this. My feet are stuck through the bottom of the plane. Help me get out.

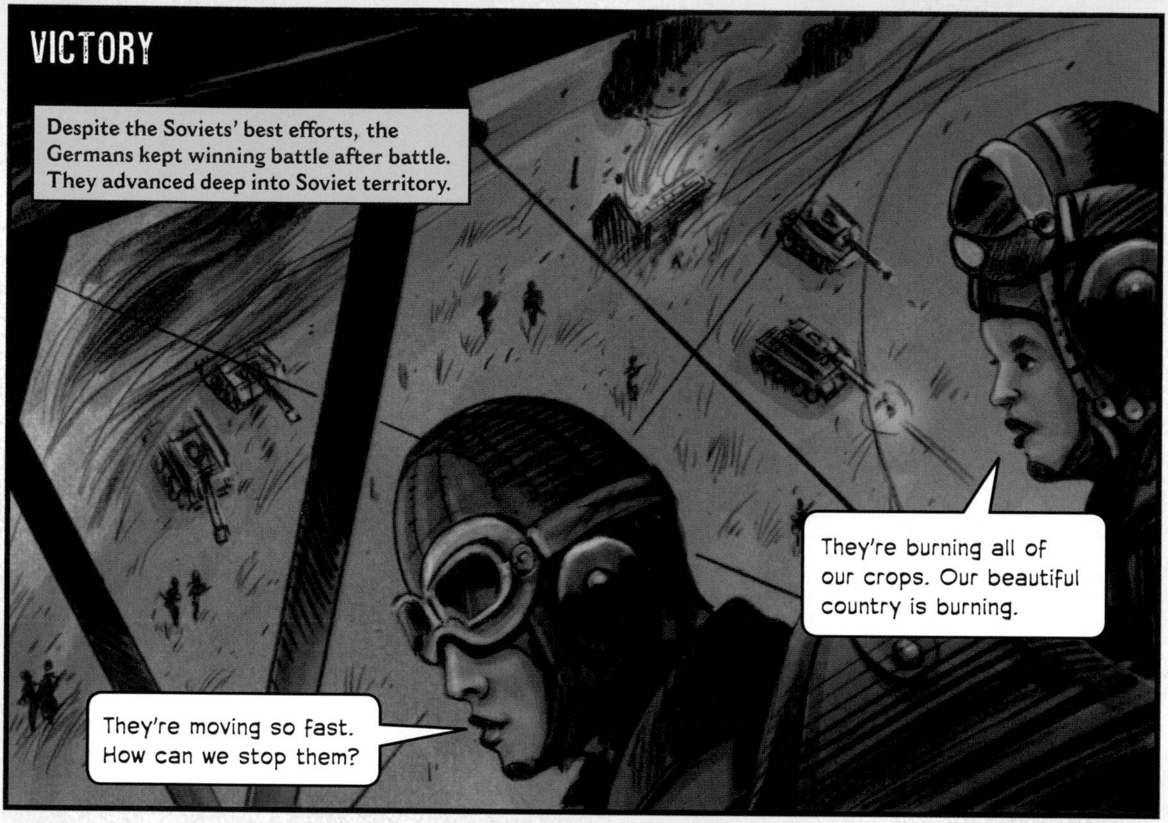
VICTORY
Despite the Soviets' best efforts, the Germans kept winning battle after battle. They advanced deep into Soviet territory.
They're burning all of our crops. Our beautiful country is burning.
They're moving so fast. How can we stop them?

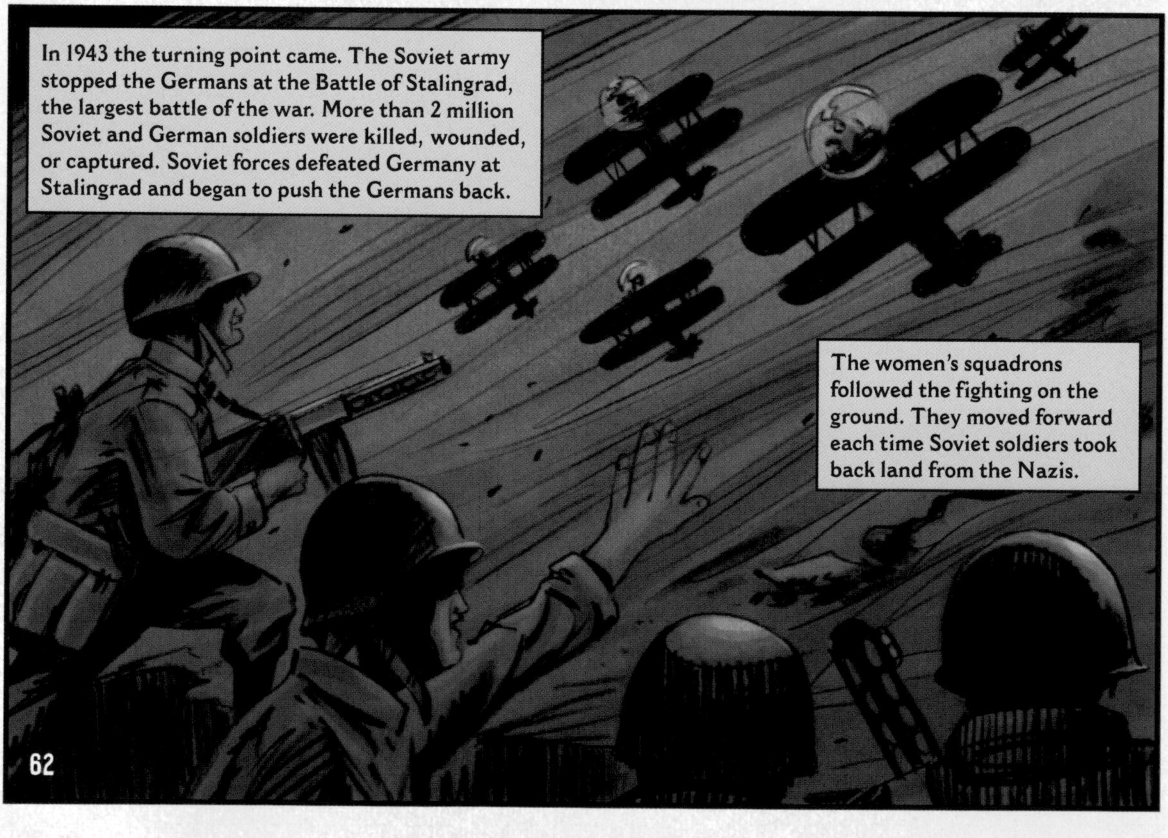
In 1943 the turning point came. The Soviet army stopped the Germans at the Battle of Stalingrad, the largest battle of the war. More than 2 million Soviet and German soldiers were killed, wounded, or captured. Soviet forces defeated Germany at Stalingrad and began to push the Germans back.
The women's squadrons followed the fighting on the ground. They moved forward each time Soviet soldiers took back land from the Nazis.

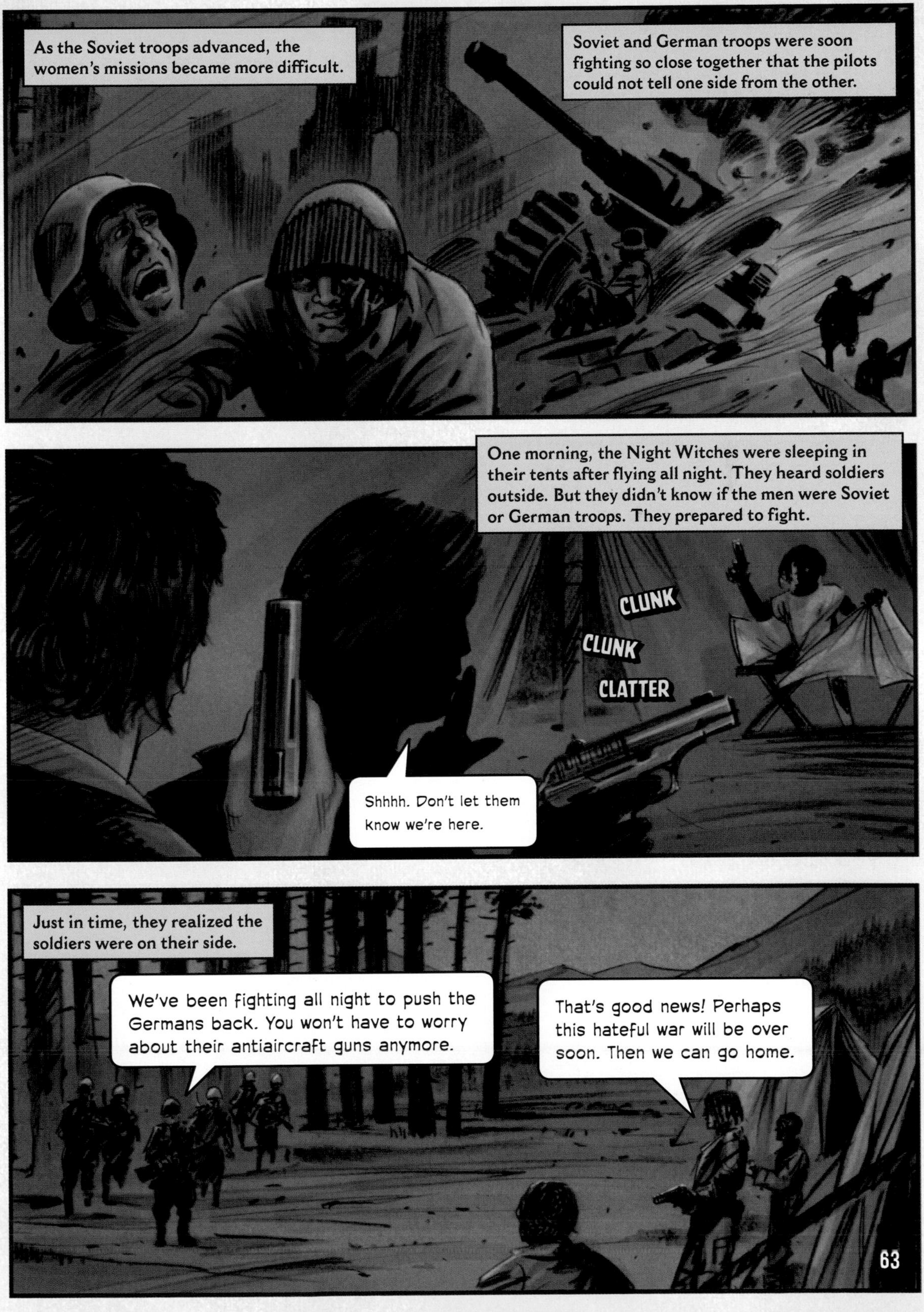
As the Soviet troops advanced, the women's missions became more difficult.
Soviet and German troops were soon fighting so close together that the pilots could not tell one side from the other.
One morning, the Night Witches were sleeping in their tents after flying all night. They heard soldiers outside. But they didn't know if the men were Soviet or German troops. They prepared to fight.
CLUNK
CLUNK
CLATTER
Shhhh. Don't let them know we're here.
Just in time, they realized the soldiers were on their side.
We've been fighting all night to push the Germans back. You won't have to worry about their antiaircraft guns anymore.
That's good news! Perhaps this hateful war will be over soon. Then we can go home.

HEROES OF THE MOTHERLAND

June 24, 1945. It was over. Nazi Germany was defeated. More than 40,000 Soviet soldiers marched through Moscow's Red Square in a great parade to celebrate the end of the war.

Members of the 46th Night Bomber Regiment took part in the parade. Many wore the Hero of the Soviet Union medal, the highest honor anyone in the Soviet military could receive.

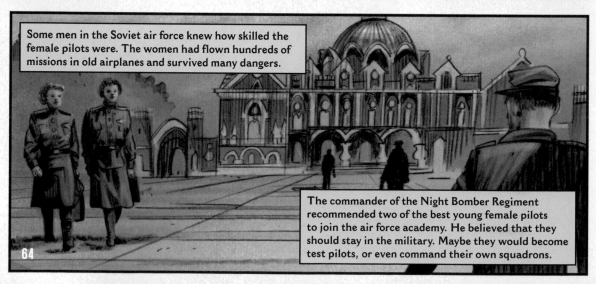

Some men in the Soviet air force knew how skilled the female pilots were. The women had flown hundreds of missions in old airplanes and survived many dangers.

The commander of the Night Bomber Regiment recommended two of the best young female pilots to join the air force academy. He believed that they should stay in the military. Maybe they would become test pilots, or even command their own squadrons.

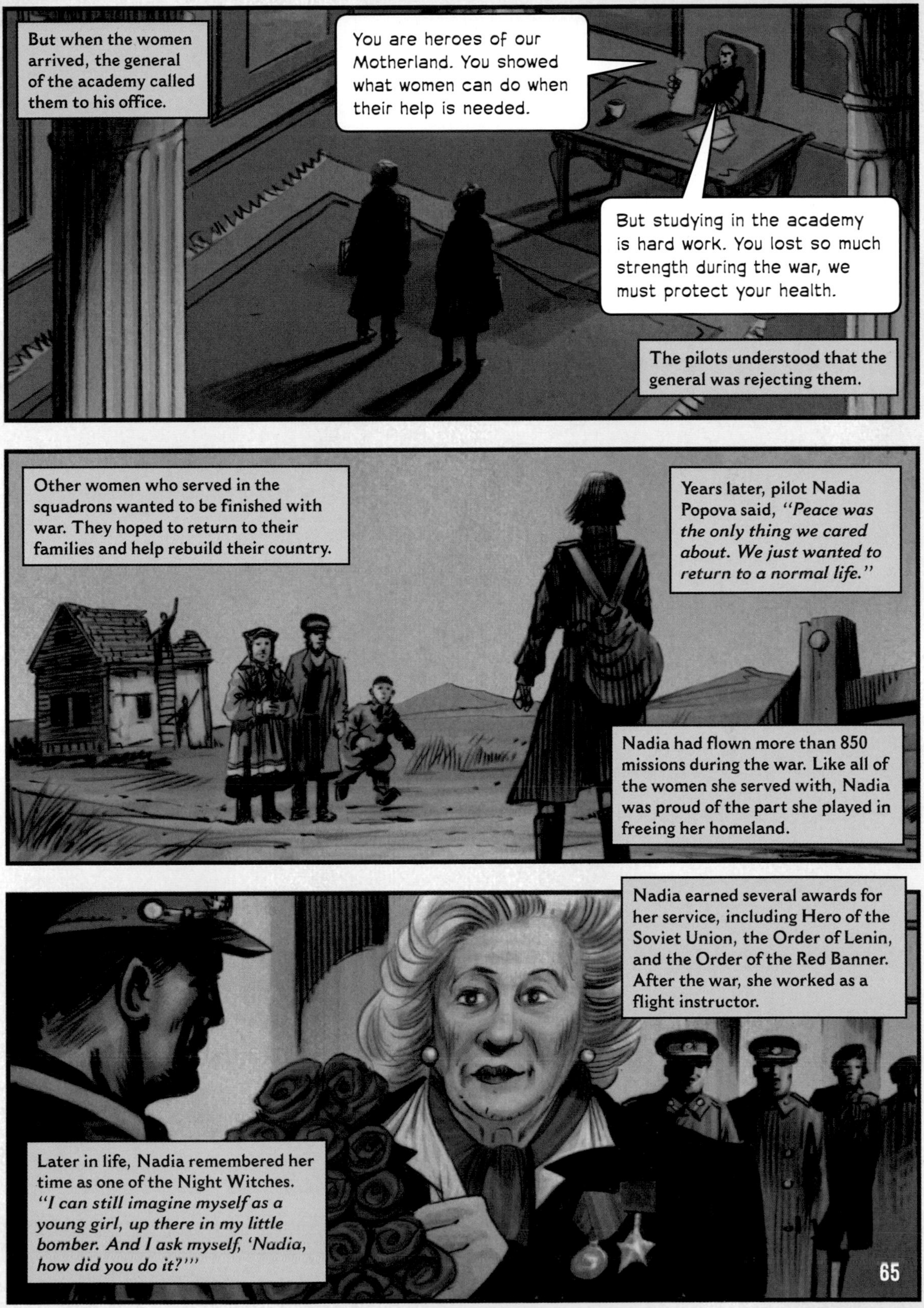
But when the women arrived, the general of the academy called them to his office.
You are heroes of our Motherland. You showed what women can do when their help is needed.
But studying in the academy is hard work. You lost so much strength during the war, we must protect your health.
The pilots understood that the general was rejecting them.
Other women who served in the squadrons wanted to be finished with war. They hoped to return to their families and help rebuild their country.
Years later, pilot Nadia Popova said, *"Peace was the only thing we cared about. We just wanted to return to a normal life."*
Nadia had flown more than 850 missions during the war. Like all of the women she served with, Nadia was proud of the part she played in freeing her homeland.
Nadia earned several awards for her service, including Hero of the Soviet Union, the Order of Lenin, and the Order of the Red Banner. After the war, she worked as a flight instructor.
Later in life, Nadia remembered her time as one of the Night Witches. *"I can still imagine myself as a young girl, up there in my little bomber. And I ask myself, 'Nadia, how did you do it?'"*

THE UNBREAKABLE ZAMPERINI

A WORLD WAR II SURVIVOR'S BRAVE STORY

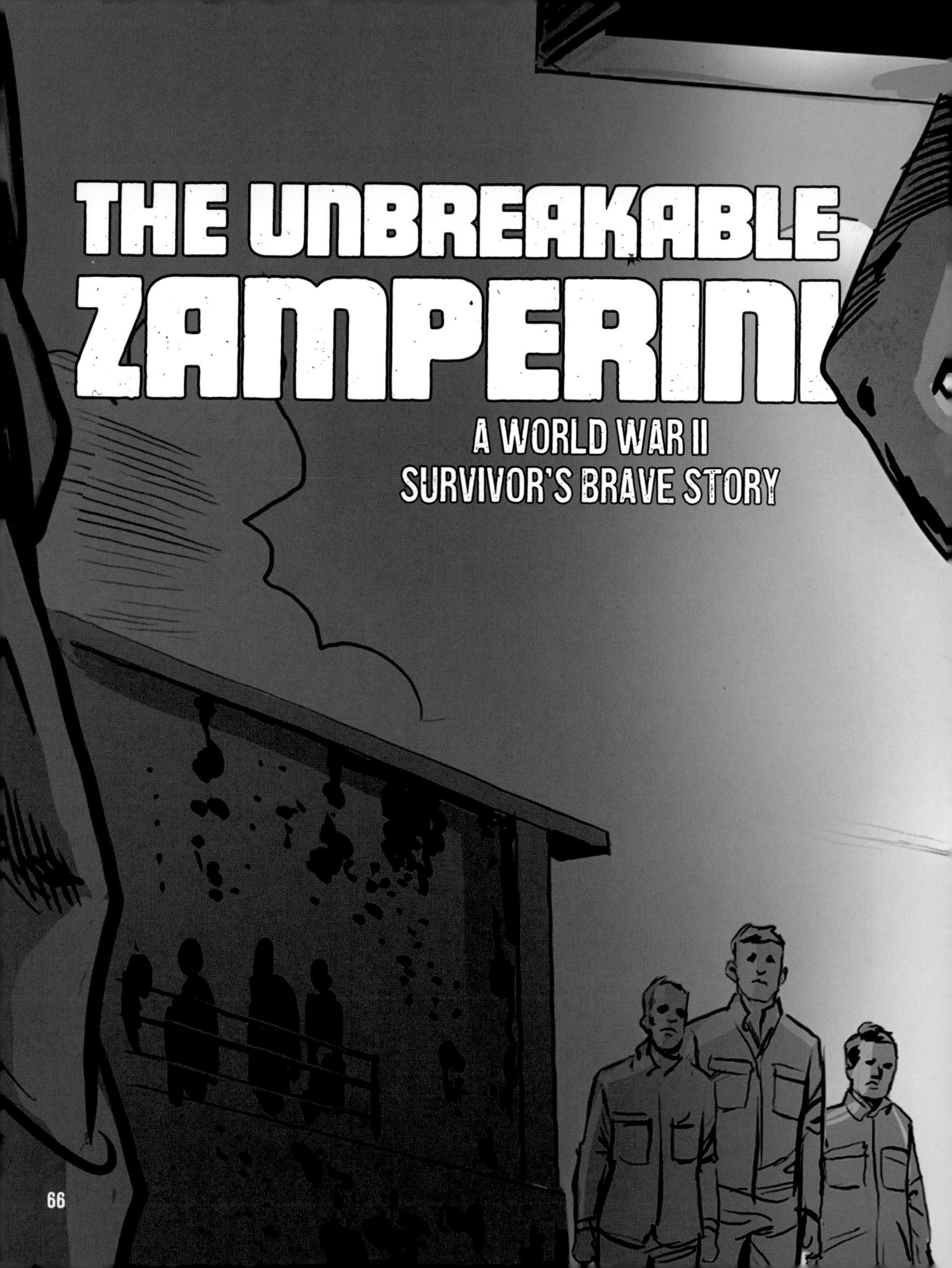

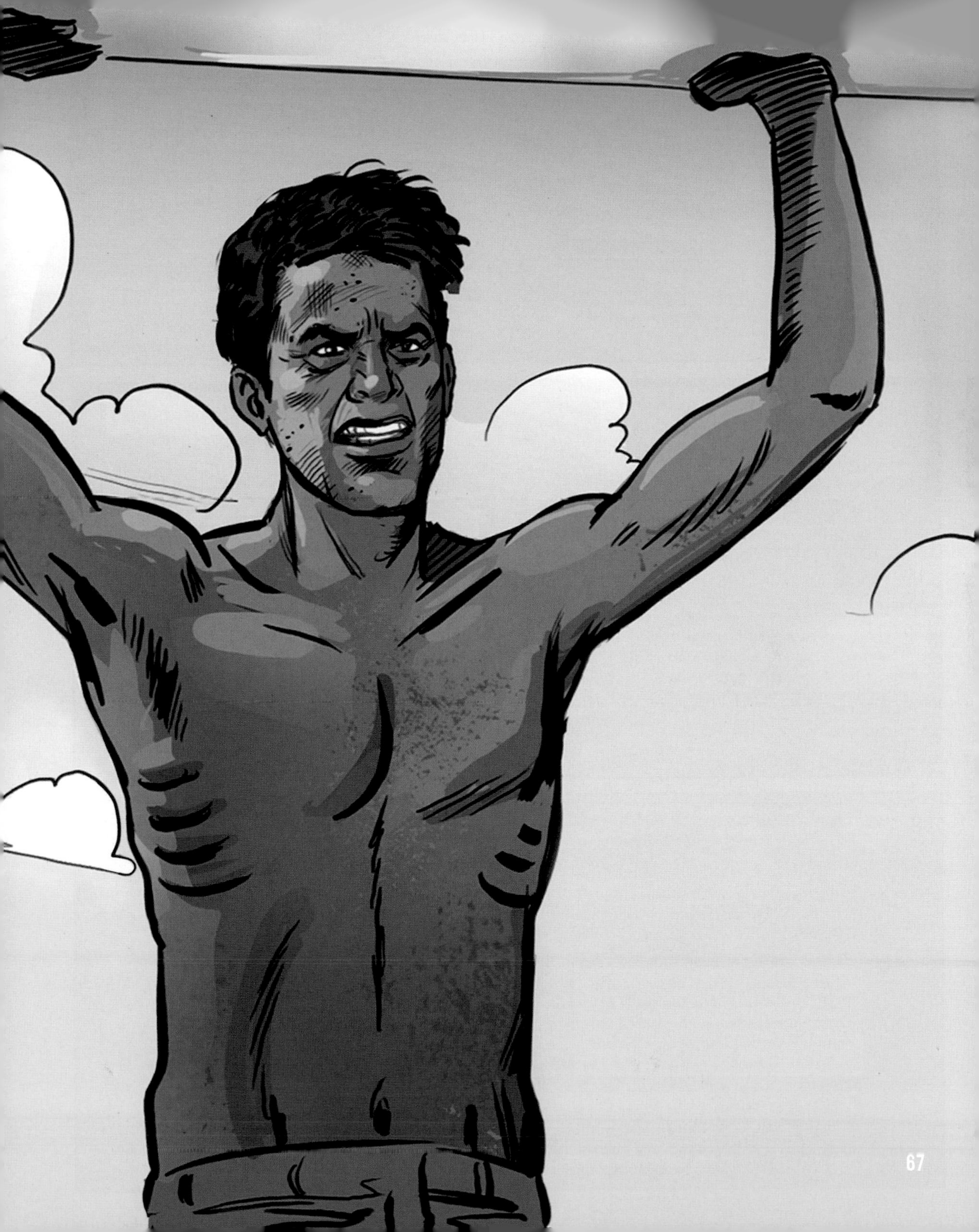

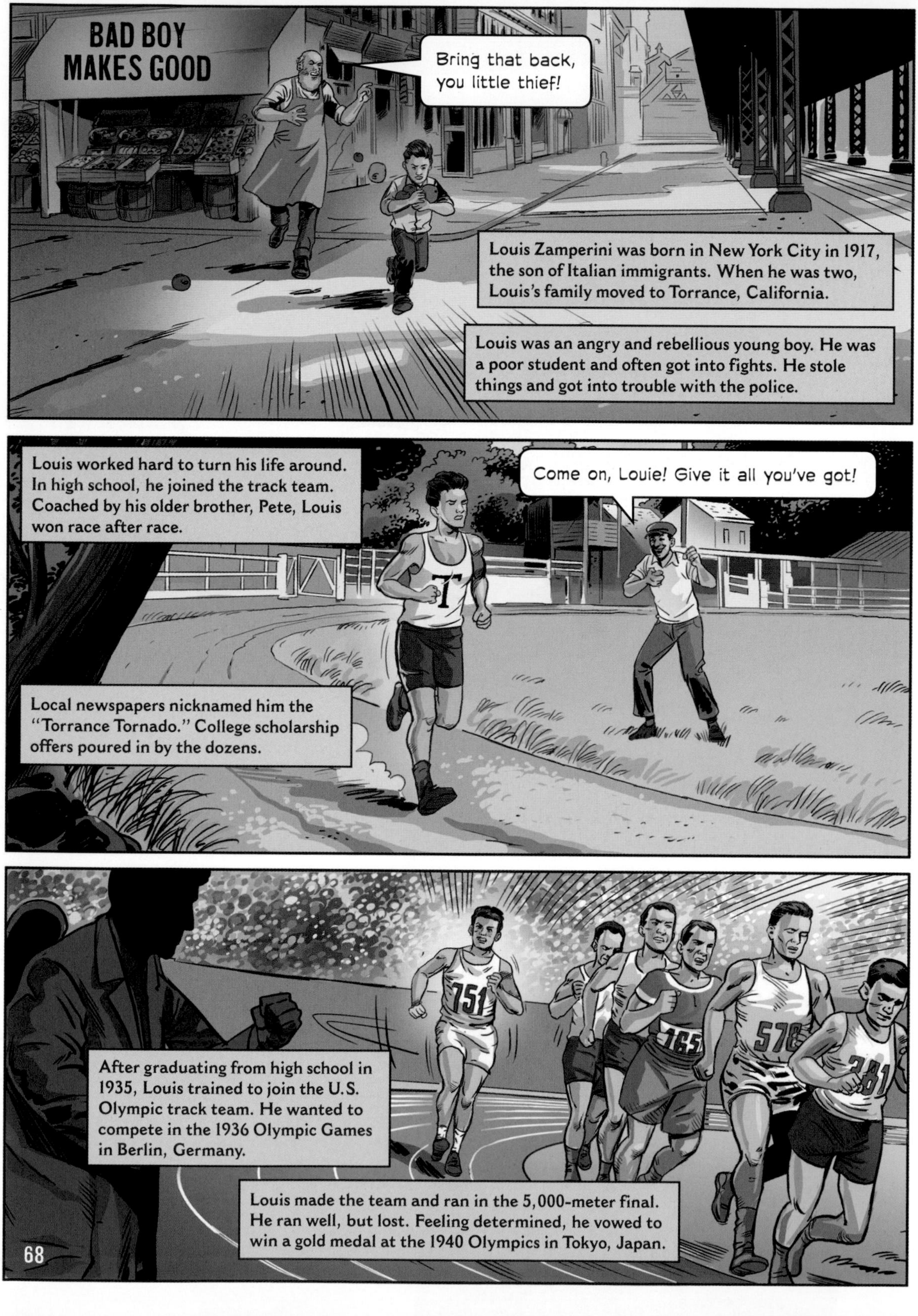
BAD BOY MAKES GOOD
Bring that back, you little thief!
Louis Zamperini was born in New York City in 1917, the son of Italian immigrants. When he was two, Louis's family moved to Torrance, California.
Louis was an angry and rebellious young boy. He was a poor student and often got into fights. He stole things and got into trouble with the police.
Louis worked hard to turn his life around. In high school, he joined the track team. Coached by his older brother, Pete, Louis won race after race.
Come on, Louie! Give it all you've got!
Local newspapers nicknamed him the "Torrance Tornado." College scholarship offers poured in by the dozens.
After graduating from high school in 1935, Louis trained to join the U.S. Olympic track team. He wanted to compete in the 1936 Olympic Games in Berlin, Germany.
Louis made the team and ran in the 5,000-meter final. He ran well, but lost. Feeling determined, he vowed to win a gold medal at the 1940 Olympics in Tokyo, Japan.

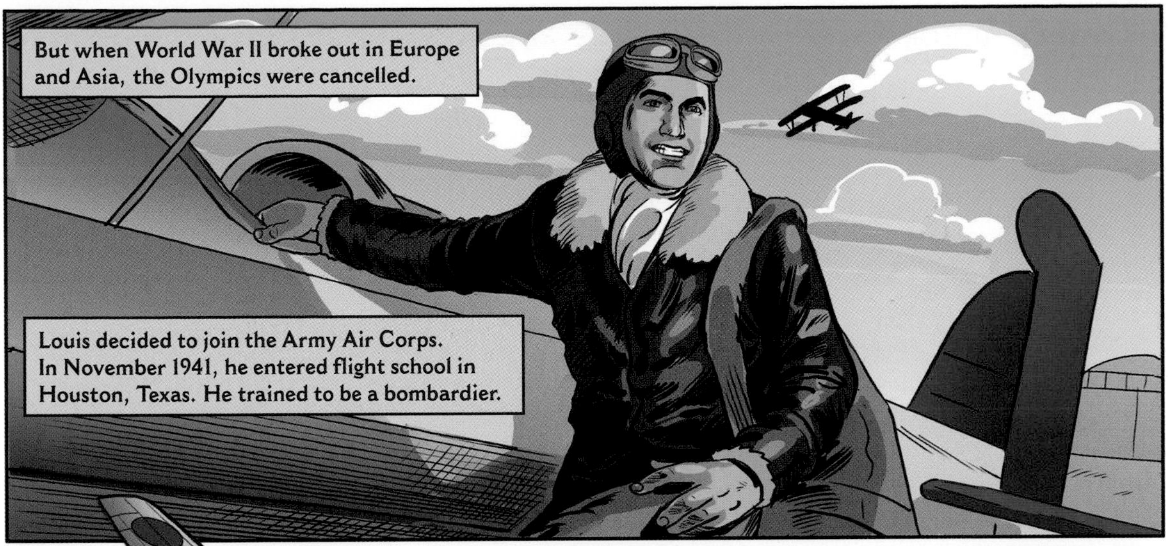
But when World War II broke out in Europe and Asia, the Olympics were cancelled.
Louis decided to join the Army Air Corps. In November 1941, he entered flight school in Houston, Texas. He trained to be a bombardier.

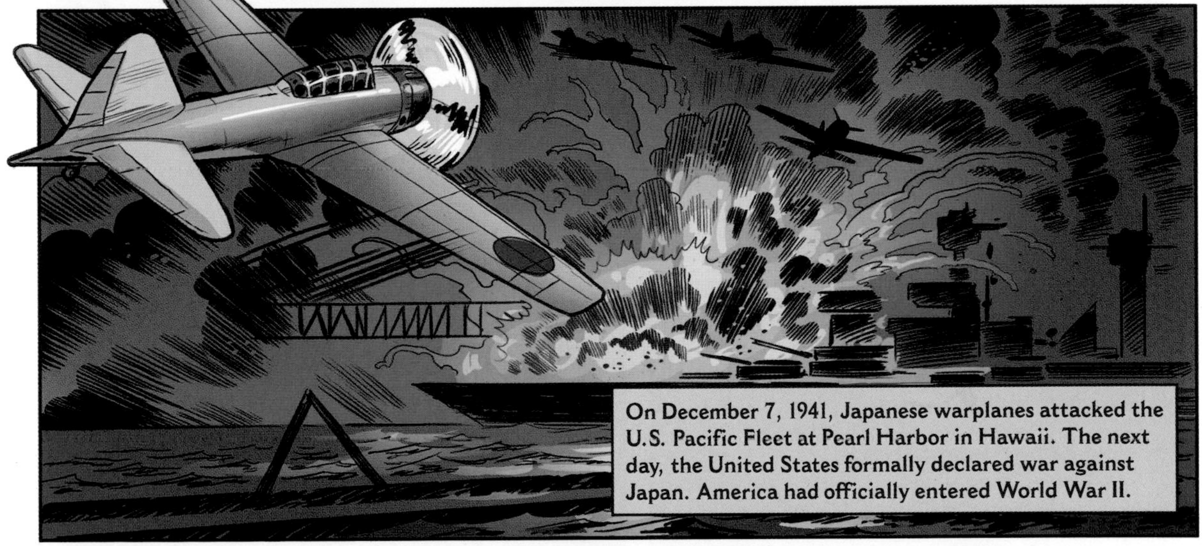
On December 7, 1941, Japanese warplanes attacked the U.S. Pacific Fleet at Pearl Harbor in Hawaii. The next day, the United States formally declared war against Japan. America had officially entered World War II.

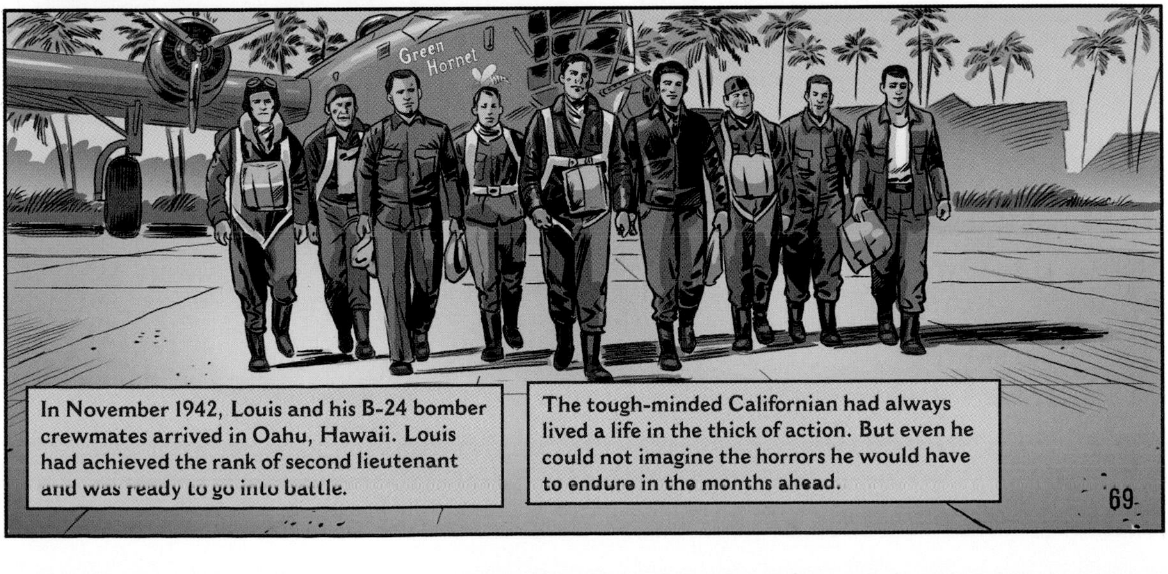
Green Hornet
In November 1942, Louis and his B-24 bomber crewmates arrived in Oahu, Hawaii. Louis had achieved the rank of second lieutenant and was ready to go into battle.
The tough-minded Californian had always lived a life in the thick of action. But even he could not imagine the horrors he would have to endure in the months ahead.

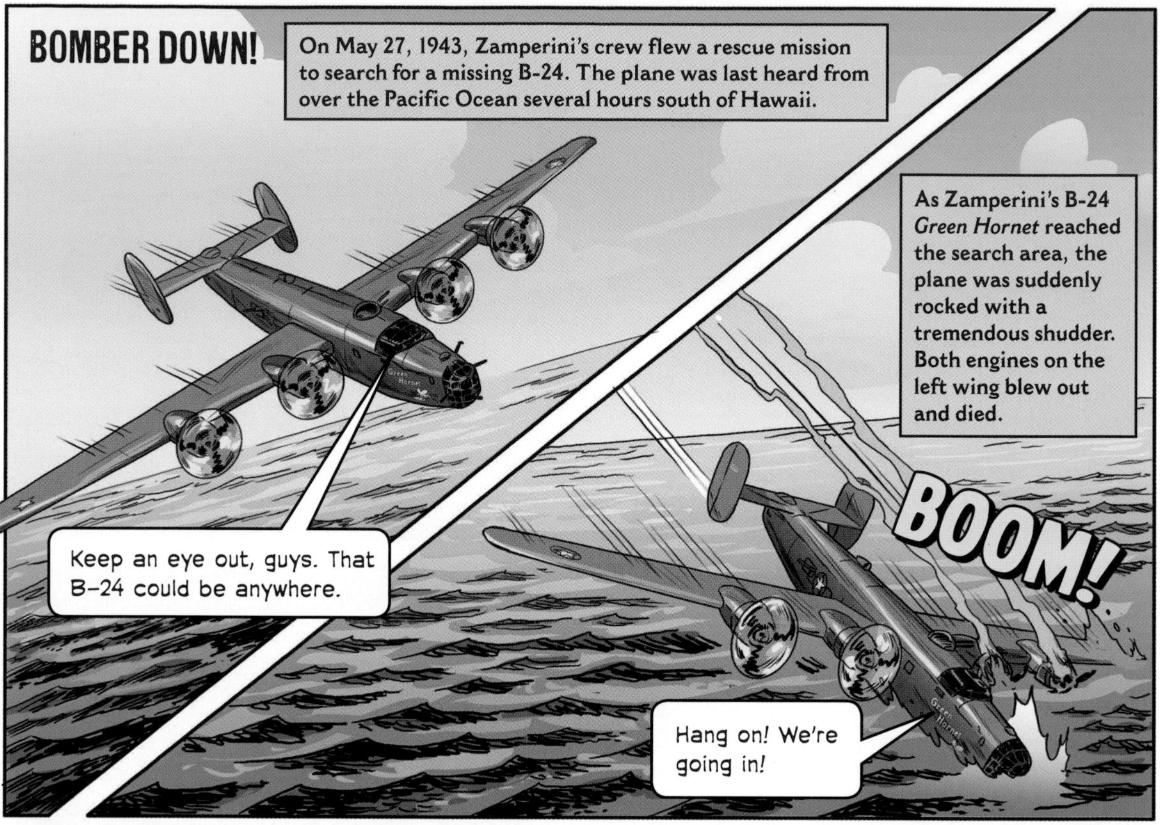
BOMBER DOWN!
On May 27, 1943, Zamperini's crew flew a rescue mission to search for a missing B-24. The plane was last heard from over the Pacific Ocean several hours south of Hawaii.
Keep an eye out, guys. That B-24 could be anywhere.
As Zamperini's B-24 *Green Hornet* reached the search area, the plane was suddenly rocked with a tremendous shudder. Both engines on the left wing blew out and died.
BOOM!
Hang on! We're going in!

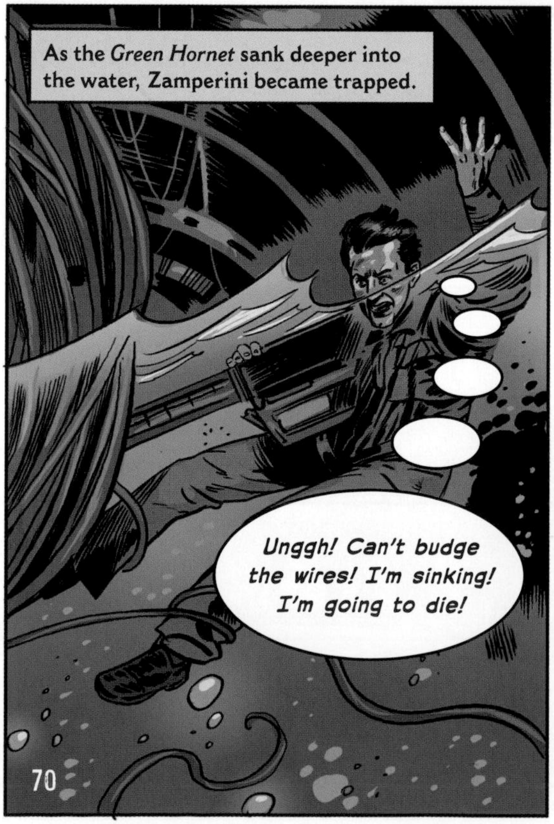
As the *Green Hornet* sank deeper into the water, Zamperini became trapped.
Ungh! Can't budge the wires! I'm sinking! I'm going to die!

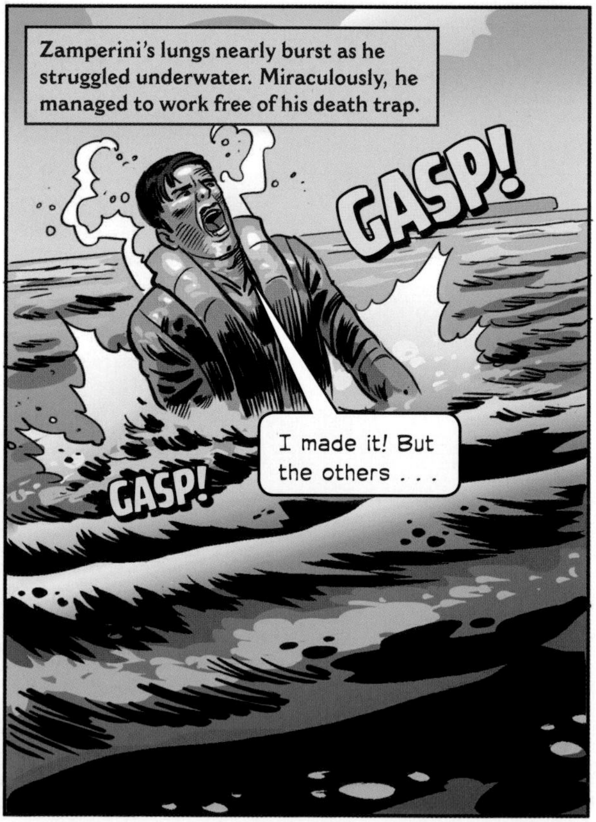
Zamperini's lungs nearly burst as he struggled underwater. Miraculously, he managed to work free of his death trap.
GASP!
I made it! But the others . . .
GASP!

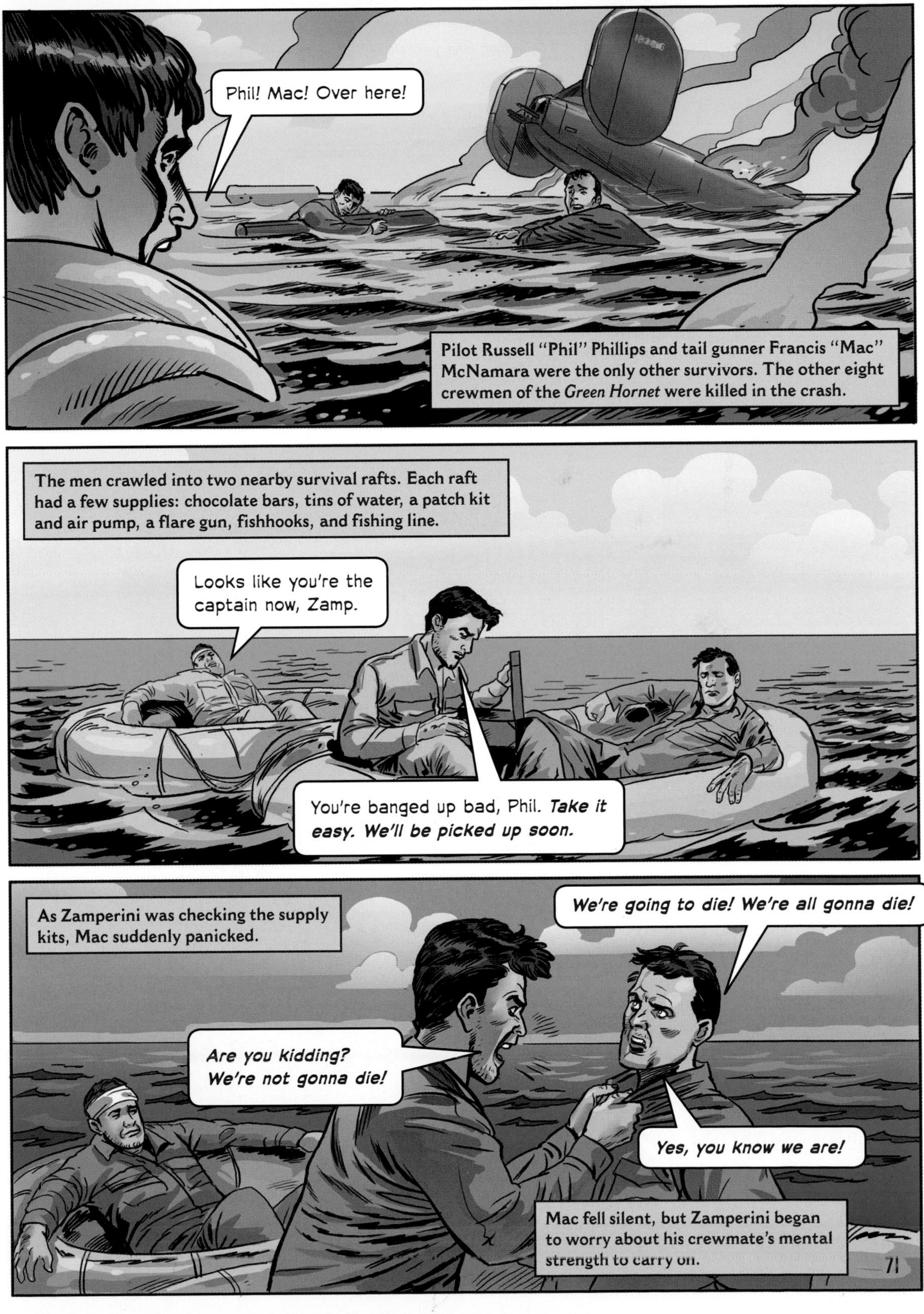
Phil! Mac! Over here!
Pilot Russell "Phil" Phillips and tail gunner Francis "Mac" McNamara were the only other survivors. The other eight crewmen of the Green Hornet were killed in the crash.
The men crawled into two nearby survival rafts. Each raft had a few supplies: chocolate bars, tins of water, a patch kit and air pump, a flare gun, fishhooks, and fishing line.
Looks like you're the captain now, Zamp.
You're banged up bad, Phil. Take it easy. We'll be picked up soon.
As Zamperini was checking the supply kits, Mac suddenly panicked.
We're going to die! We're all gonna die!
Are you kidding? We're not gonna die!
Yes, you know we are!
Mac fell silent, but Zamperini began to worry about his crewmate's mental strength to carry on.

The next morning, Zamperini discovered that the chocolate bars were gone. Mac had eaten them all.

What did you do? What did you do?!

I-- I--

We're three together-- we've got to work together!

By the third day, the three men had no food. And they had already drunk their small supply of water.

At the first rainfall, Zamperini used the canvas air pump cases to collect and save the water.

See how it's done, Mac? Nice and easy . . . so we don't lose a drop.

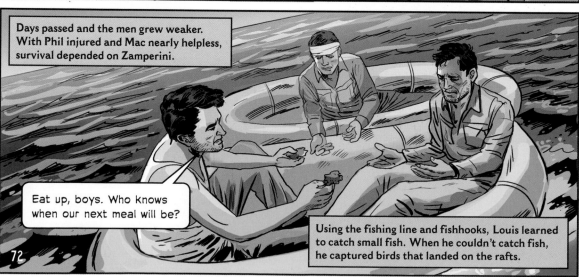

Days passed and the men grew weaker. With Phil injured and Mac nearly helpless, survival depended on Zamperini.

Eat up, boys. Who knows when our next meal will be?

Using the fishing line and fishhooks, Louis learned to catch small fish. When he couldn't catch fish, he captured birds that landed on the rafts.

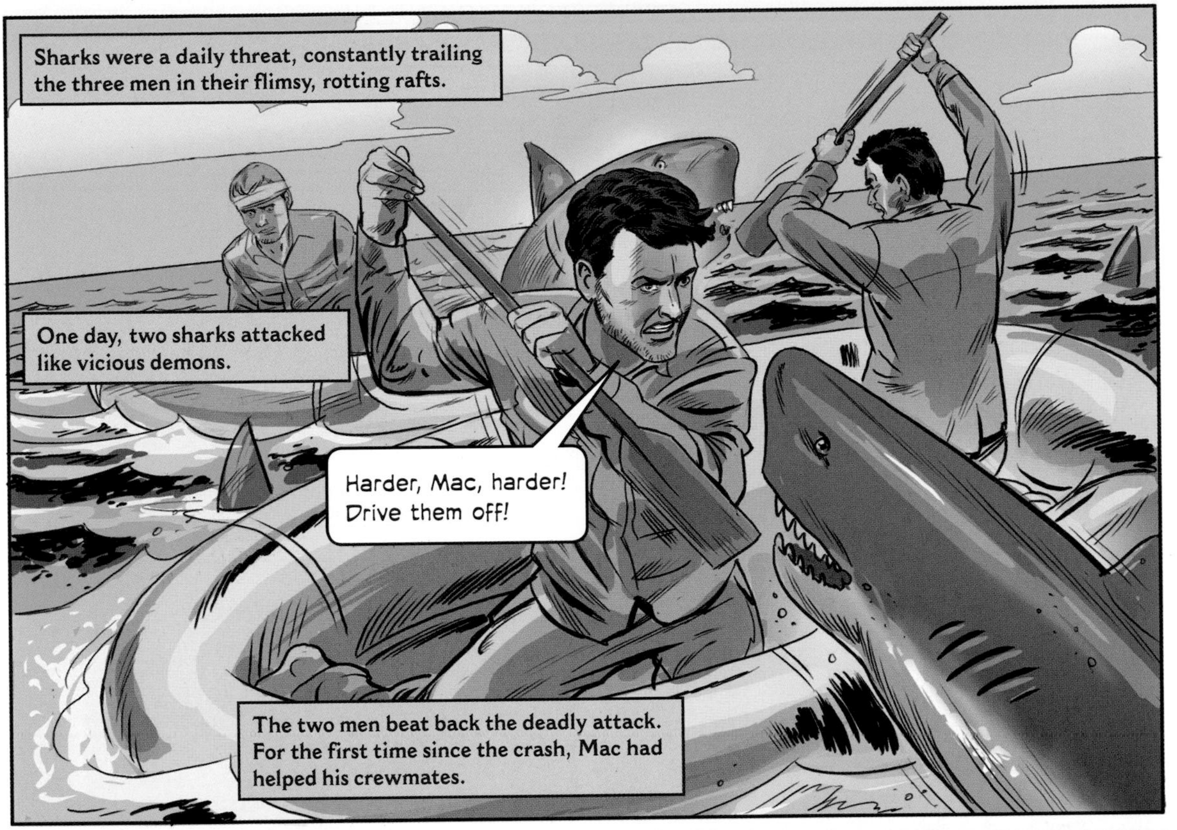
Sharks were a daily threat, constantly trailing the three men in their flimsy, rotting rafts.
One day, two sharks attacked like vicious demons.
Harder, Mac, harder! Drive them off!
The two men beat back the deadly attack. For the first time since the crash, Mac had helped his crewmates.

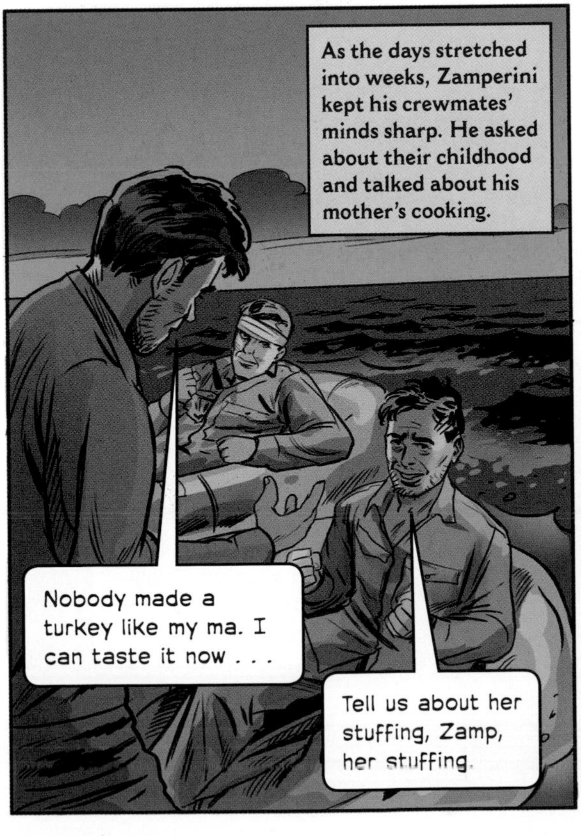
As the days stretched into weeks, Zamperini kept his crewmates' minds sharp. He asked about their childhood and talked about his mother's cooking.
Nobody made a turkey like my ma. I can taste it now . . .
Tell us about her stuffing, Zamp, her stuffing.

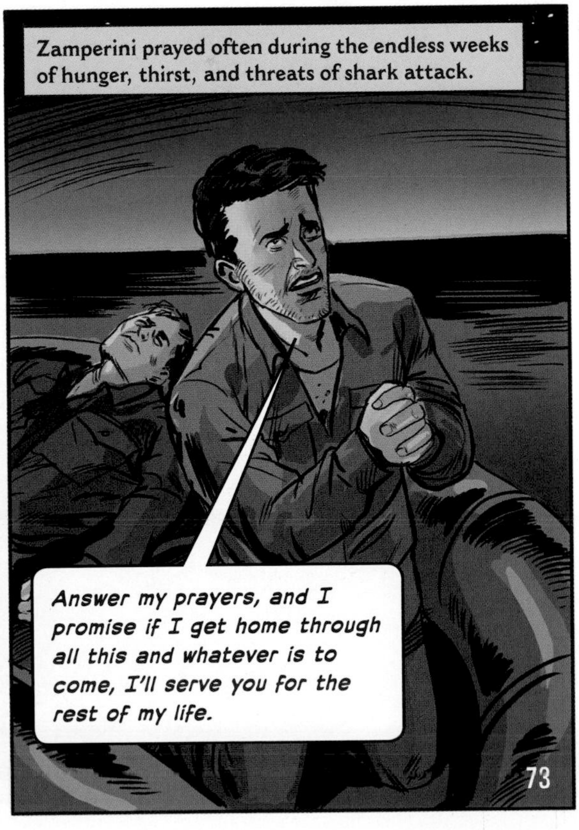
Zamperini prayed often during the endless weeks of hunger, thirst, and threats of shark attack.
Answer my prayers, and I promise if I get home through all this and whatever is to come, I'll serve you for the rest of my life.

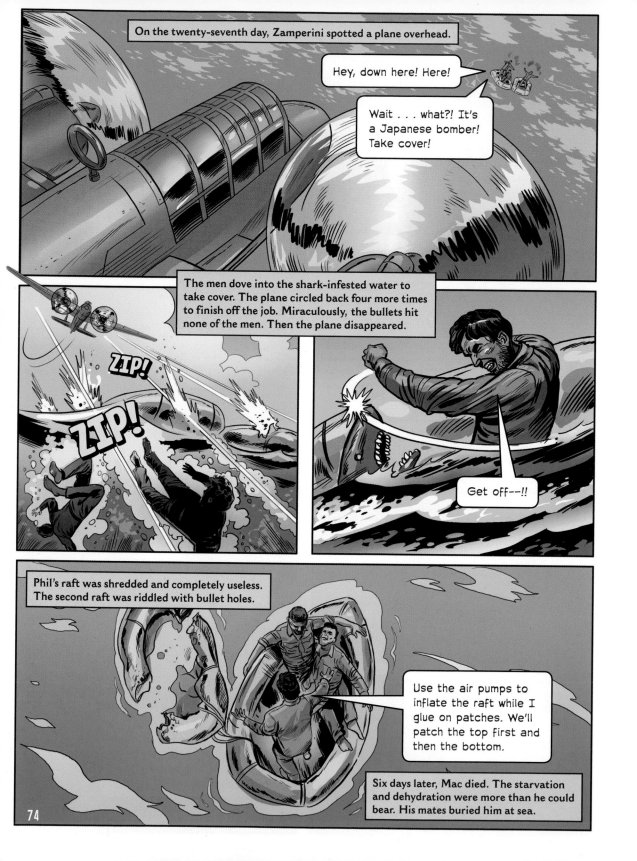

On the twenty-seventh day, Zamperini spotted a plane overhead.

Hey, down here! Here!

Wait . . . what?! It's a Japanese bomber! Take cover!

The men dove into the shark-infested water to take cover. The plane circled back four more times to finish off the job. Miraculously, the bullets hit none of the men. Then the plane disappeared.

ZIP!

ZIP!

Get off--!!

Phil's raft was shredded and completely useless. The second raft was riddled with bullet holes.

Use the air pumps to inflate the raft while I glue on patches. We'll patch the top first and then the bottom.

Six days later, Mac died. The starvation and dehydration were more than he could bear. His mates buried him at sea.

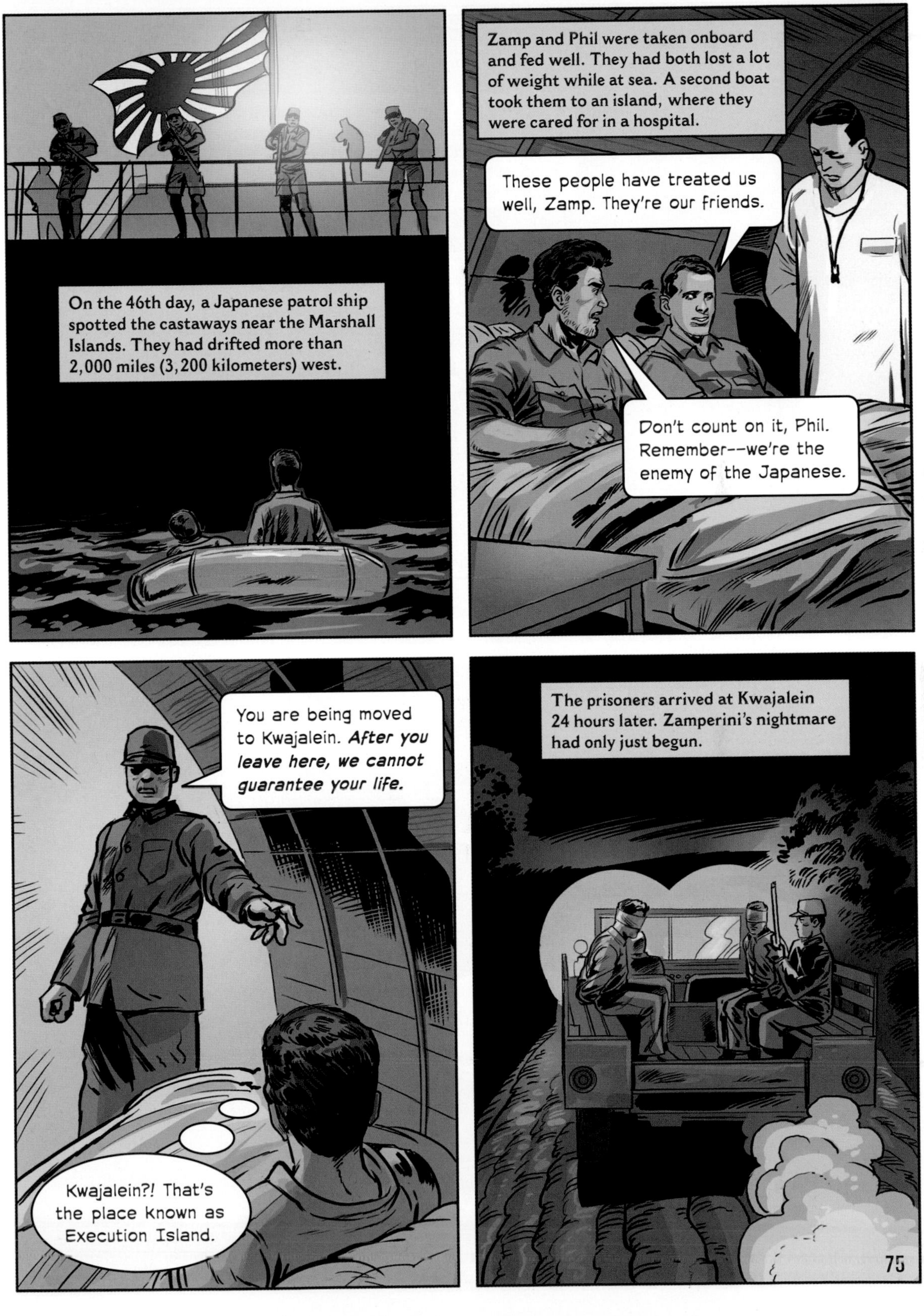
On the 46th day, a Japanese patrol ship spotted the castaways near the Marshall Islands. They had drifted more than 2,000 miles (3,200 kilometers) west.
Zamp and Phil were taken onboard and fed well. They had both lost a lot of weight while at sea. A second boat took them to an island, where they were cared for in a hospital.
These people have treated us well, Zamp. They're our friends.
Don't count on it, Phil. Remember--we're the enemy of the Japanese.
You are being moved to Kwajalein. *After you leave here, we cannot guarantee your life.*
Kwajalein?! That's the place known as Execution Island.
The prisoners arrived at Kwajalein 24 hours later. Zamperini's nightmare had only just begun.

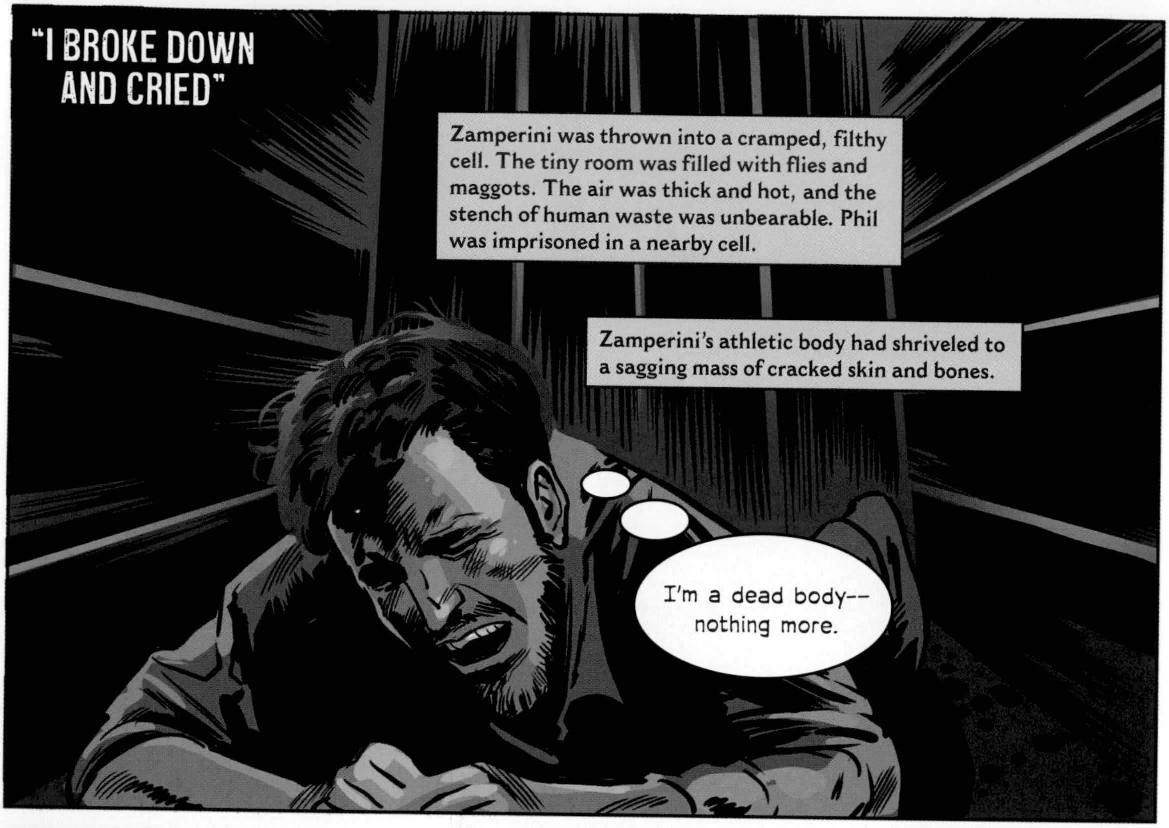
"I BROKE DOWN AND CRIED"
Zamperini was thrown into a cramped, filthy cell. The tiny room was filled with flies and maggots. The air was thick and hot, and the stench of human waste was unbearable. Phil was imprisoned in a nearby cell.
Zamperini's athletic body had shriveled to a sagging mass of cracked skin and bones.
I'm a dead body--nothing more.

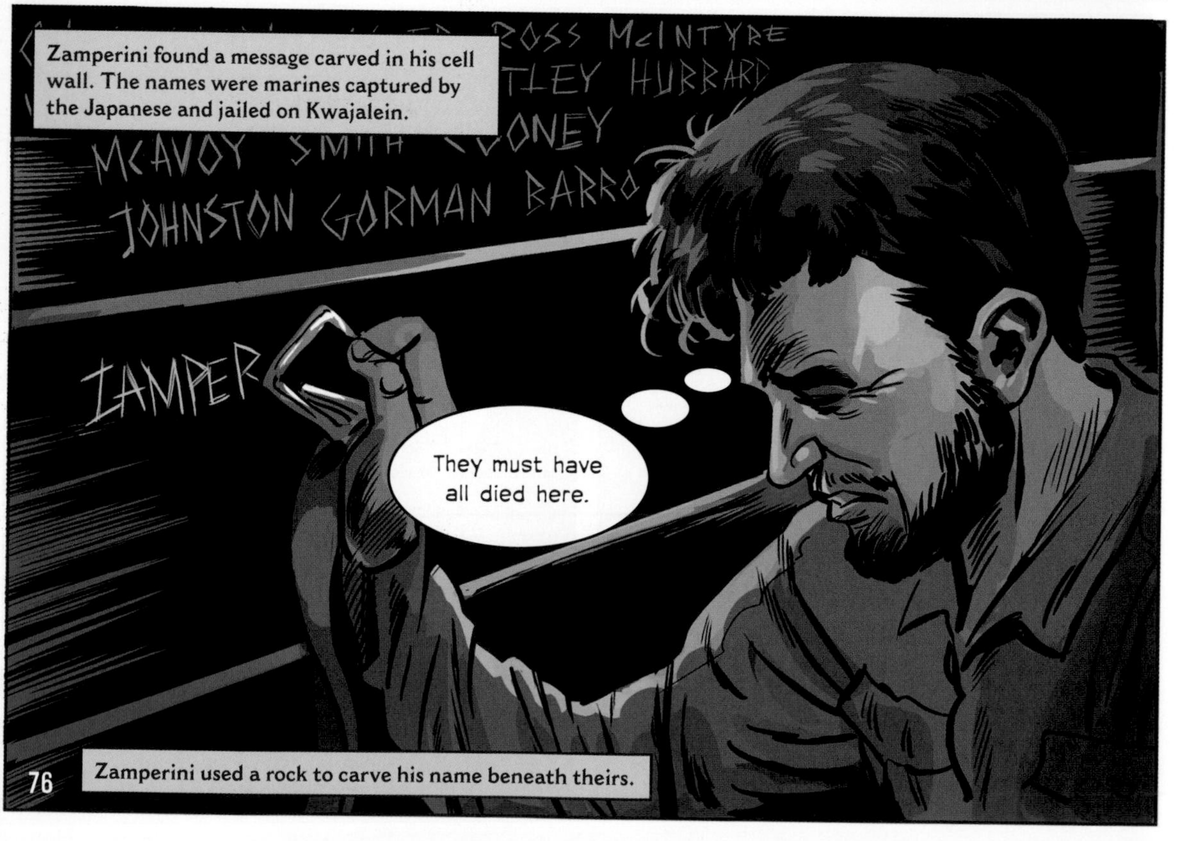
Zamperini found a message carved in his cell wall. The names were marines captured by the Japanese and jailed on Kwajalein.
McAVOY SMITH
JOHNSTON GORMAN
ZAMPER
They must have all died here.
Zamperini used a rock to carve his name beneath theirs.

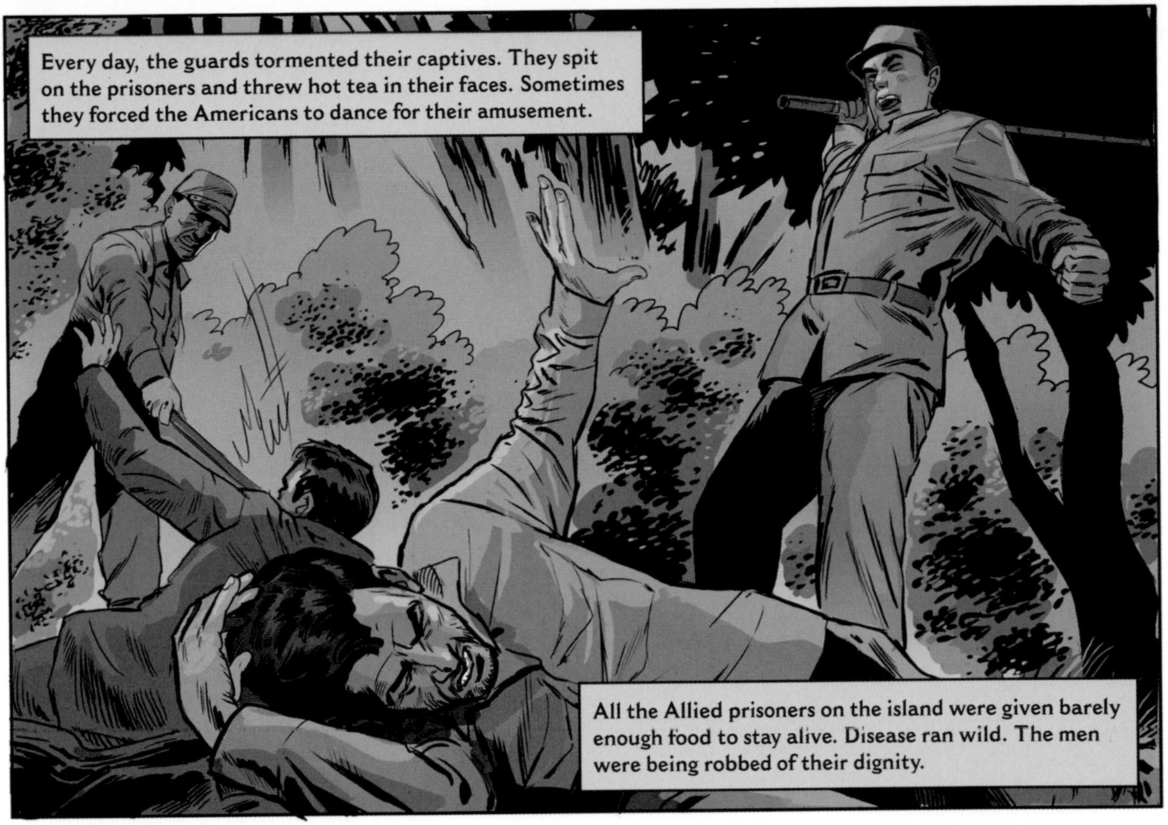
Every day, the guards tormented their captives. They spit on the prisoners and threw hot tea in their faces. Sometimes they forced the Americans to dance for their amusement.
All the Allied prisoners on the island were given barely enough food to stay alive. Disease ran wild. The men were being robbed of their dignity.

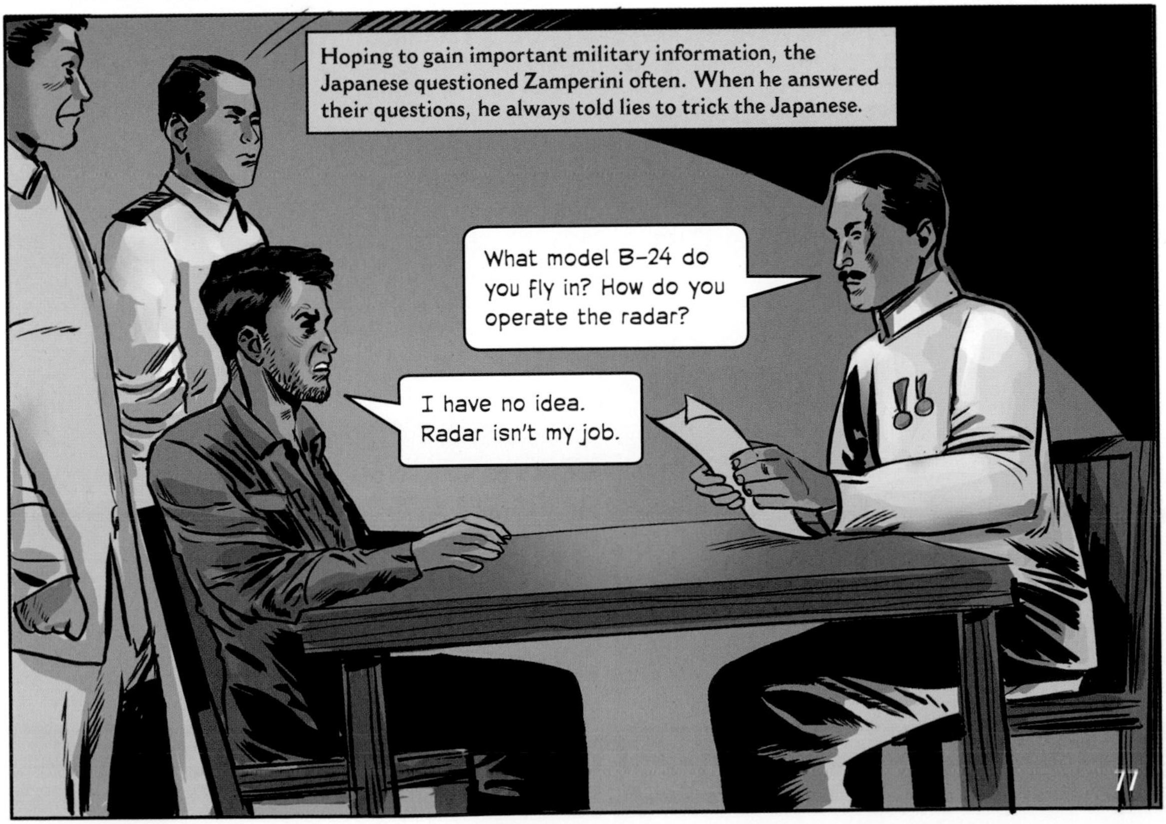
Hoping to gain important military information, the Japanese questioned Zamperini often. When he answered their questions, he always told lies to trick the Japanese.
What model B-24 do you fly in? How do you operate the radar?
I have no idea. Radar isn't my job.

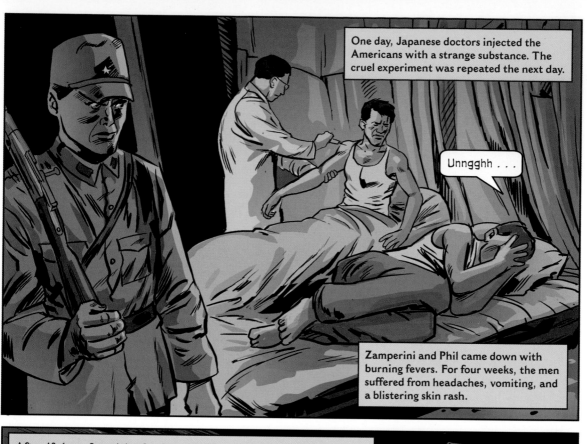

One day, Japanese doctors injected the Americans with a strange substance. The cruel experiment was repeated the next day.

Unngghh . . .

Zamperini and Phil came down with burning fevers. For four weeks, the men suffered from headaches, vomiting, and a blistering skin rash.

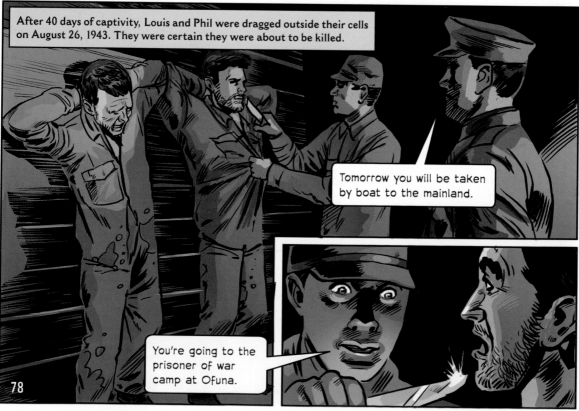

After 40 days of captivity, Louis and Phil were dragged outside their cells on August 26, 1943. They were certain they were about to be killed.

Tomorrow you will be taken by boat to the mainland.

You're going to the prisoner of war camp at Ofuna.

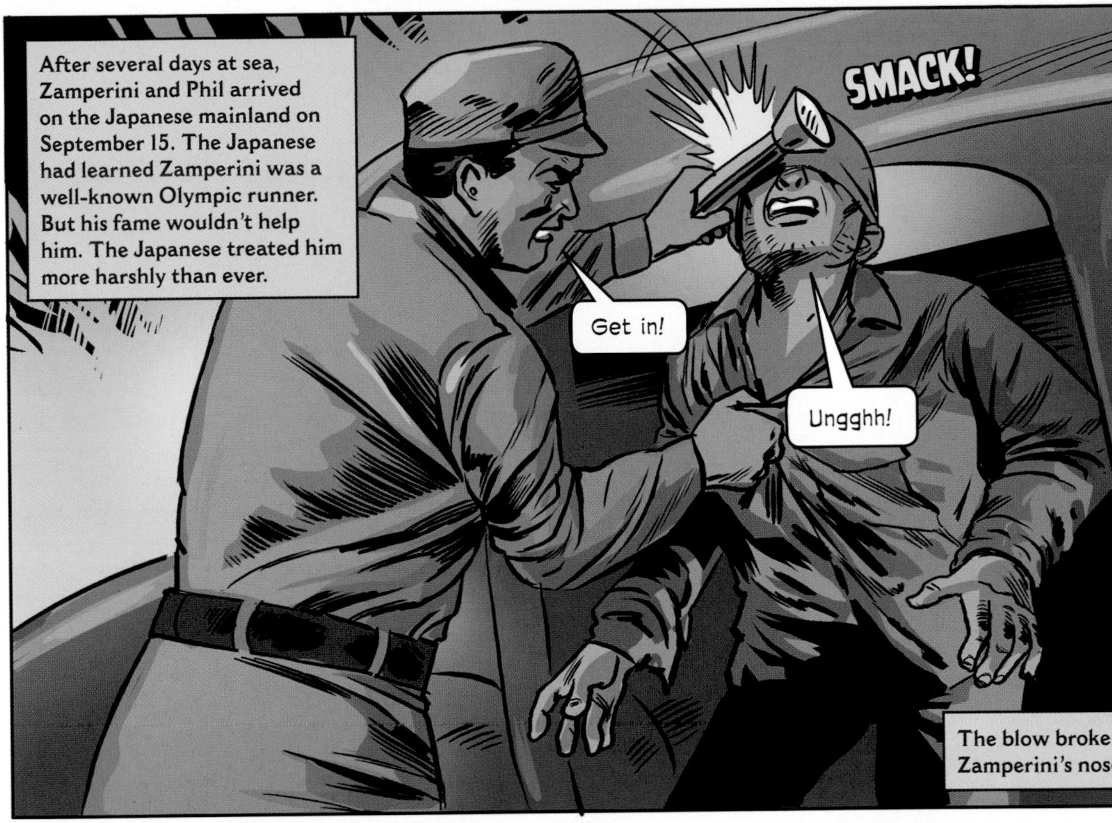
After several days at sea, Zamperini and Phil arrived on the Japanese mainland on September 15. The Japanese had learned Zamperini was a well-known Olympic runner. But his fame wouldn't help him. The Japanese treated him more harshly than ever.
SMACK!
Get in!
Ungghh!
The blow broke Zamperini's nose.

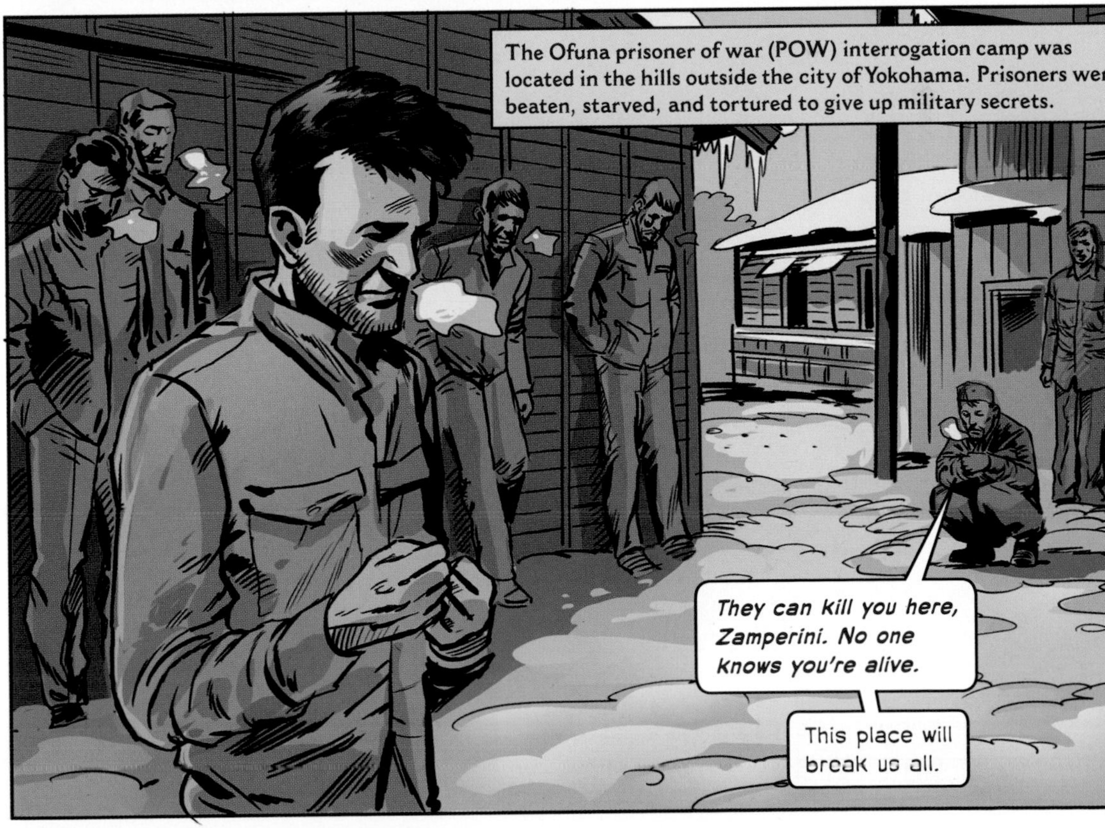
The Ofuna prisoner of war (POW) interrogation camp was located in the hills outside the city of Yokohama. Prisoners were beaten, starved, and tortured to give up military secrets.
They can kill you here, Zamperini. No one knows you're alive.
This place will break us all.

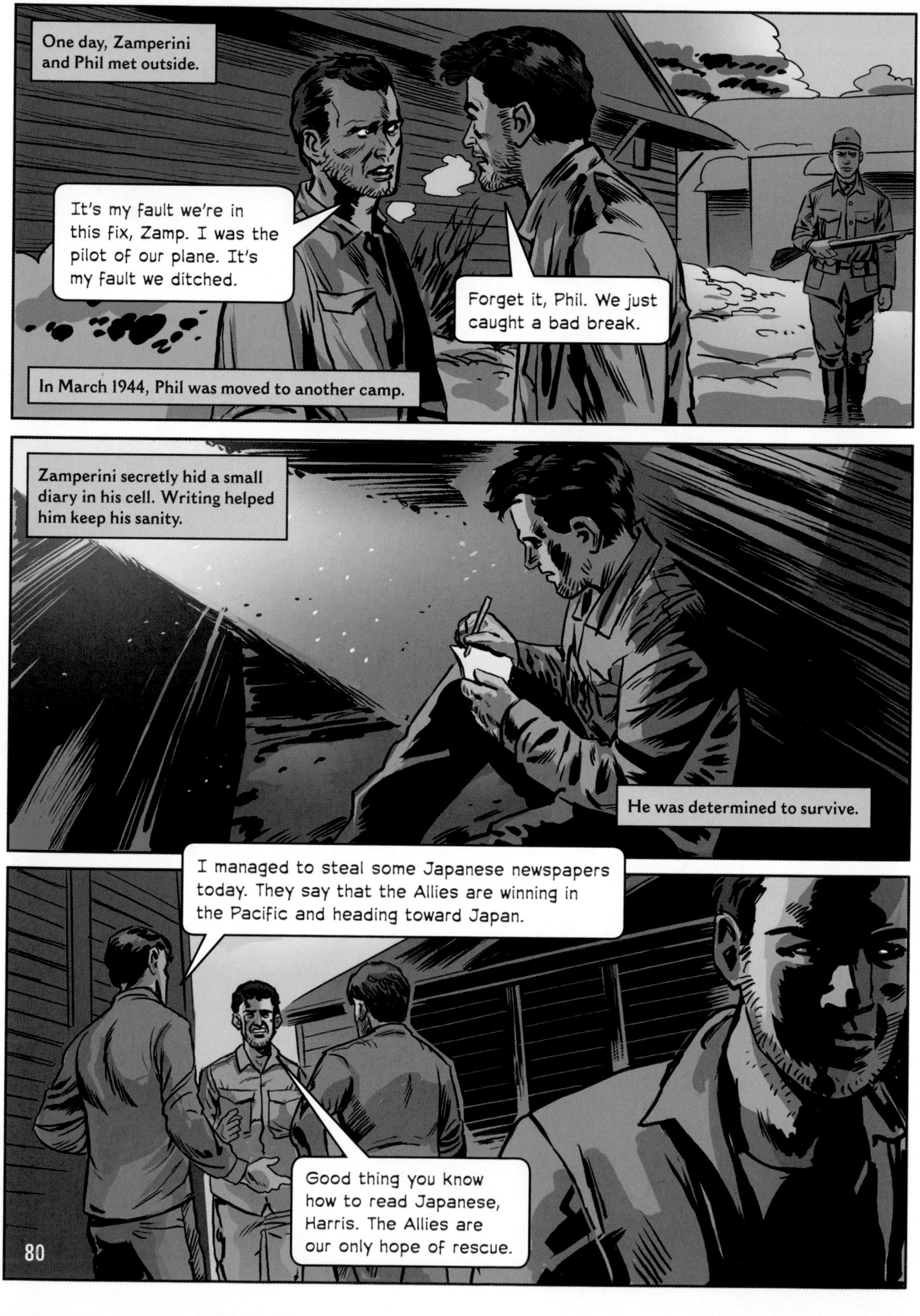
One day, Zamperini and Phil met outside.
It's my fault we're in this fix, Zamp. I was the pilot of our plane. It's my fault we ditched.
Forget it, Phil. We just caught a bad break.
In March 1944, Phil was moved to another camp.
Zamperini secretly hid a small diary in his cell. Writing helped him keep his sanity.
He was determined to survive.
I managed to steal some Japanese newspapers today. They say that the Allies are winning in the Pacific and heading toward Japan.
Good thing you know how to read Japanese, Harris. The Allies are our only hope of rescue.

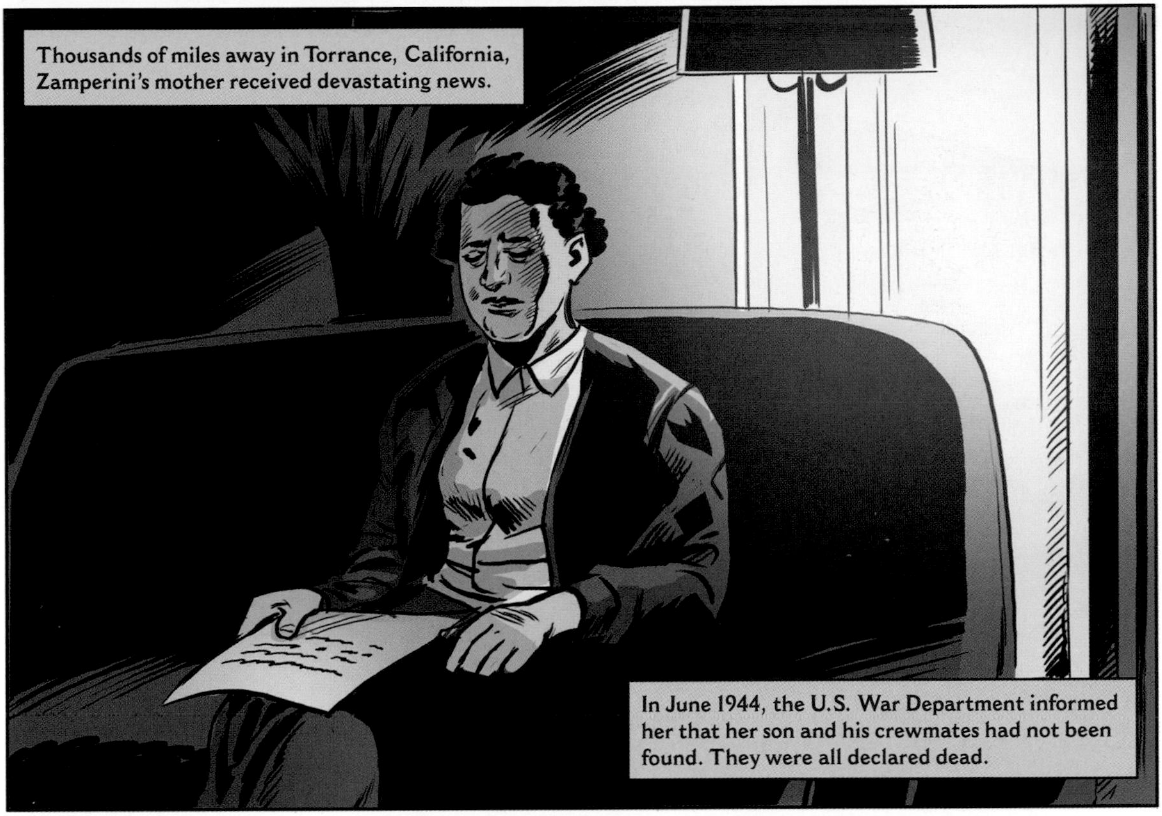
Thousands of miles away in Torrance, California, Zamperini's mother received devastating news.
In June 1944, the U.S. War Department informed her that her son and his crewmates had not been found. They were all declared dead.

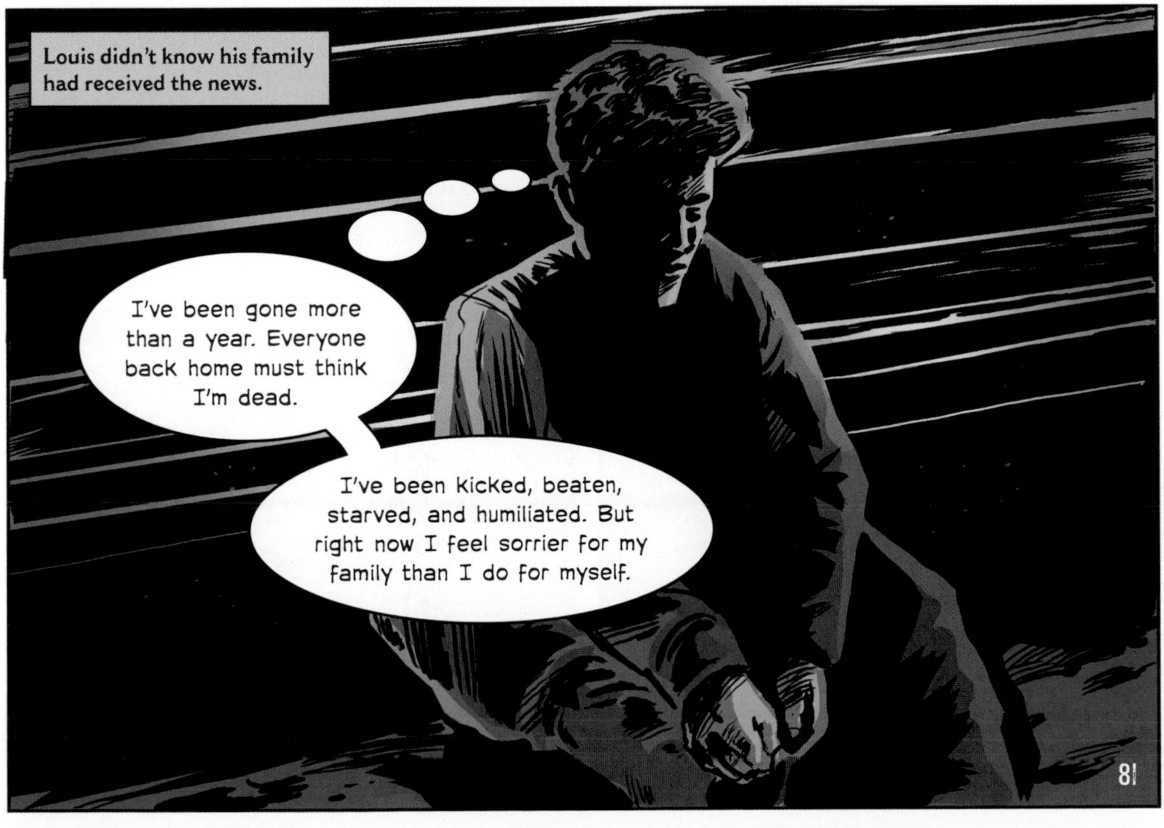
Louis didn't know his family had received the news.
I've been gone more than a year. Everyone back home must think I'm dead.
I've been kicked, beaten, starved, and humiliated. But right now I feel sorrier for my family than I do for myself.

TORTURE AND TORMENT

On September 30, 1944, Louis was transferred to the Omori POW camp, which lay on a man-made island in Tokyo Bay. The camp was "home" to about 600 Allied prisoners.

Name!

Zamperini.

Hmmm . . .

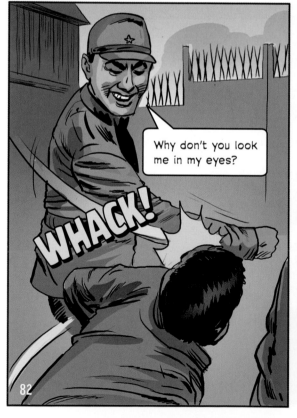

Why don't you look me in my eyes?

WHACK!

Zamperini stubbornly raised his eyes to face the man.

Don't look me in my eyes!

WHACK!

He's crazy!

Louis immediately hated the man—and feared him.

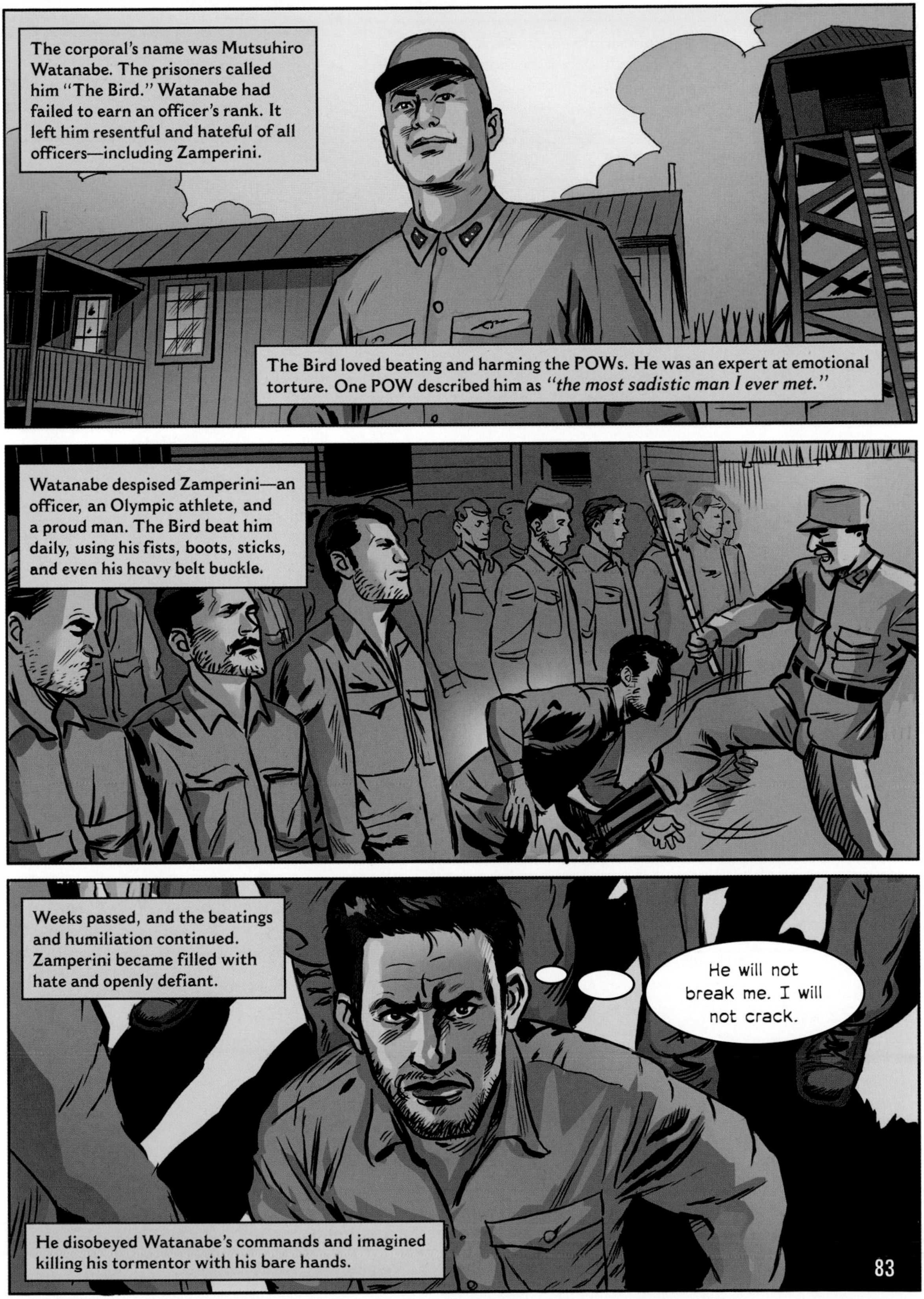
The corporal's name was Mutsuhiro Watanabe. The prisoners called him "The Bird." Watanabe had failed to earn an officer's rank. It left him resentful and hateful of all officers—including Zamperini.
The Bird loved beating and harming the POWs. He was an expert at emotional torture. One POW described him as *"the most sadistic man I ever met."*
Watanabe despised Zamperini—an officer, an Olympic athlete, and a proud man. The Bird beat him daily, using his fists, boots, sticks, and even his heavy belt buckle.
Weeks passed, and the beatings and humiliation continued. Zamperini became filled with hate and openly defiant.
He will not break me. I will not crack.
He disobeyed Watanabe's commands and imagined killing his tormentor with his bare hands.

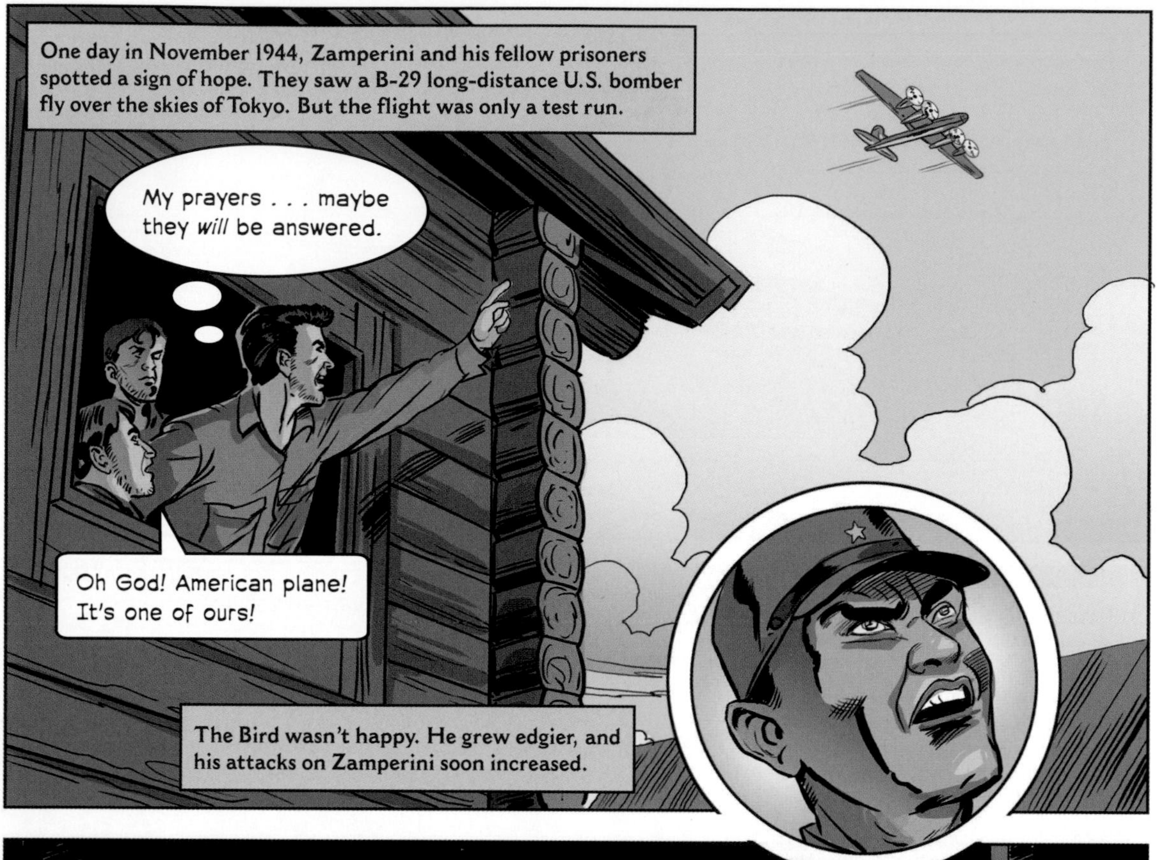
One day in November 1944, Zamperini and his fellow prisoners spotted a sign of hope. They saw a B-29 long-distance U.S. bomber fly over the skies of Tokyo. But the flight was only a test run.
My prayers . . . maybe they *will* be answered.
Oh God! American plane! It's one of ours!
The Bird wasn't happy. He grew edgier, and his attacks on Zamperini soon increased.

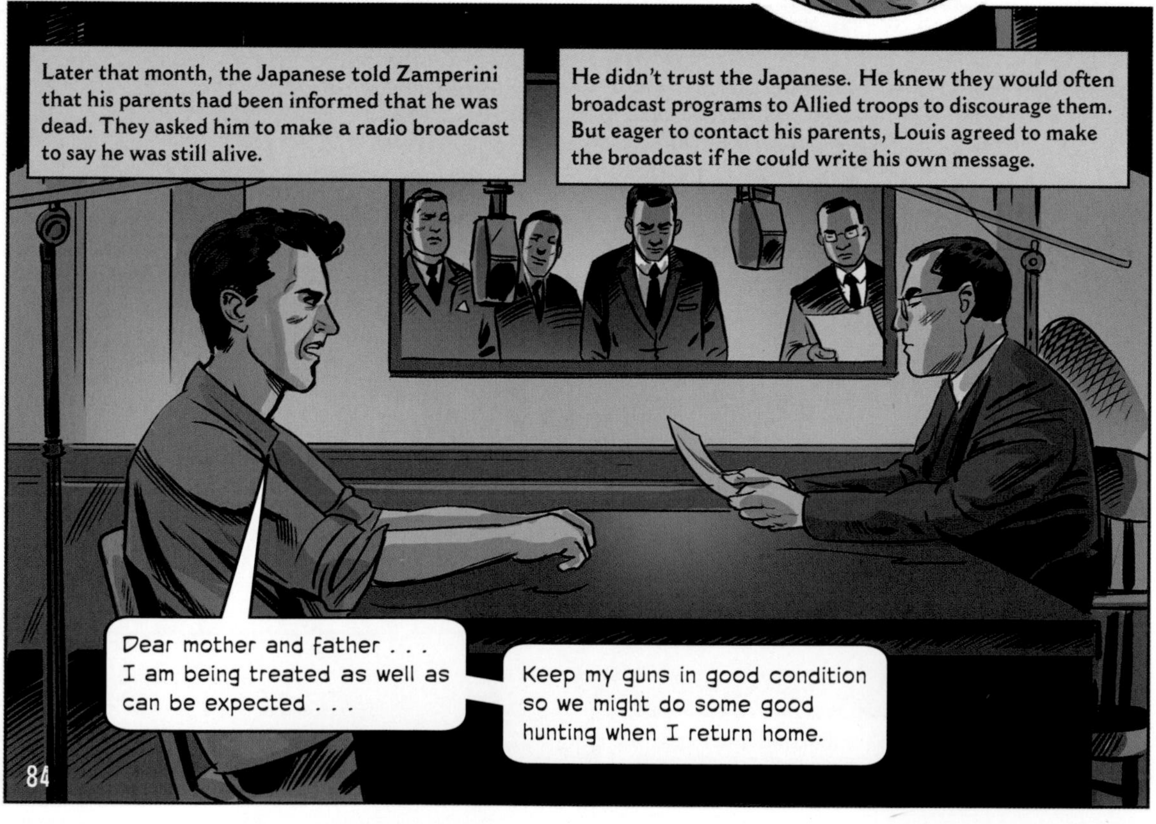
Later that month, the Japanese told Zamperini that his parents had been informed that he was dead. They asked him to make a radio broadcast to say he was still alive.
He didn't trust the Japanese. He knew they would often broadcast programs to Allied troops to discourage them. But eager to contact his parents, Louis agreed to make the broadcast if he could write his own message.
Dear mother and father . . . I am being treated as well as can be expected . . .
Keep my guns in good condition so we might do some good hunting when I return home.

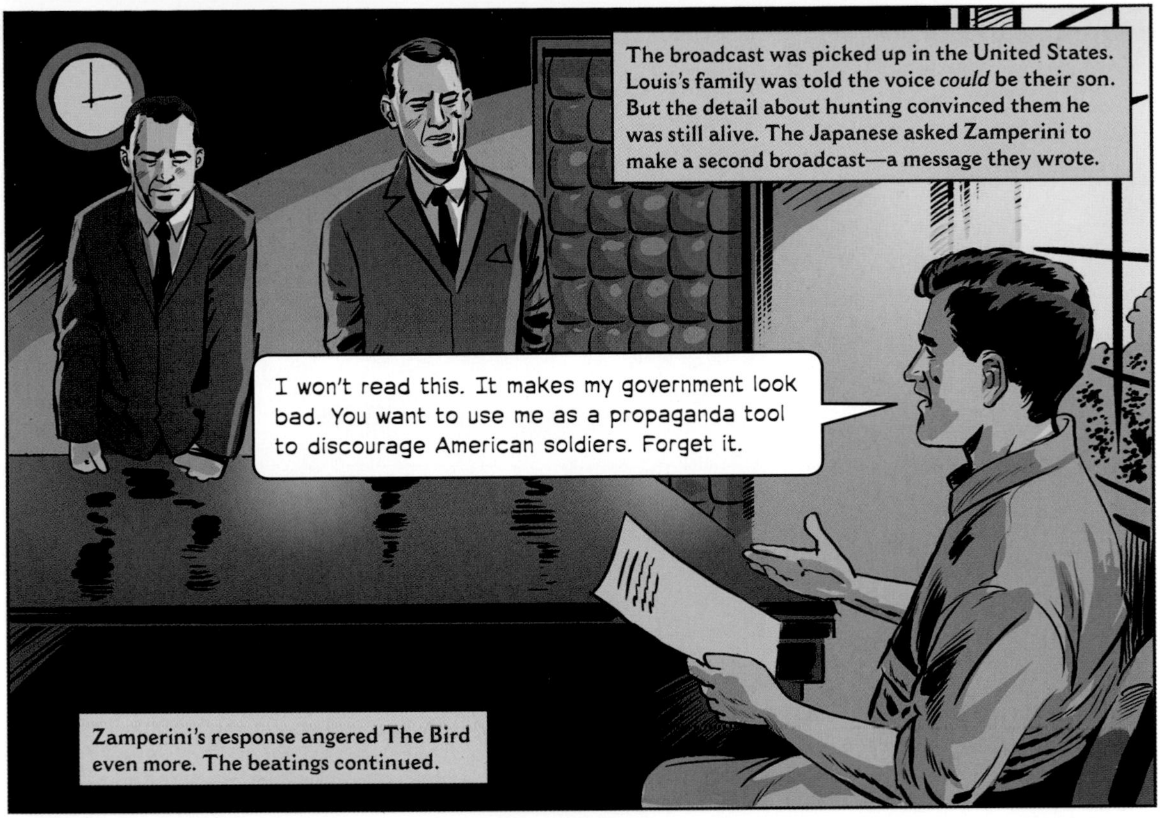

The broadcast was picked up in the United States. Louis's family was told the voice *could* be their son. But the detail about hunting convinced them he was still alive. The Japanese asked Zamperini to make a second broadcast—a message they wrote.
I won't read this. It makes my government look bad. You want to use me as a propaganda tool to discourage American soldiers. Forget it.
Zamperini's response angered The Bird even more. The beatings continued.

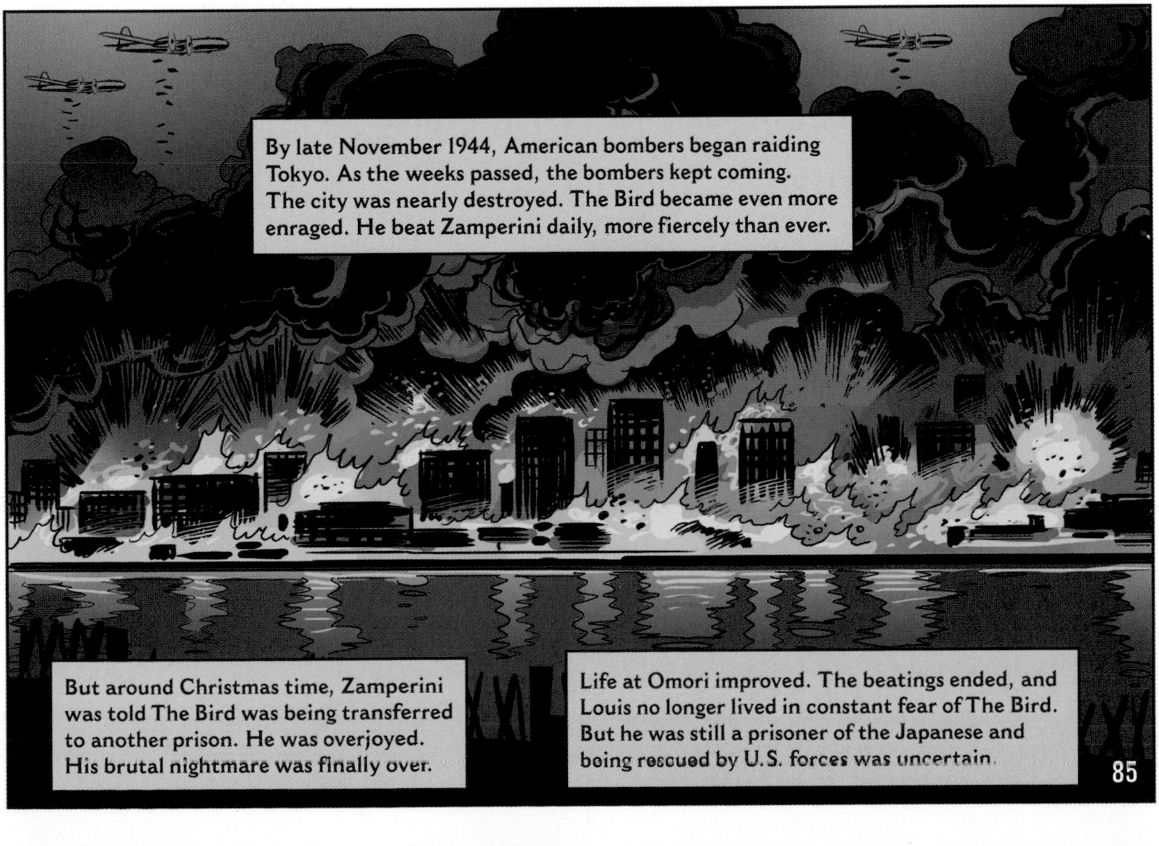

By late November 1944, American bombers began raiding Tokyo. As the weeks passed, the bombers kept coming. The city was nearly destroyed. The Bird became even more enraged. He beat Zamperini daily, more fiercely than ever.
But around Christmas time, Zamperini was told The Bird was being transferred to another prison. He was overjoyed. His brutal nightmare was finally over.
Life at Omori improved. The beatings ended, and Louis no longer lived in constant fear of The Bird. But he was still a prisoner of the Japanese and being rescued by U.S. forces was uncertain.

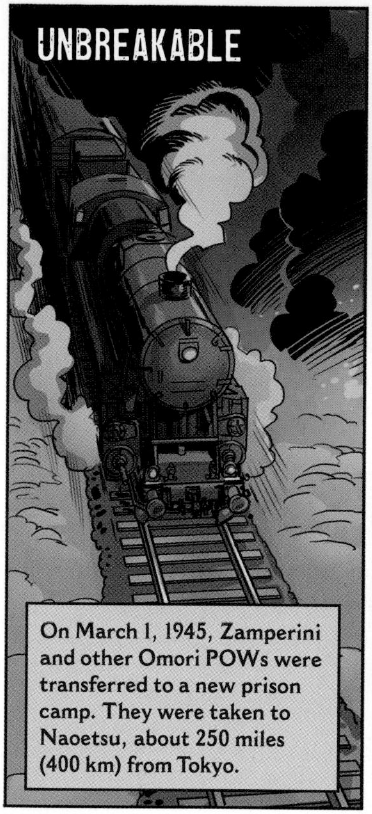
On March 1, 1945, Zamperini and other Omori POWs were transferred to a new prison camp. They were taken to Naoetsu, about 250 miles (400 km) from Tokyo.

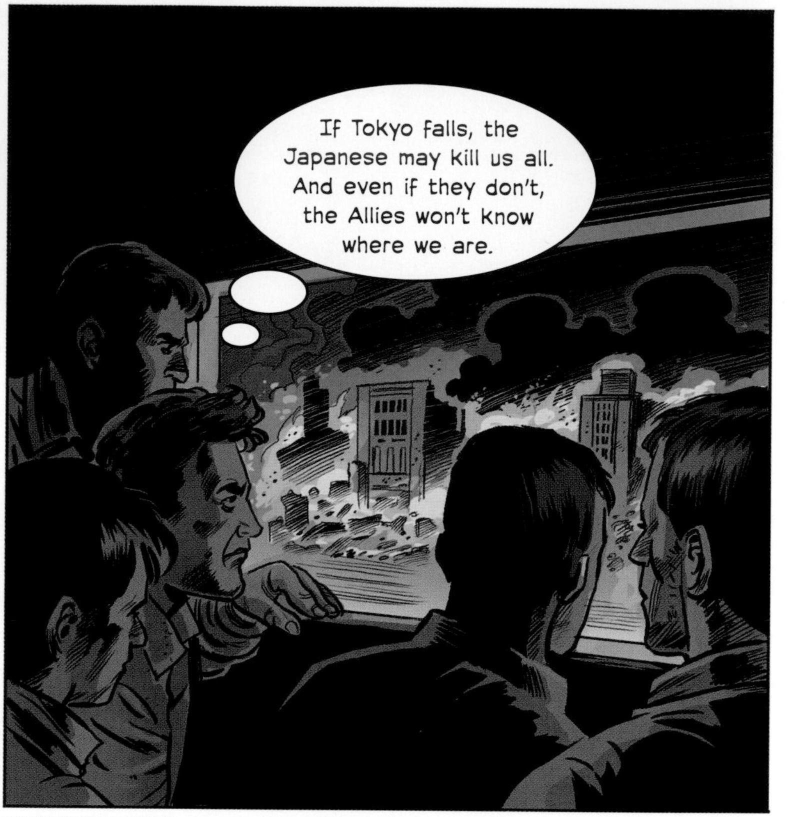
If Tokyo falls, the Japanese may kill us all. And even if they don't, the Allies won't know where we are.

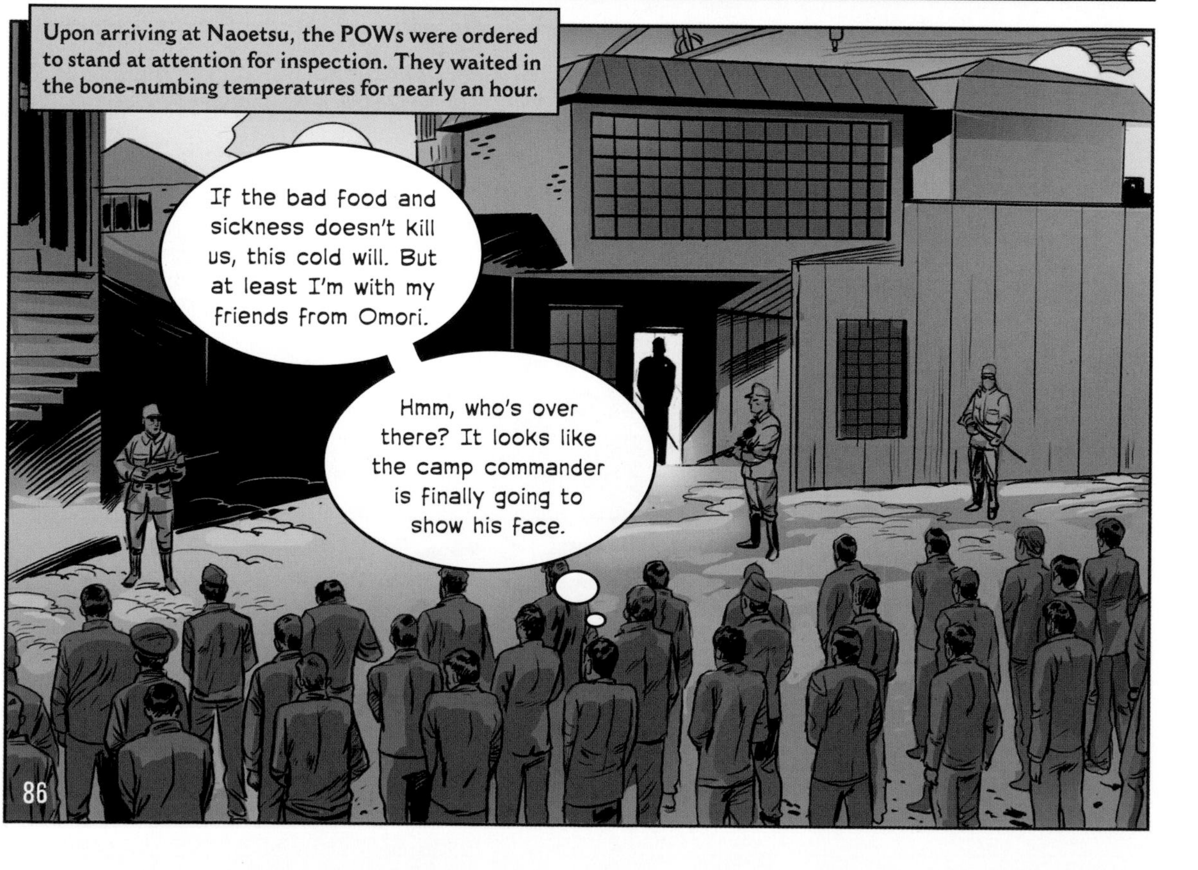
Upon arriving at Naoetsu, the POWs were ordered to stand at attention for inspection. They waited in the bone-numbing temperatures for nearly an hour.
If the bad food and sickness doesn't kill us, this cold will. But at least I'm with my friends from Omori.
Hmm, who's over there? It looks like the camp commander is finally going to show his face.

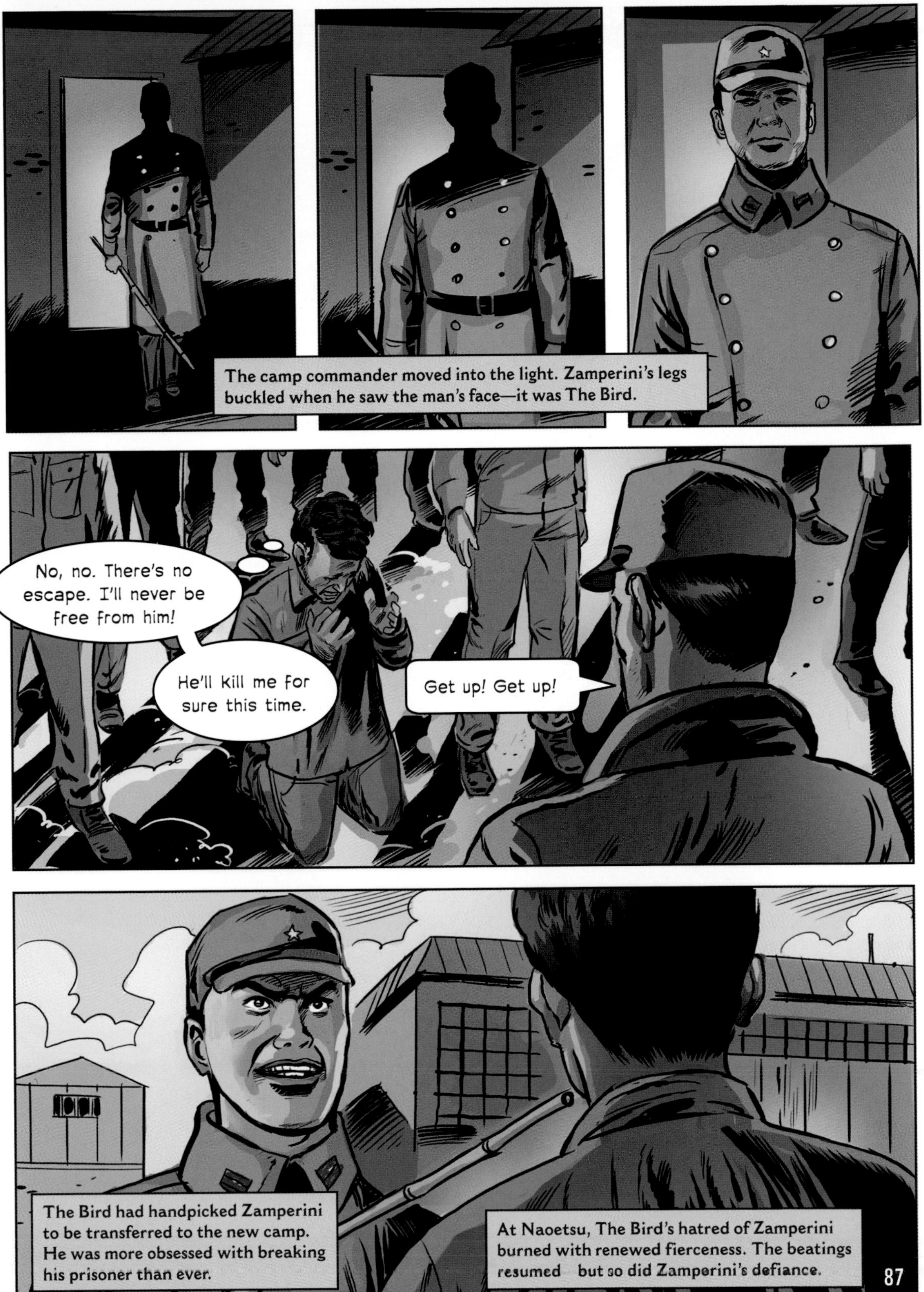
The camp commander moved into the light. Zamperini's legs buckled when he saw the man's face—it was The Bird.
No, no. There's no escape. I'll never be free from him!
He'll kill me for sure this time.
Get up! Get up!
The Bird had handpicked Zamperini to be transferred to the new camp. He was more obsessed with breaking his prisoner than ever.
At Naoetsu, The Bird's hatred of Zamperini burned with renewed fierceness. The beatings resumed but so did Zamperini's defiance.

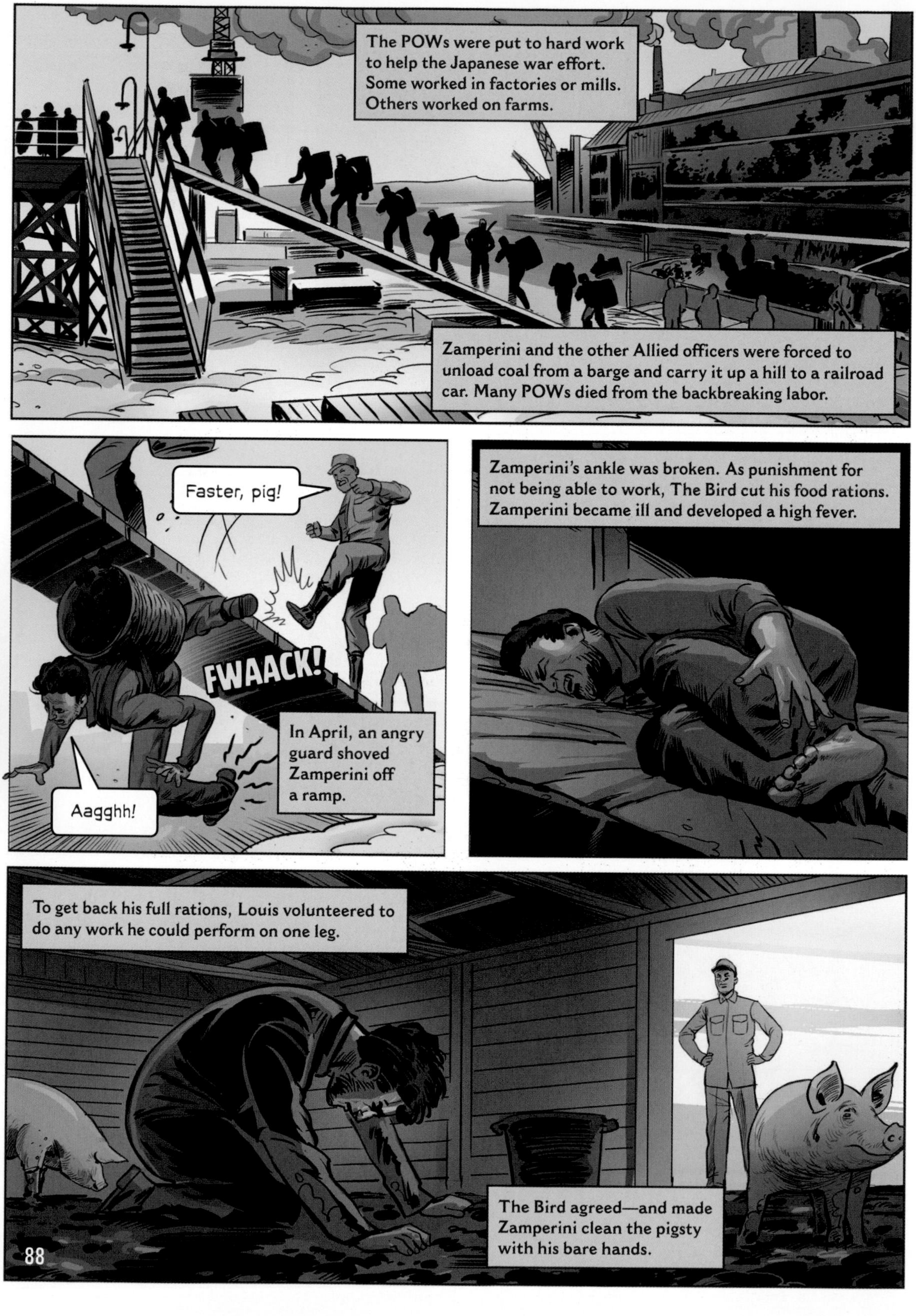
The POWs were put to hard work to help the Japanese war effort. Some worked in factories or mills. Others worked on farms.
Zamperini and the other Allied officers were forced to unload coal from a barge and carry it up a hill to a railroad car. Many POWs died from the backbreaking labor.
Faster, pig!
FWAACK!
Aagghh!
In April, an angry guard shoved Zamperini off a ramp.
Zamperini's ankle was broken. As punishment for not being able to work, The Bird cut his food rations. Zamperini became ill and developed a high fever.
To get back his full rations, Louis volunteered to do any work he could perform on one leg.
The Bird agreed—and made Zamperini clean the pigsty with his bare hands.

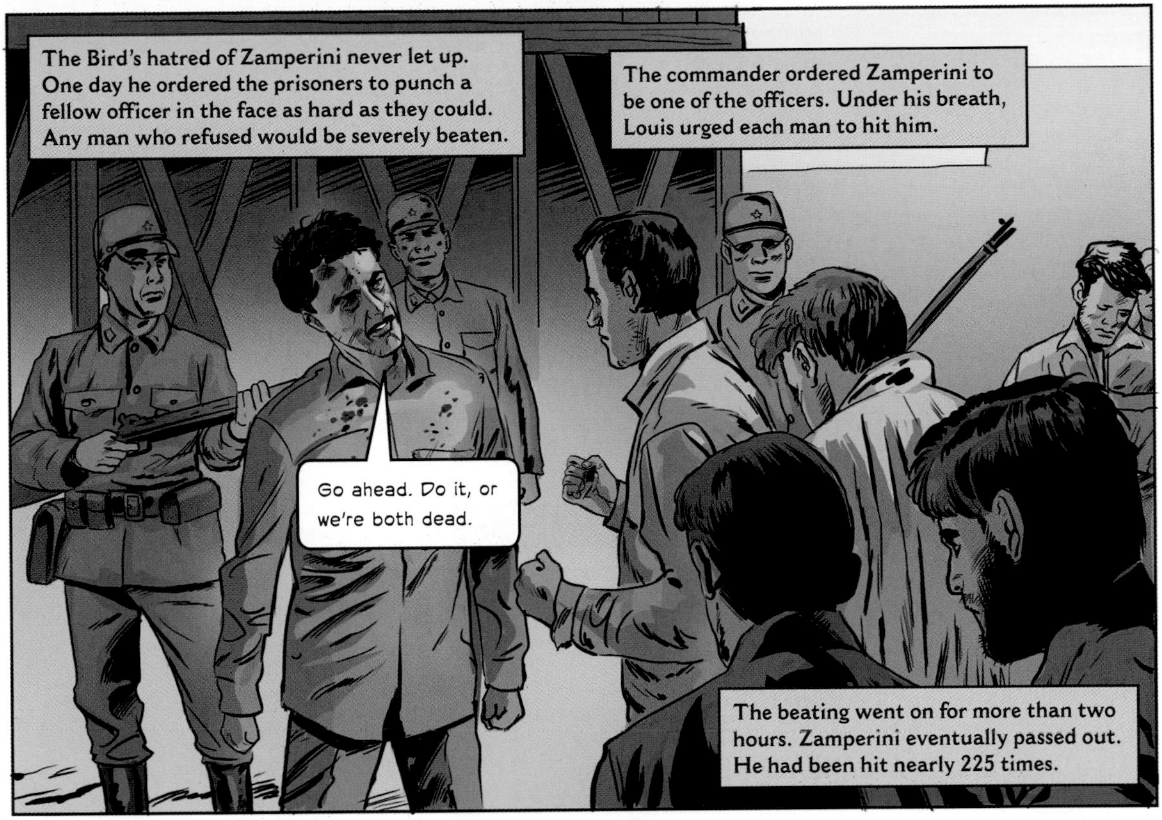
The Bird's hatred of Zamperini never let up. One day he ordered the prisoners to punch a fellow officer in the face as hard as they could. Any man who refused would be severely beaten.
The commander ordered Zamperini to be one of the officers. Under his breath, Louis urged each man to hit him.
Go ahead. Do it, or we're both dead.
The beating went on for more than two hours. Zamperini eventually passed out. He had been hit nearly 225 times.

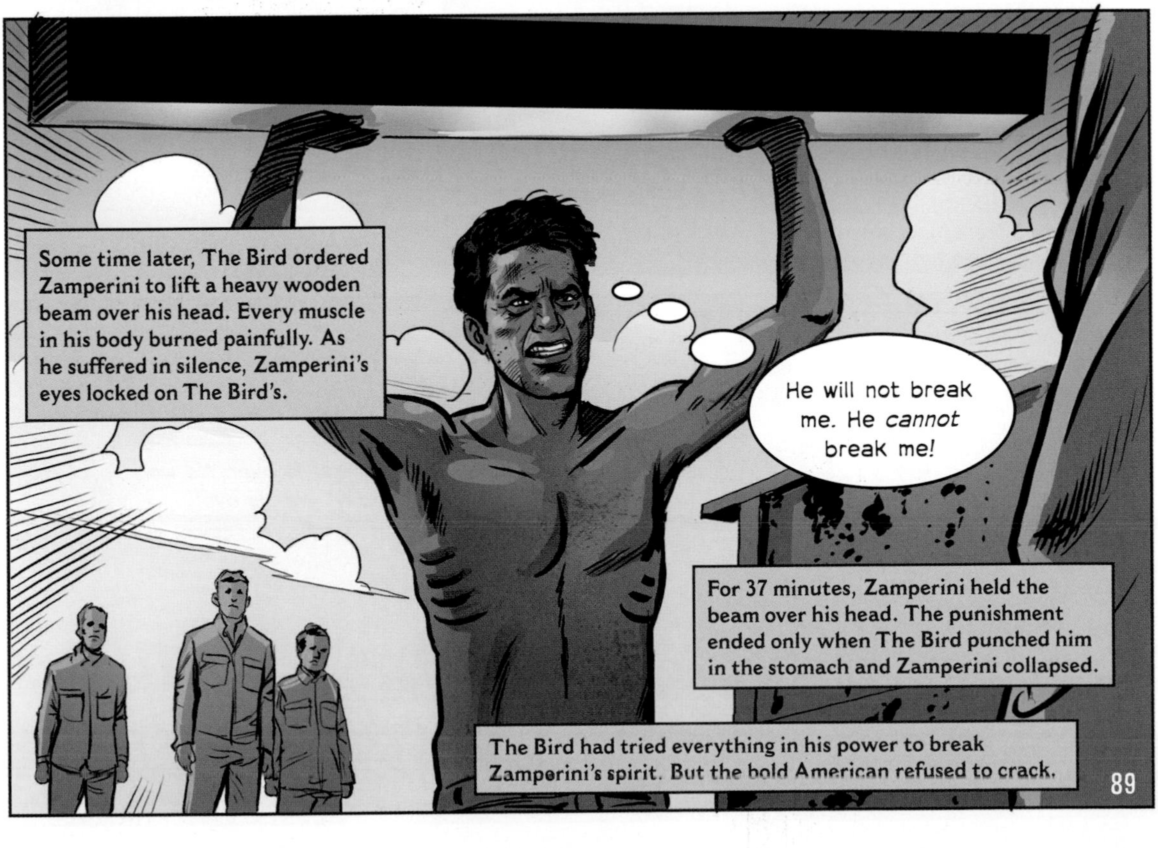
Some time later, The Bird ordered Zamperini to lift a heavy wooden beam over his head. Every muscle in his body burned painfully. As he suffered in silence, Zamperini's eyes locked on The Bird's.
He will not break me. He *cannot* break me!
For 37 minutes, Zamperini held the beam over his head. The punishment ended only when The Bird punched him in the stomach and Zamperini collapsed.
The Bird had tried everything in his power to break Zamperini's spirit. But the bold American refused to crack.

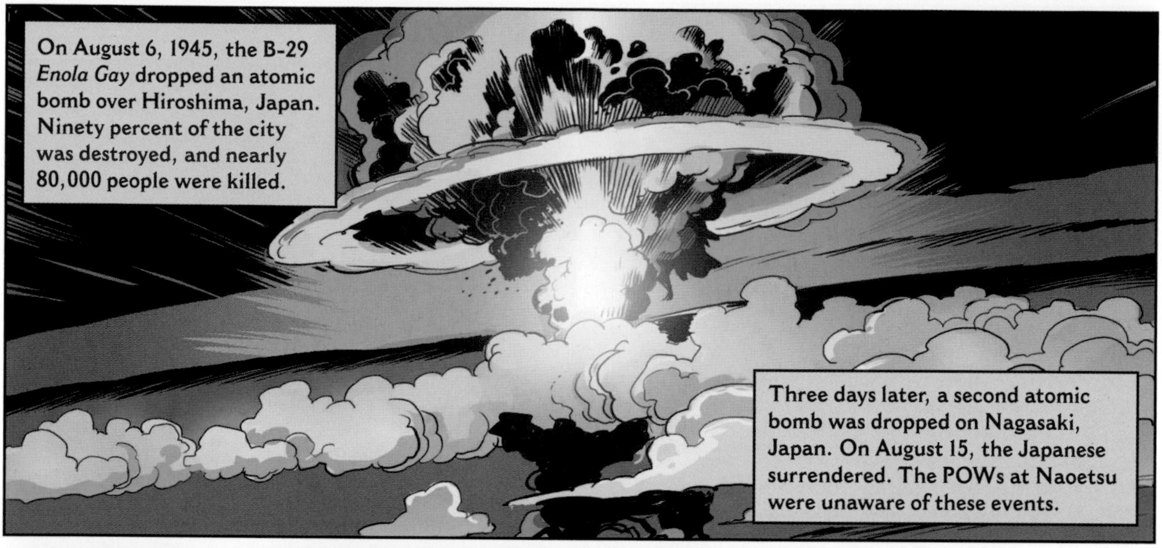
On August 6, 1945, the B-29 *Enola Gay* dropped an atomic bomb over Hiroshima, Japan. Ninety percent of the city was destroyed, and nearly 80,000 people were killed.
Three days later, a second atomic bomb was dropped on Nagasaki, Japan. On August 15, the Japanese surrendered. The POWs at Naoetsu were unaware of these events.

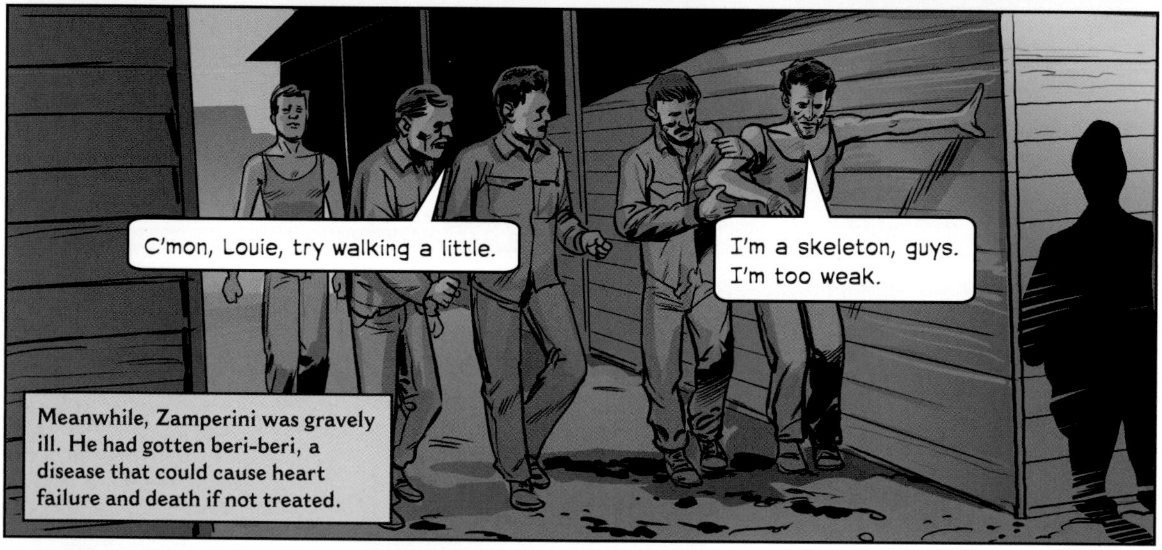
C'mon, Louie, try walking a little.
I'm a skeleton, guys. I'm too weak.
Meanwhile, Zamperini was gravely ill. He had gotten beri-beri, a disease that could cause heart failure and death if not treated.

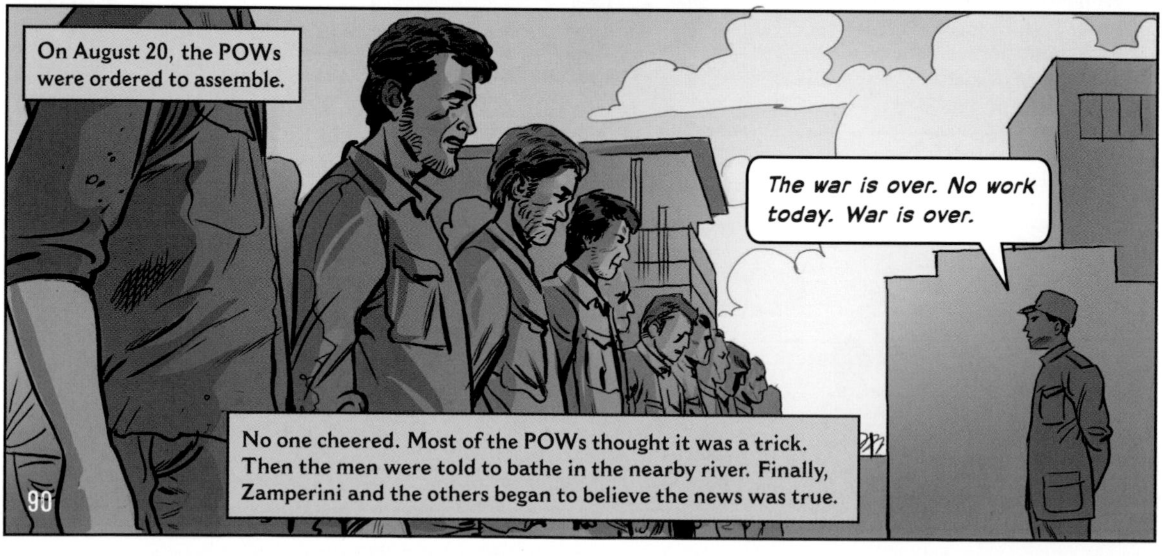
On August 20, the POWs were ordered to assemble.
The war is over. No work today. War is over.
No one cheered. Most of the POWs thought it was a trick. Then the men were told to bathe in the nearby river. Finally, Zamperini and the others began to believe the news was true.

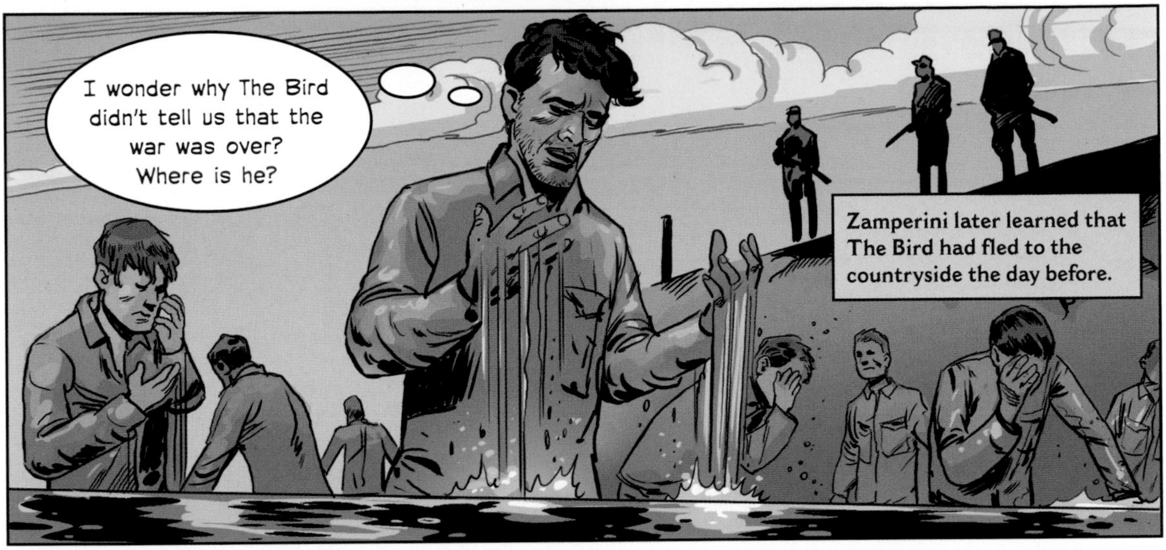
I wonder why The Bird didn't tell us that the war was over? Where is he?
Zamperini later learned that The Bird had fled to the countryside the day before.

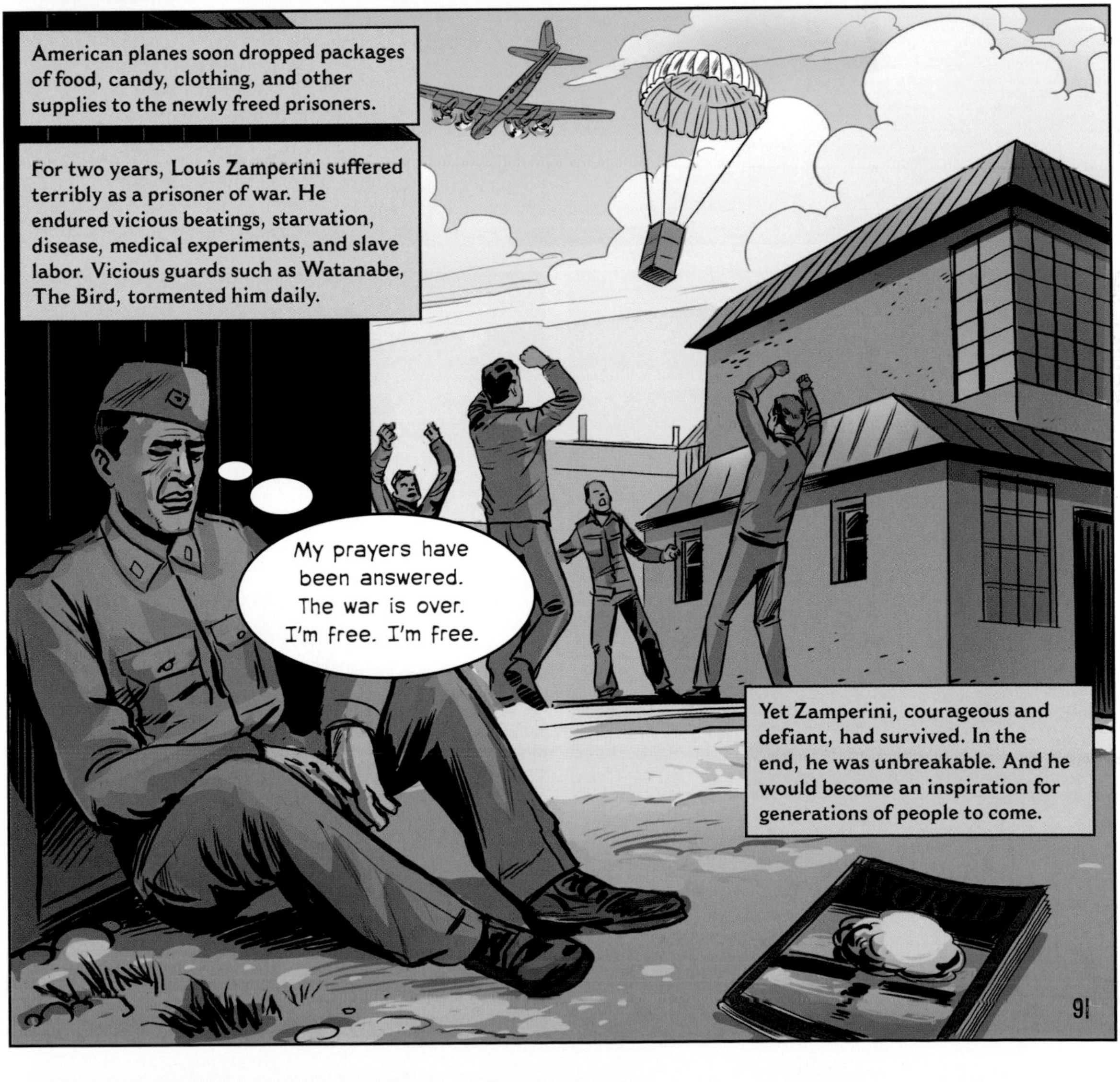
American planes soon dropped packages of food, candy, clothing, and other supplies to the newly freed prisoners.
For two years, Louis Zamperini suffered terribly as a prisoner of war. He endured vicious beatings, starvation, disease, medical experiments, and slave labor. Vicious guards such as Watanabe, The Bird, tormented him daily.
My prayers have been answered. The war is over. I'm free. I'm free.
Yet Zamperini, courageous and defiant, had survived. In the end, he was unbreakable. And he would become an inspiration for generations of people to come.

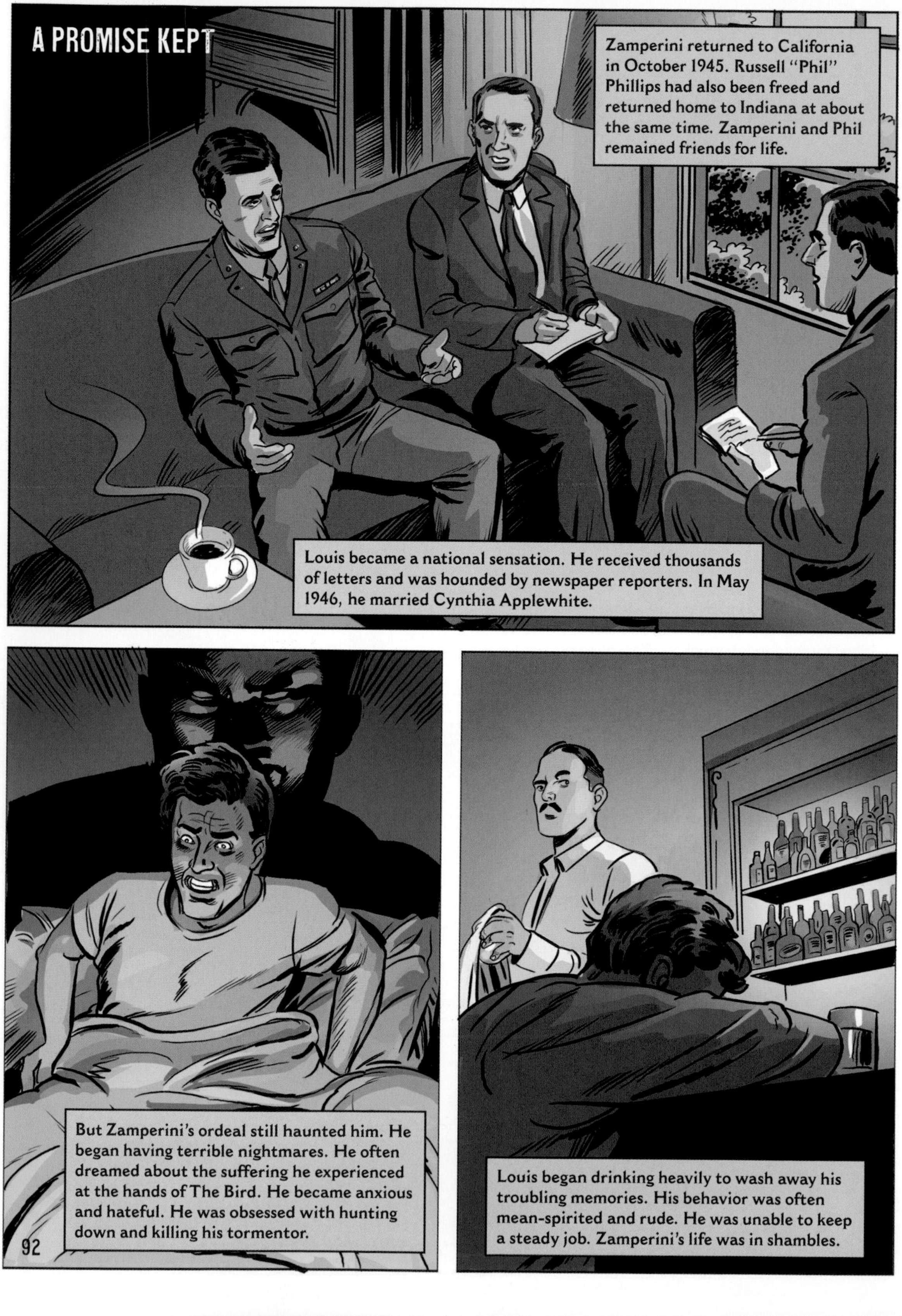
A PROMISE KEPT
Zamperini returned to California in October 1945. Russell "Phil" Phillips had also been freed and returned home to Indiana at about the same time. Zamperini and Phil remained friends for life.
Louis became a national sensation. He received thousands of letters and was hounded by newspaper reporters. In May 1946, he married Cynthia Applewhite.
But Zamperini's ordeal still haunted him. He began having terrible nightmares. He often dreamed about the suffering he experienced at the hands of The Bird. He became anxious and hateful. He was obsessed with hunting down and killing his tormentor.
Louis began drinking heavily to wash away his troubling memories. His behavior was often mean-spirited and rude. He was unable to keep a steady job. Zamperini's life was in shambles.

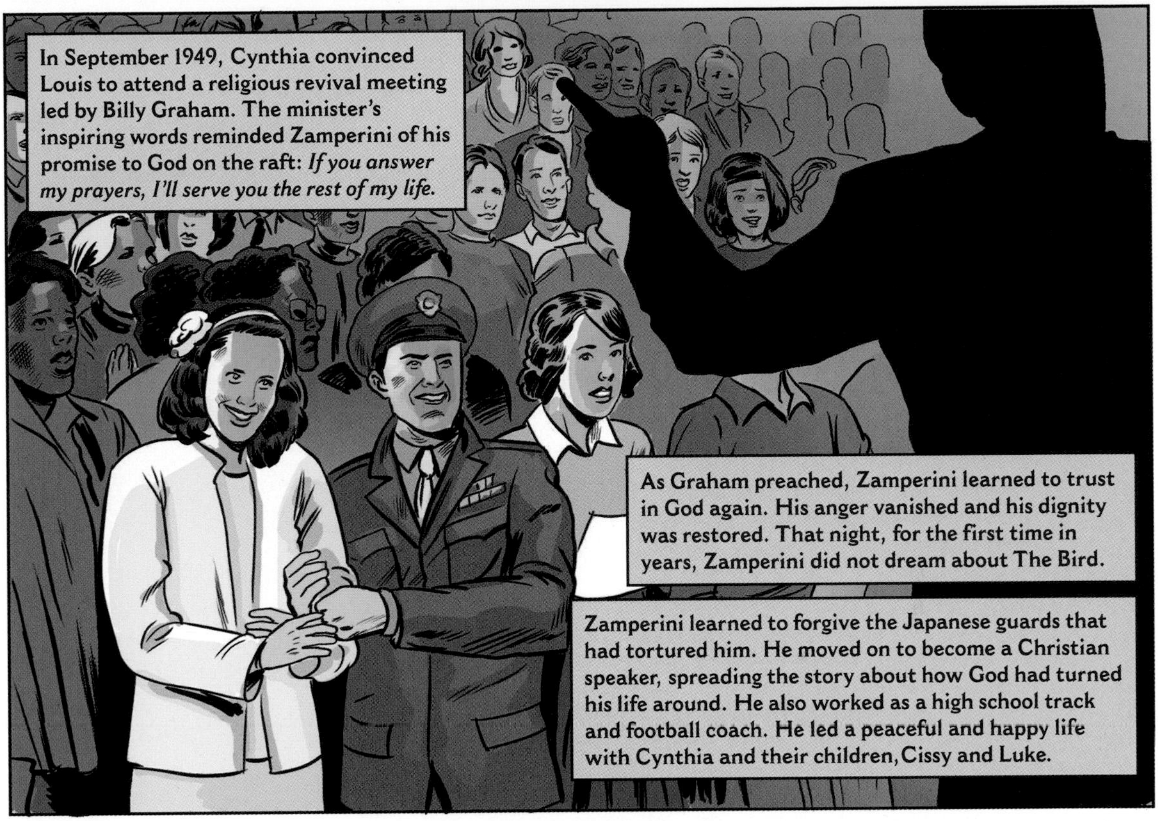
In September 1949, Cynthia convinced Louis to attend a religious revival meeting led by Billy Graham. The minister's inspiring words reminded Zamperini of his promise to God on the raft: *If you answer my prayers, I'll serve you the rest of my life.*
As Graham preached, Zamperini learned to trust in God again. His anger vanished and his dignity was restored. That night, for the first time in years, Zamperini did not dream about The Bird.
Zamperini learned to forgive the Japanese guards that had tortured him. He moved on to become a Christian speaker, spreading the story about how God had turned his life around. He also worked as a high school track and football coach. He led a peaceful and happy life with Cynthia and their children, Cissy and Luke.

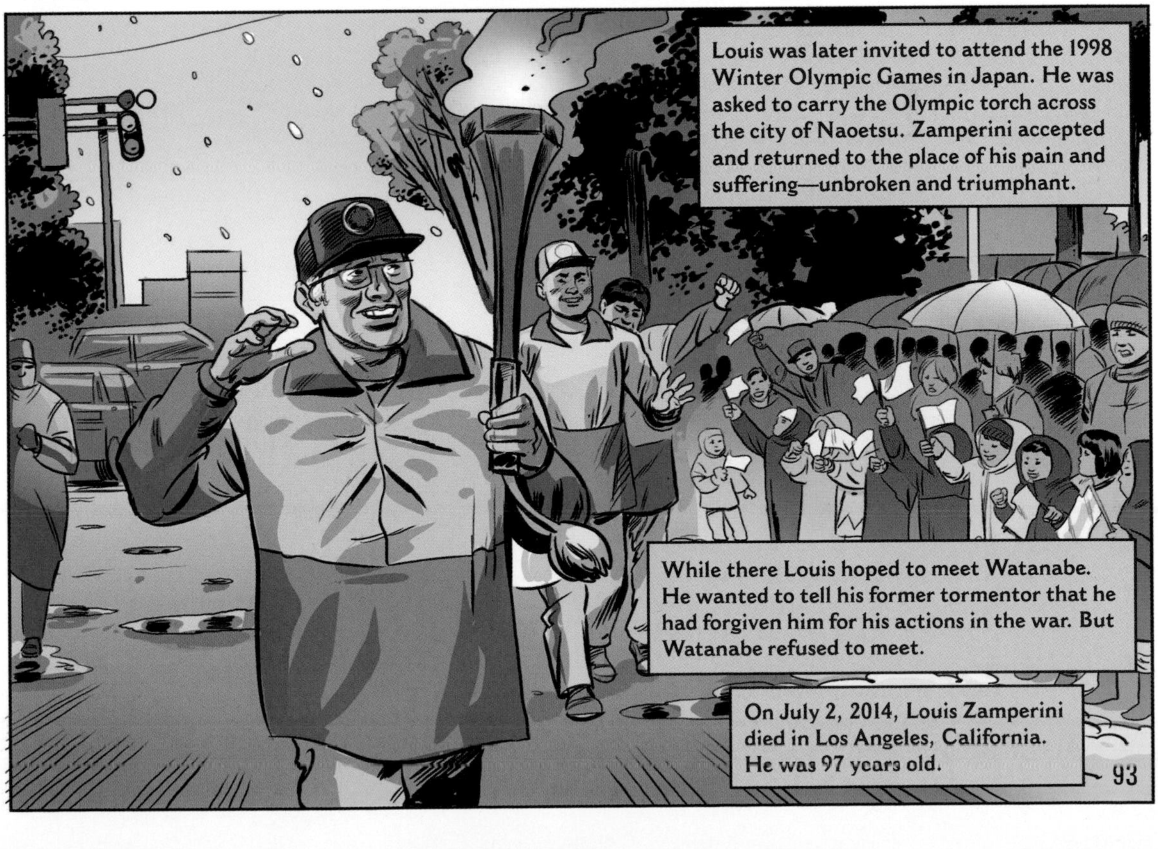
Louis was later invited to attend the 1998 Winter Olympic Games in Japan. He was asked to carry the Olympic torch across the city of Naoetsu. Zamperini accepted and returned to the place of his pain and suffering—unbroken and triumphant.
While there Louis hoped to meet Watanabe. He wanted to tell his former tormentor that he had forgiven him for his actions in the war. But Watanabe refused to meet.
On July 2, 2014, Louis Zamperini died in Los Angeles, California. He was 97 years old.

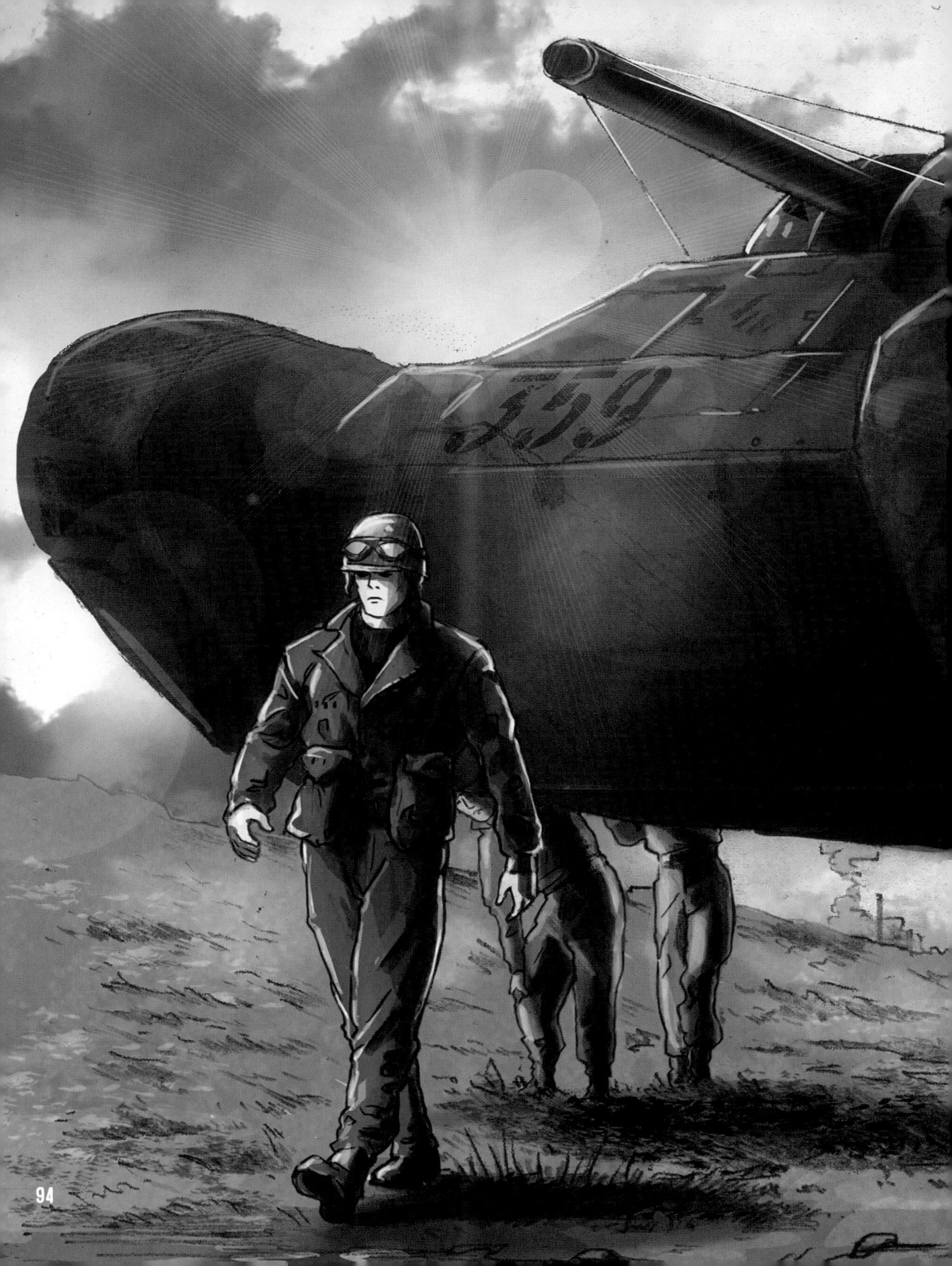
559

U.S. GHOST ARMY

THE MASTER ILLUSIONISTS OF WORLD WAR II

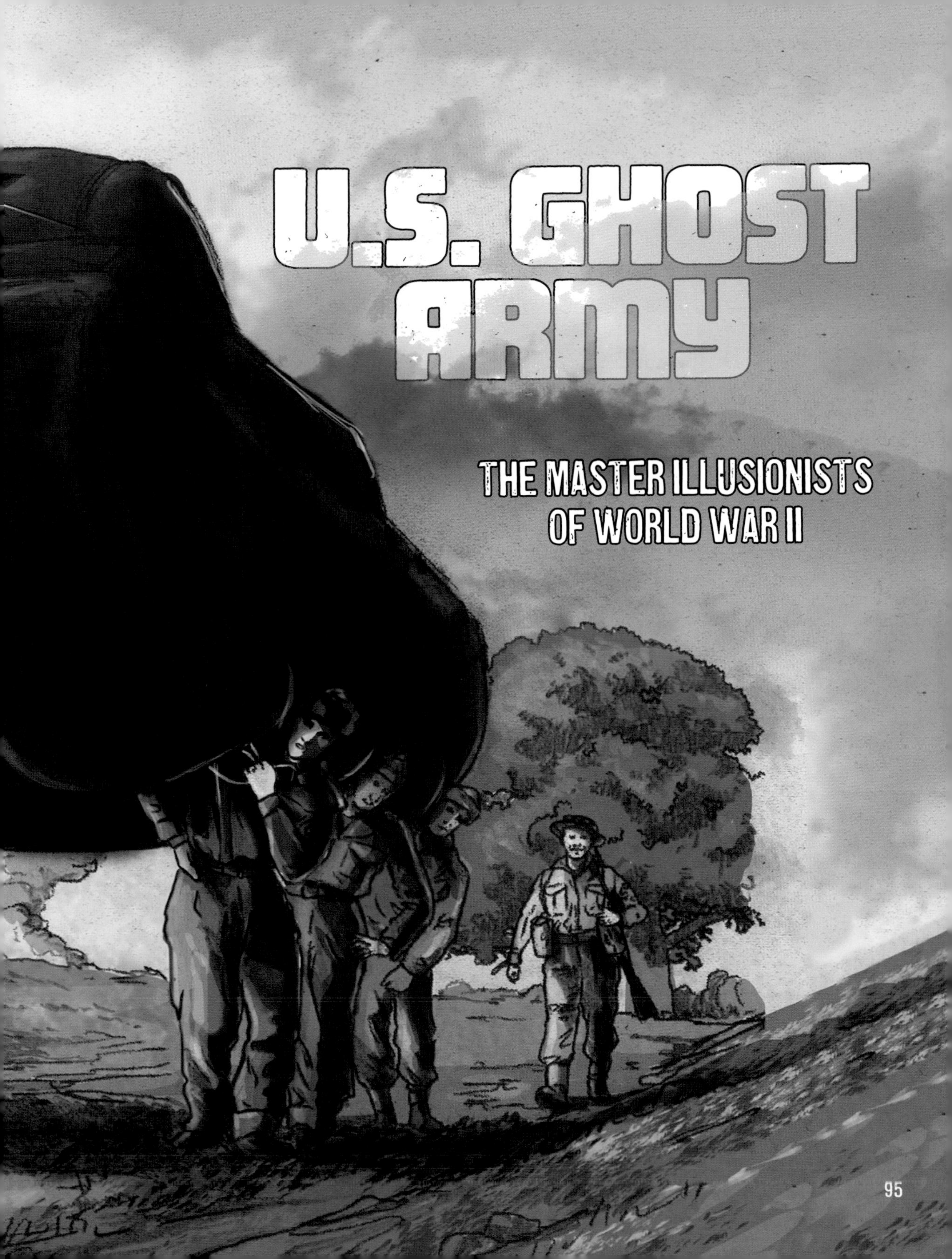

MASTERS OF DECEPTION

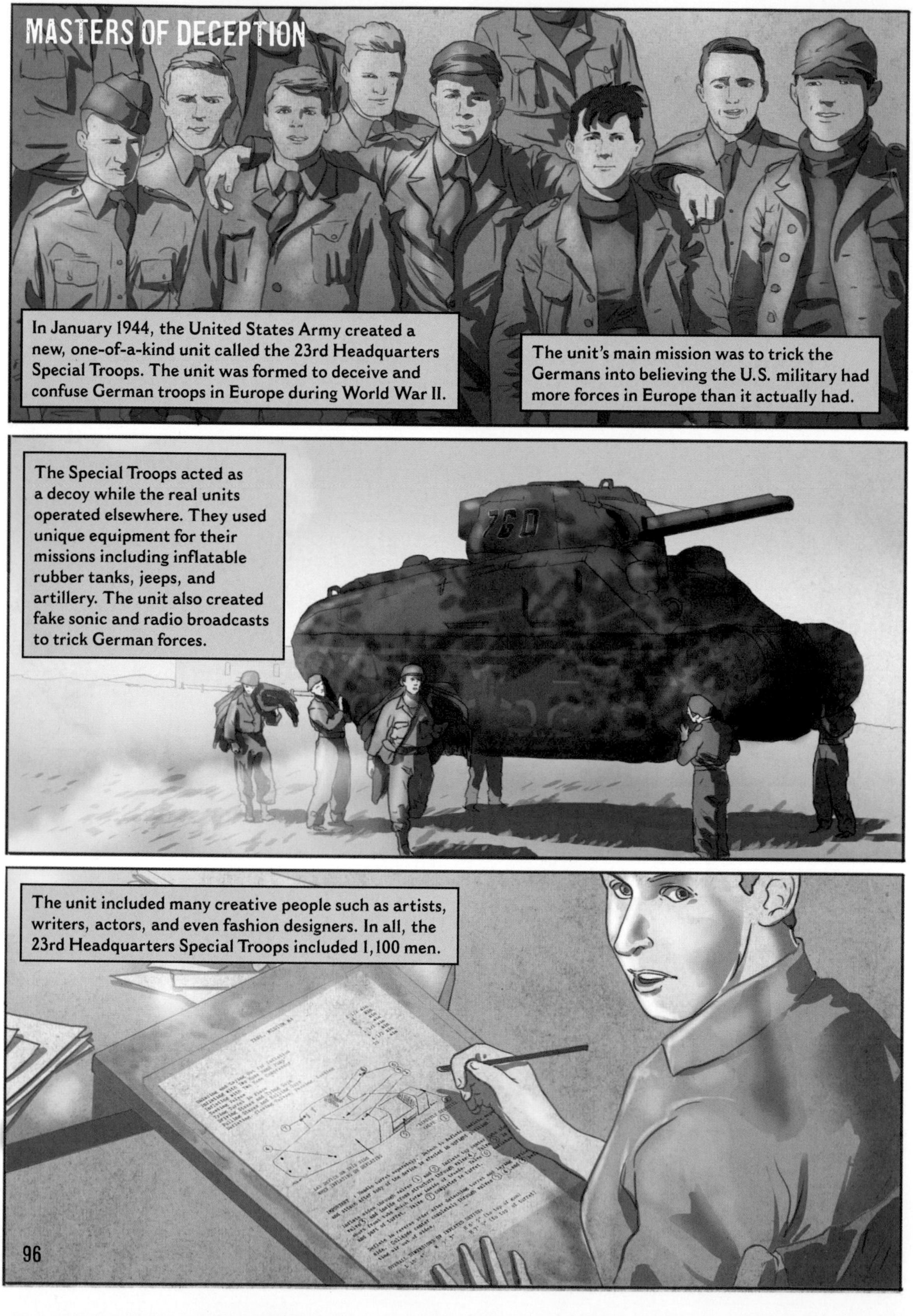
In January 1944, the United States Army created a new, one-of-a-kind unit called the 23rd Headquarters Special Troops. The unit was formed to deceive and confuse German troops in Europe during World War II.
The unit's main mission was to trick the Germans into believing the U.S. military had more forces in Europe than it actually had.
The Special Troops acted as a decoy while the real units operated elsewhere. They used unique equipment for their missions including inflatable rubber tanks, jeeps, and artillery. The unit also created fake sonic and radio broadcasts to trick German forces.
The unit included many creative people such as artists, writers, actors, and even fashion designers. In all, the 23rd Headquarters Special Troops included 1,100 men.

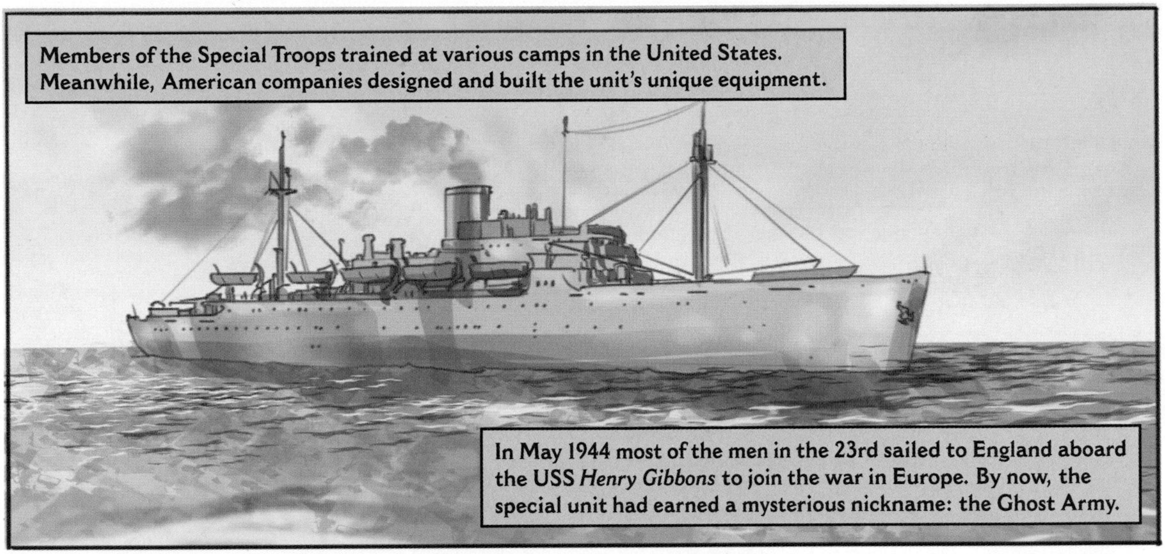
Members of the Special Troops trained at various camps in the United States. Meanwhile, American companies designed and built the unit's unique equipment.
In May 1944 most of the men in the 23rd sailed to England aboard the USS *Henry Gibbons* to join the war in Europe. By now, the special unit had earned a mysterious nickname: the Ghost Army.

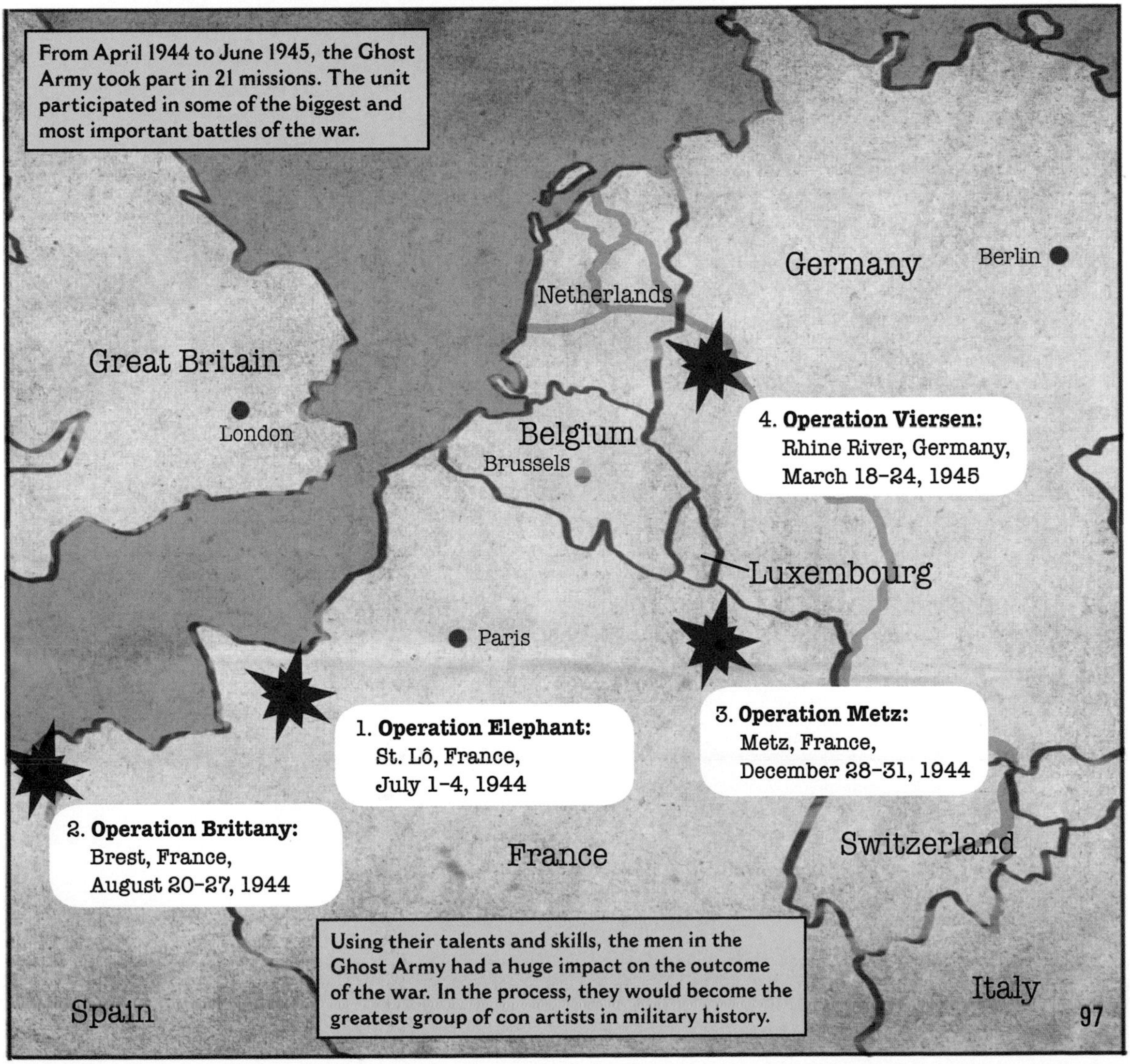
From April 1944 to June 1945, the Ghost Army took part in 21 missions. The unit participated in some of the biggest and most important battles of the war.
Germany
Berlin
Netherlands
Great Britain
London
Belgium
Brussels
4. **Operation Viersen:** Rhine River, Germany, March 18-24, 1945
Luxembourg
Paris
1. **Operation Elephant:** St. Lô, France, July 1-4, 1944
3. **Operation Metz:** Metz, France, December 28-31, 1944
2. **Operation Brittany:** Brest, France, August 20-27, 1944
France
Switzerland
Using their talents and skills, the men in the Ghost Army had a huge impact on the outcome of the war. In the process, they would become the greatest group of con artists in military history.
Spain
Italy

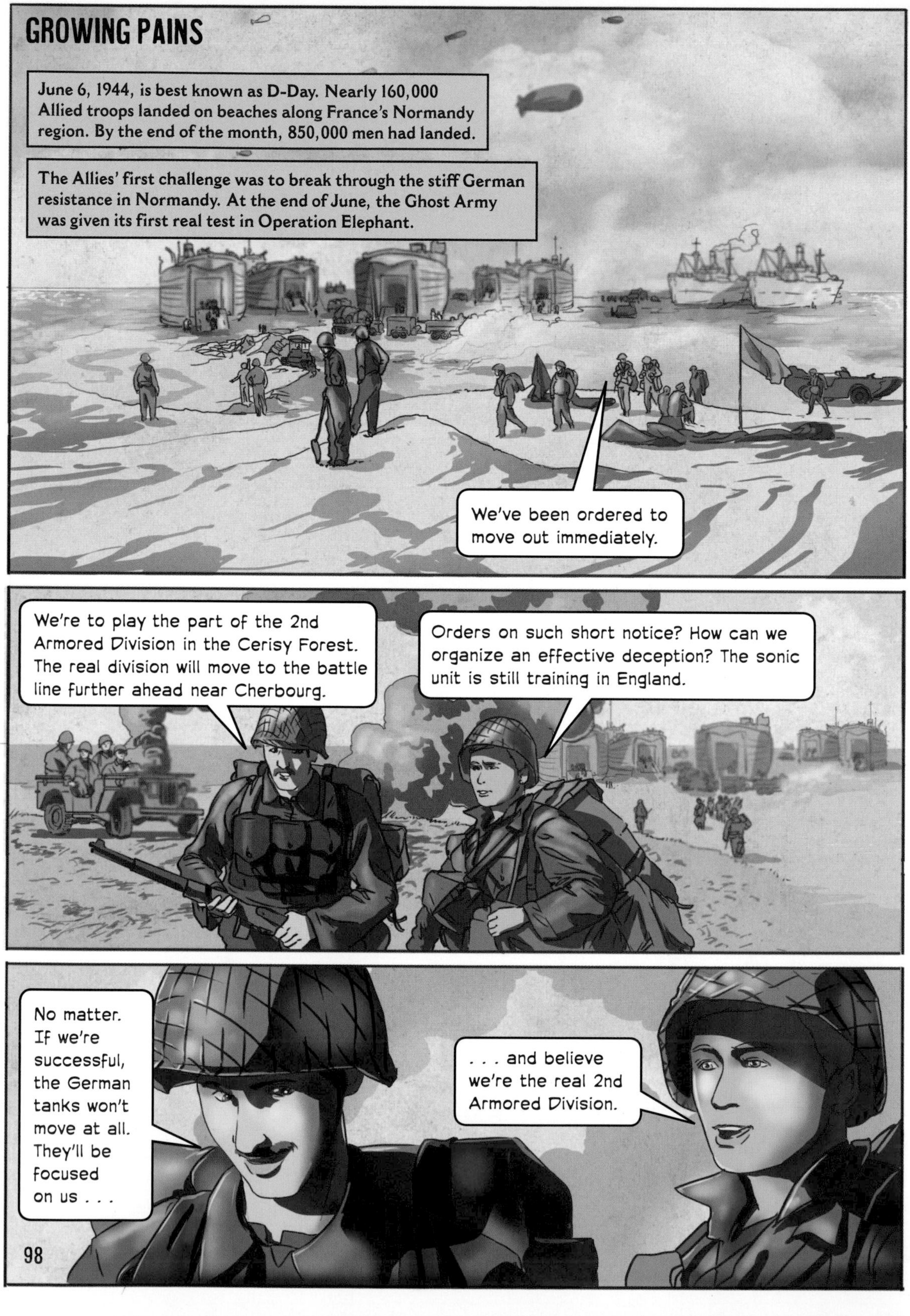
GROWING PAINS
June 6, 1944, is best known as D-Day. Nearly 160,000 Allied troops landed on beaches along France's Normandy region. By the end of the month, 850,000 men had landed.
The Allies' first challenge was to break through the stiff German resistance in Normandy. At the end of June, the Ghost Army was given its first real test in Operation Elephant.
We've been ordered to move out immediately.
We're to play the part of the 2nd Armored Division in the Cerisy Forest. The real division will move to the battle line further ahead near Cherbourg.
Orders on such short notice? How can we organize an effective deception? The sonic unit is still training in England.
No matter. If we're successful, the German tanks won't move at all. They'll be focused on us . . .
. . . and believe we're the real 2nd Armored Division.

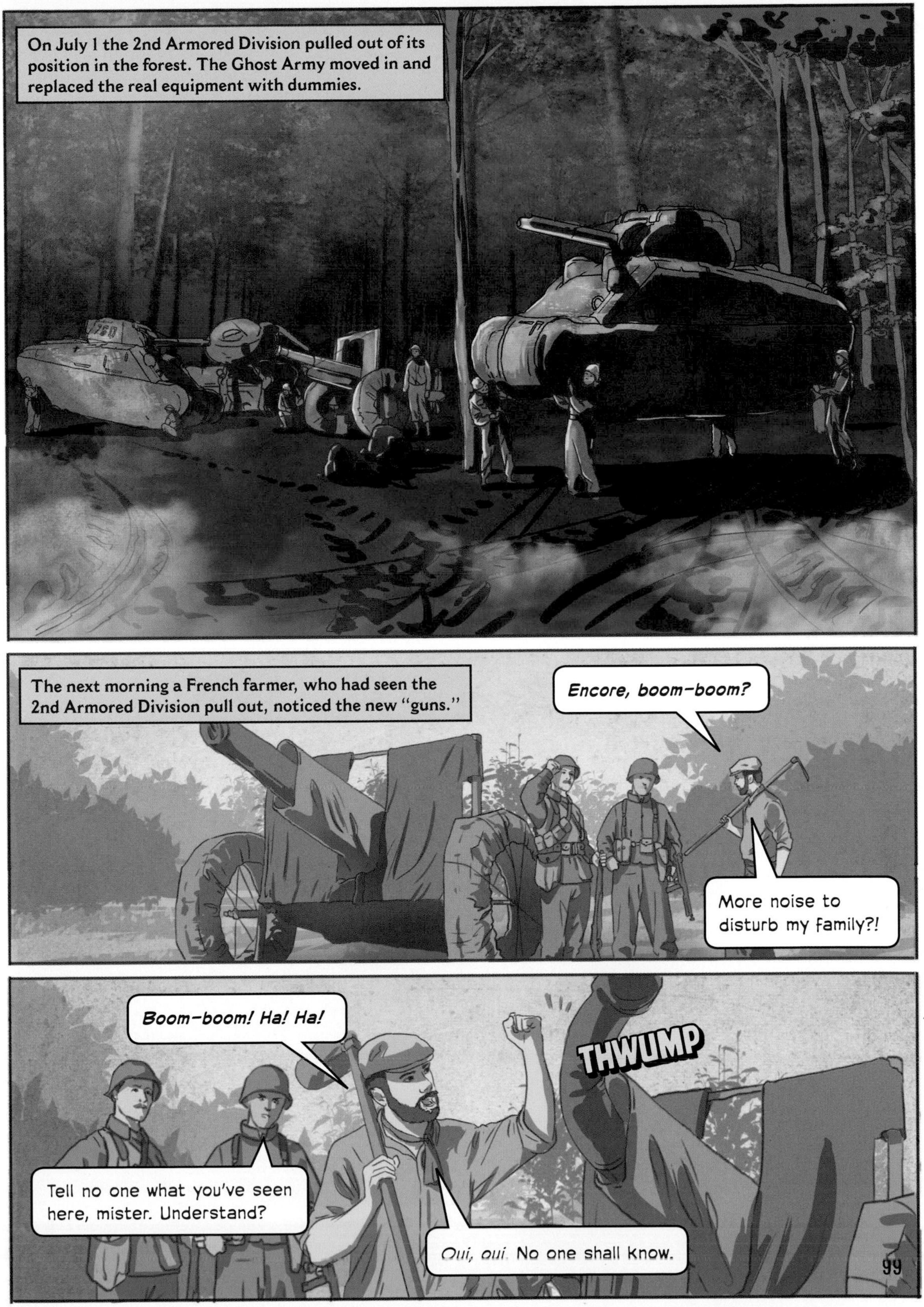
On July 1 the 2nd Armored Division pulled out of its position in the forest. The Ghost Army moved in and replaced the real equipment with dummies.
The next morning a French farmer, who had seen the 2nd Armored Division pull out, noticed the new "guns."
Encore, boom-boom?
More noise to disturb my family?!
Boom-boom! Ha! Ha!
THWUMP
Tell no one what you've seen here, mister. Understand?
Oui, oui. No one shall know.

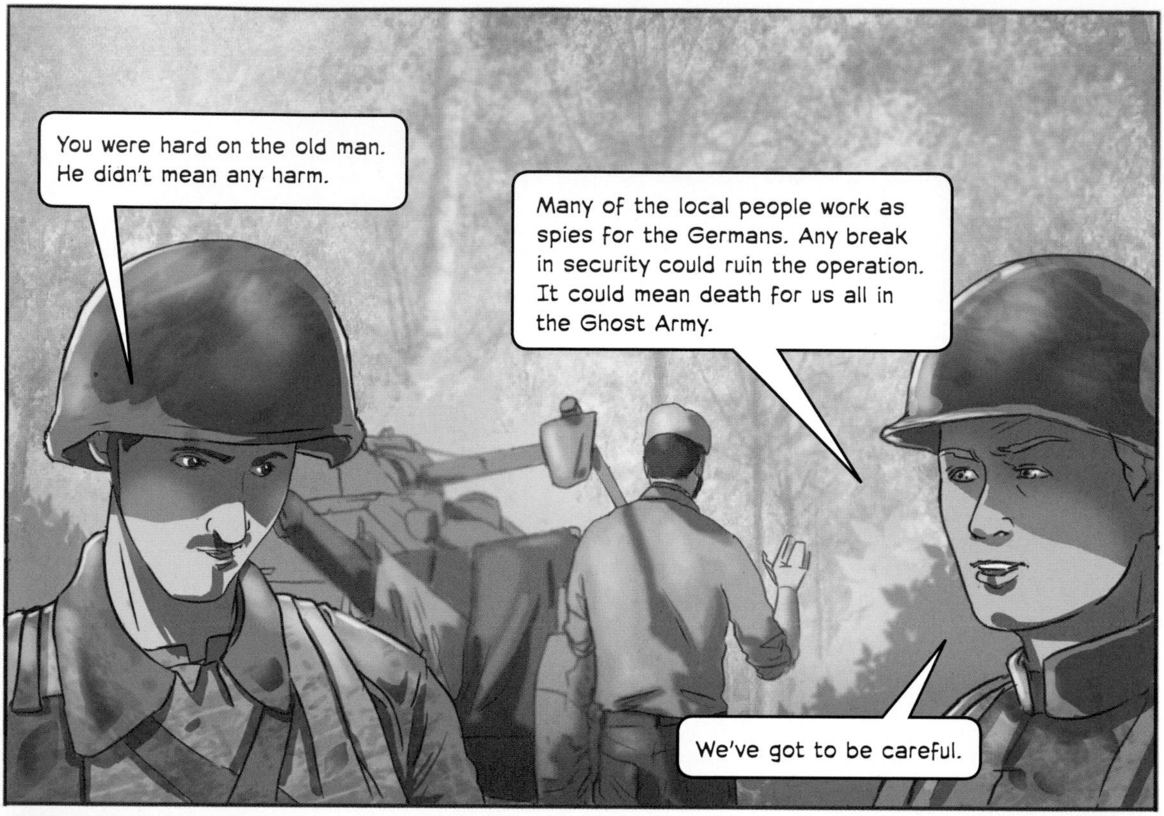
You were hard on the old man. He didn't mean any harm.
Many of the local people work as spies for the Germans. Any break in security could ruin the operation. It could mean death for us all in the Ghost Army.
We've got to be careful.

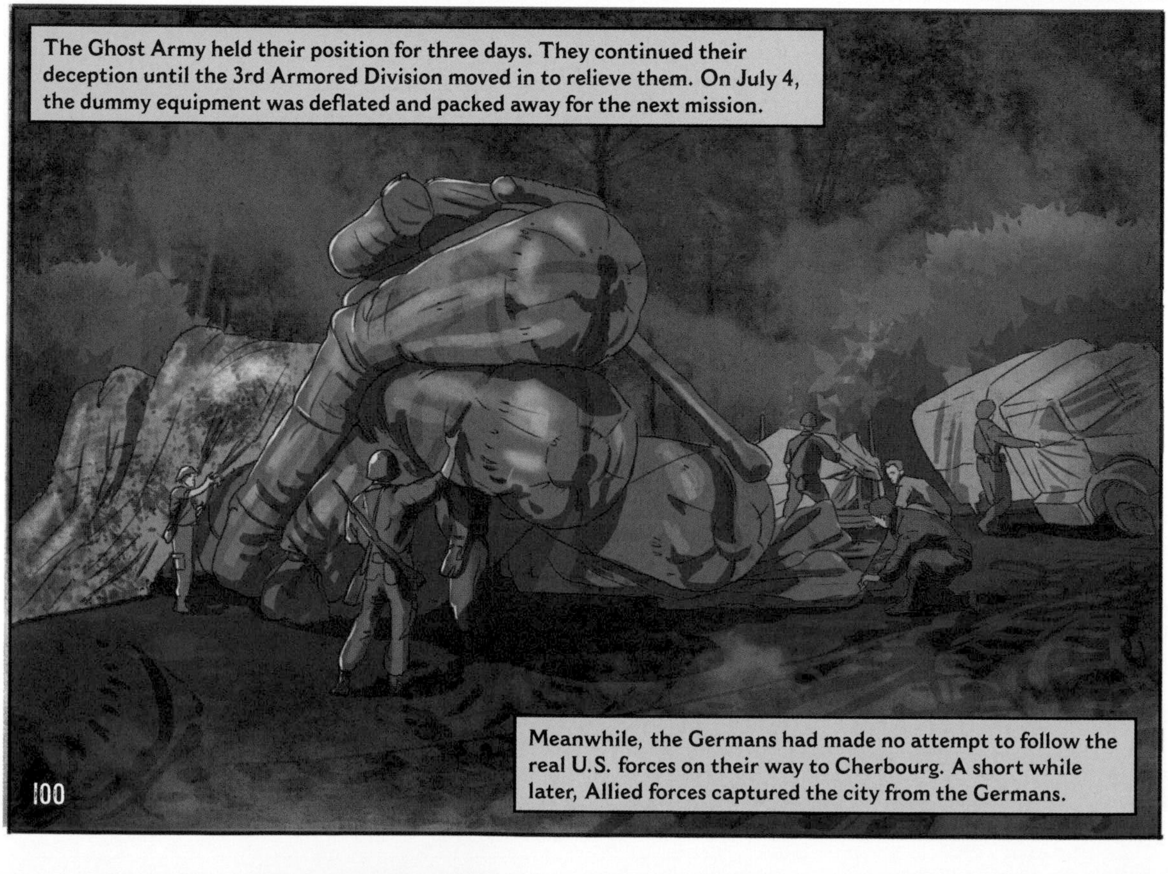
The Ghost Army held their position for three days. They continued their deception until the 3rd Armored Division moved in to relieve them. On July 4, the dummy equipment was deflated and packed away for the next mission.
Meanwhile, the Germans had made no attempt to follow the real U.S. forces on their way to Cherbourg. A short while later, Allied forces captured the city from the Germans.

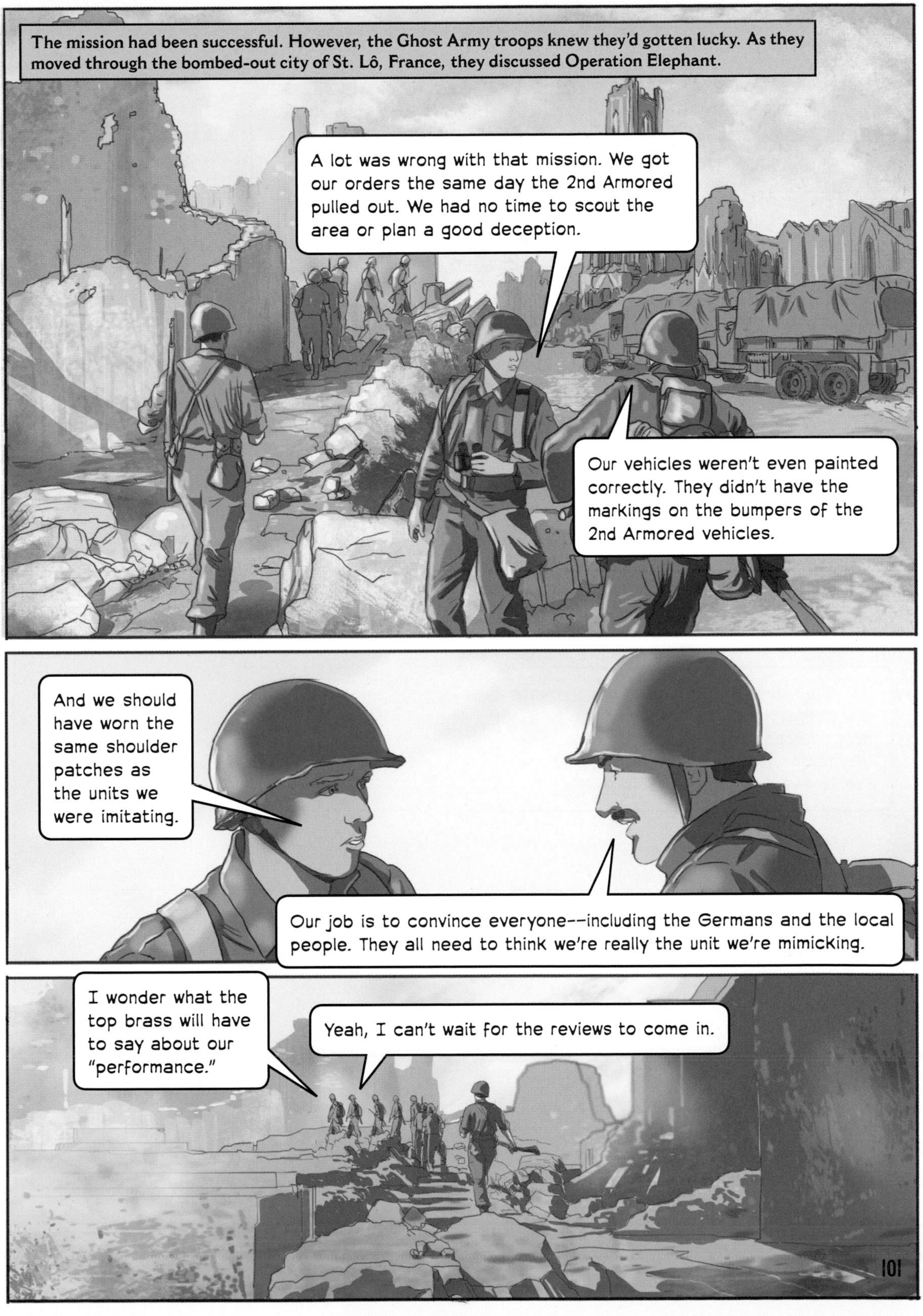
The mission had been successful. However, the Ghost Army troops knew they'd gotten lucky. As they moved through the bombed-out city of St. Lô, France, they discussed Operation Elephant.
A lot was wrong with that mission. We got our orders the same day the 2nd Armored pulled out. We had no time to scout the area or plan a good deception.
Our vehicles weren't even painted correctly. They didn't have the markings on the bumpers of the 2nd Armored vehicles.
And we should have worn the same shoulder patches as the units we were imitating.
Our job is to convince everyone--including the Germans and the local people. They all need to think we're really the unit we're mimicking.
I wonder what the top brass will have to say about our "performance."
Yeah, I can't wait for the reviews to come in.

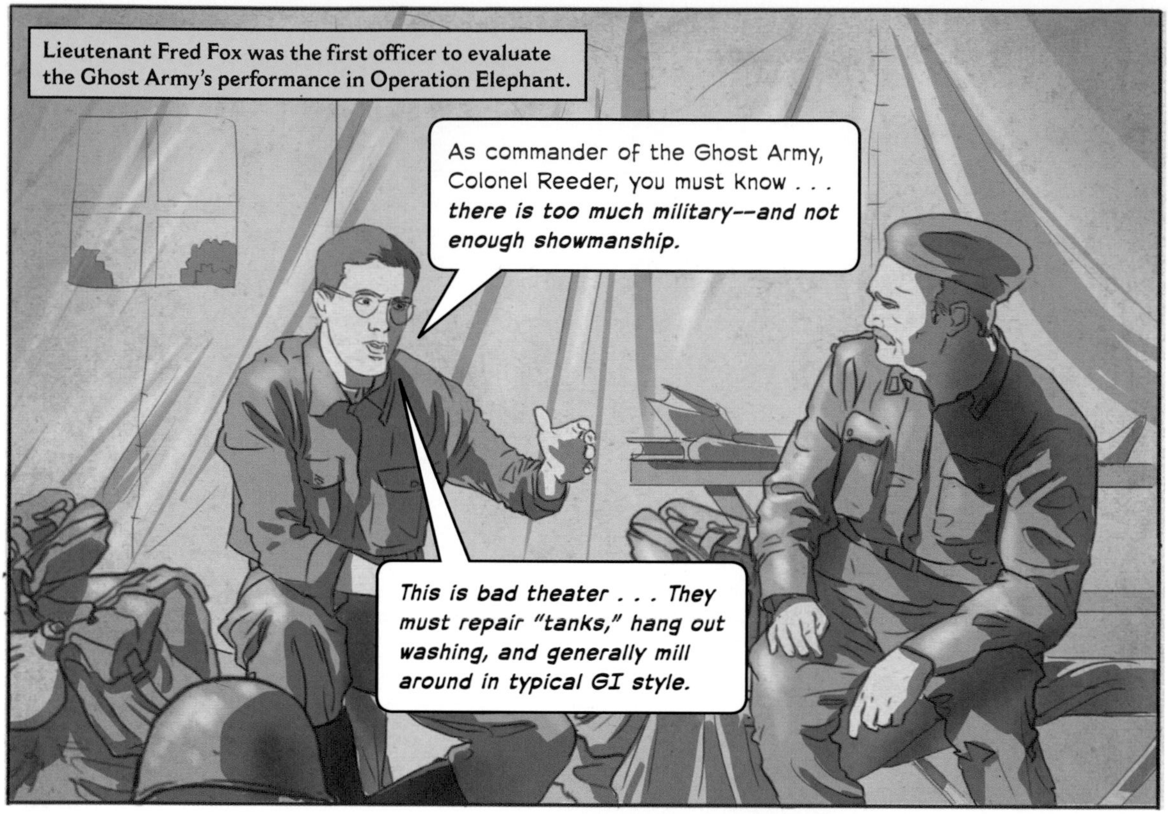
Lieutenant Fred Fox was the first officer to evaluate the Ghost Army's performance in Operation Elephant.
As commander of the Ghost Army, Colonel Reeder, you must know . . . *there is too much military--and not enough showmanship.*
This is bad theater . . . They must repair "tanks," hang out washing, and generally mill around in typical GI style.

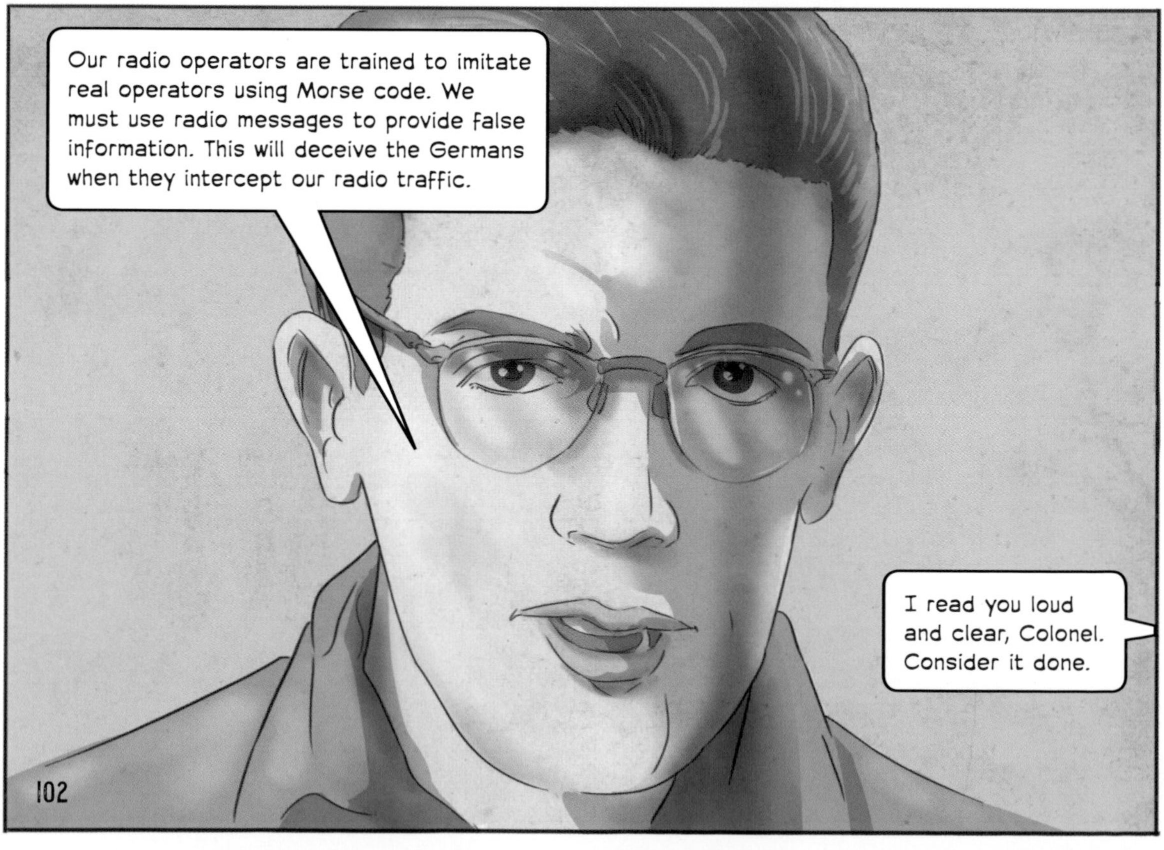
Our radio operators are trained to imitate real operators using Morse code. We must use radio messages to provide false information. This will deceive the Germans when they intercept our radio traffic.
I read you loud and clear, Colonel. Consider it done.

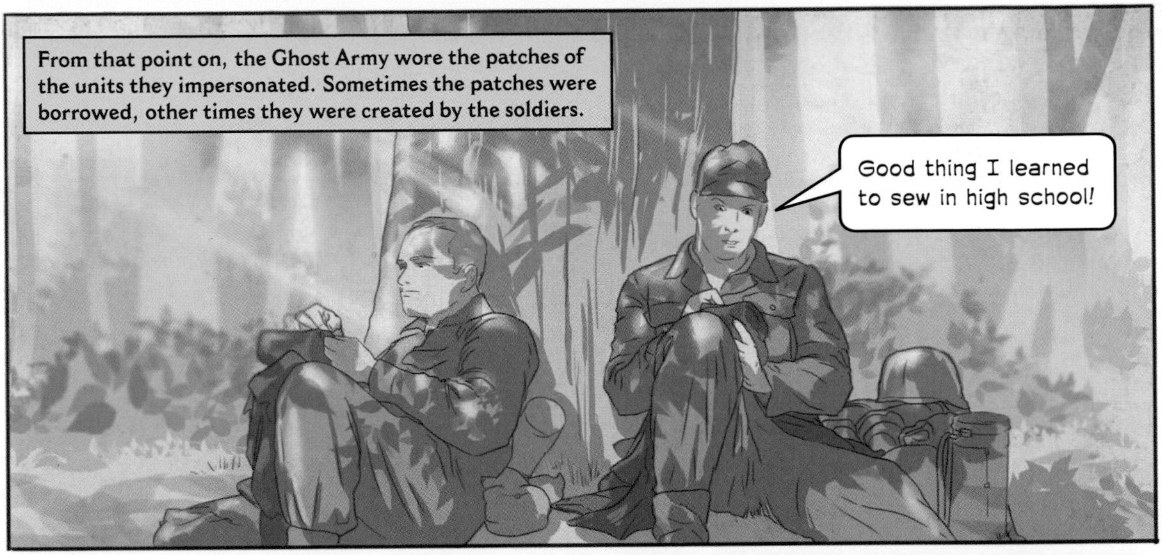
From that point on, the Ghost Army wore the patches of the units they impersonated. Sometimes the patches were borrowed, other times they were created by the soldiers.
Good thing I learned to sew in high school!

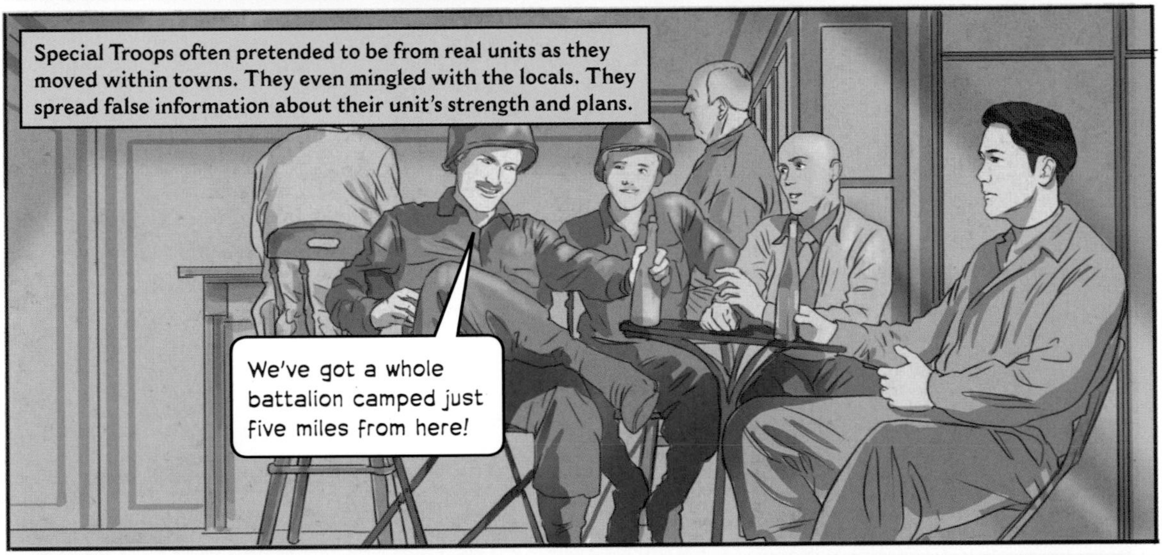
Special Troops often pretended to be from real units as they moved within towns. They even mingled with the locals. They spread false information about their unit's strength and plans.
We've got a whole battalion camped just five miles from here!

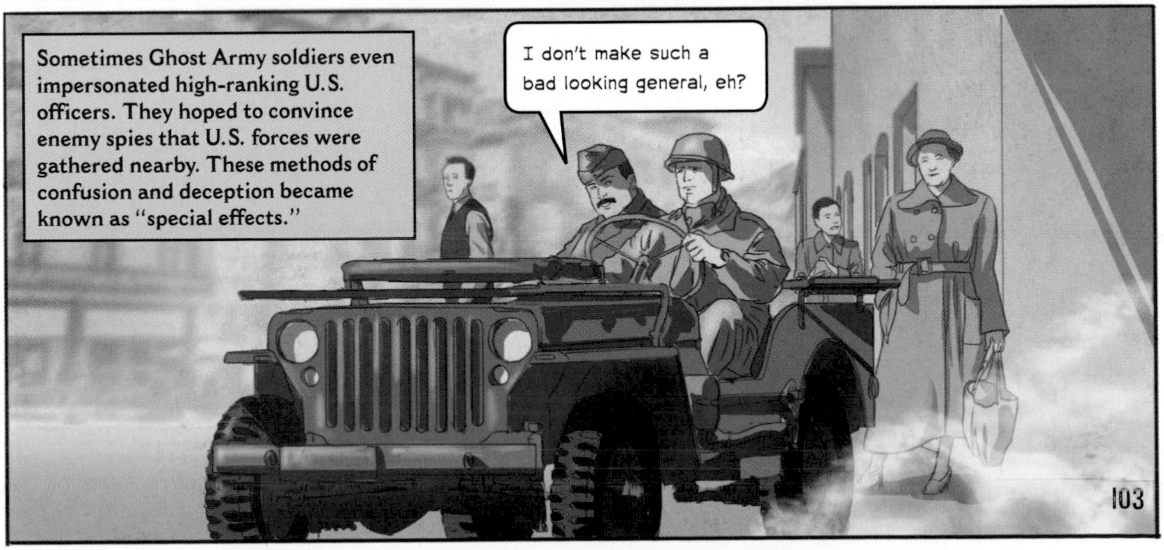
Sometimes Ghost Army soldiers even impersonated high-ranking U.S. officers. They hoped to convince enemy spies that U.S. forces were gathered nearby. These methods of confusion and deception became known as "special effects."
I don't make such a bad looking general, eh?

OPERATION BRITTANY: DEADLY SHOW AT BREST

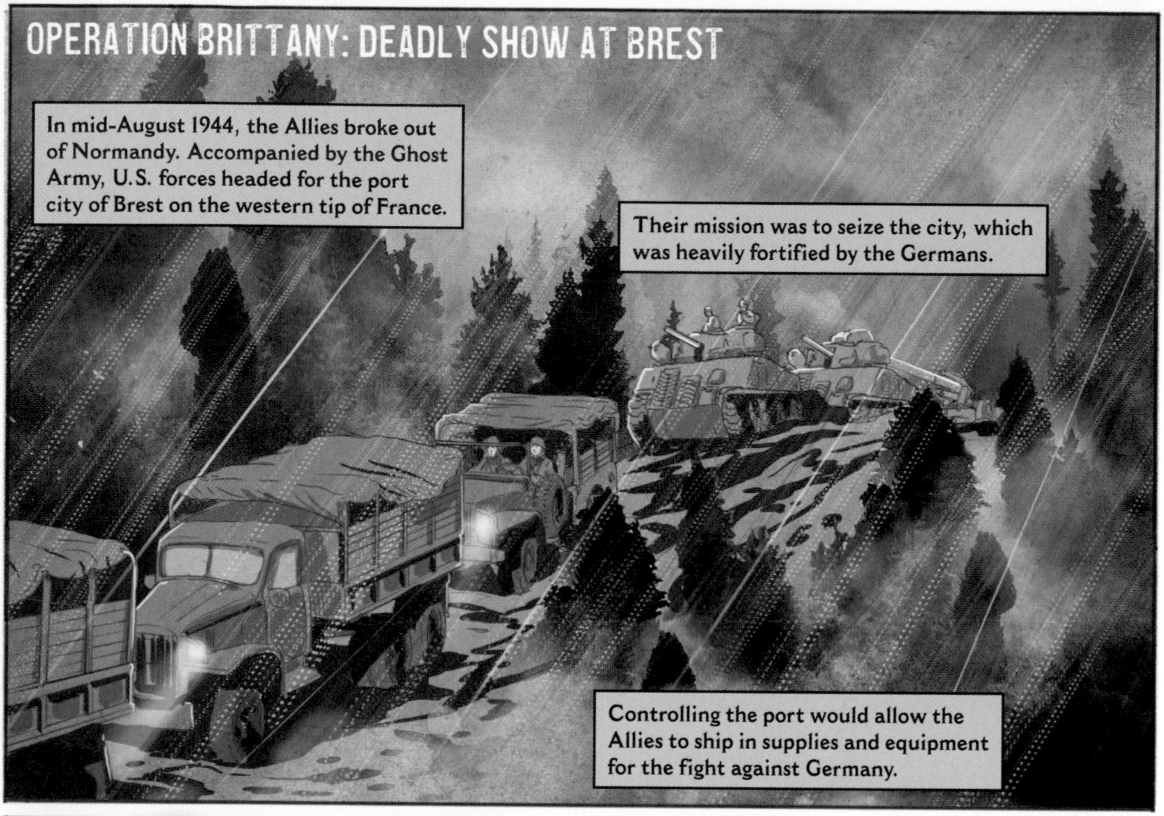
In mid-August 1944, the Allies broke out of Normandy. Accompanied by the Ghost Army, U.S. forces headed for the port city of Brest on the western tip of France.
Their mission was to seize the city, which was heavily fortified by the Germans.
Controlling the port would allow the Allies to ship in supplies and equipment for the fight against Germany.

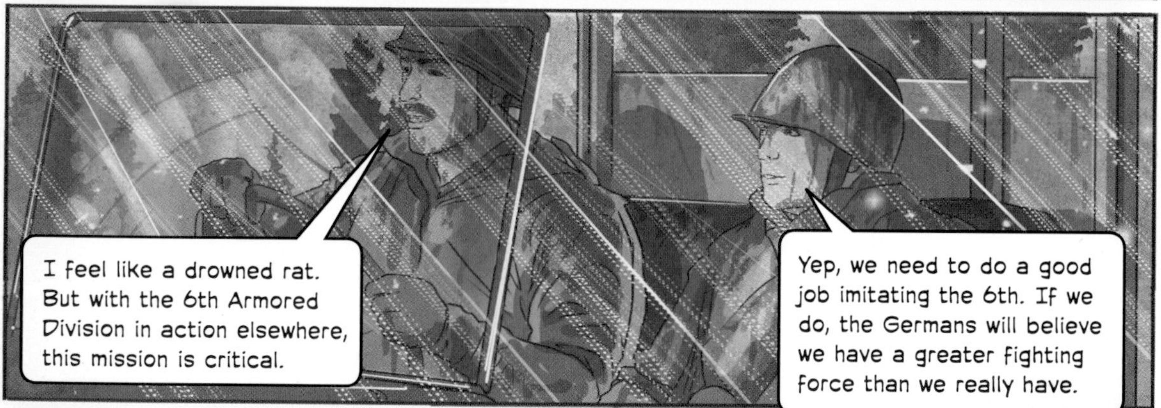
I feel like a drowned rat. But with the 6th Armored Division in action elsewhere, this mission is critical.
Yep, we need to do a good job imitating the 6th. If we do, the Germans will believe we have a greater fighting force than we really have.

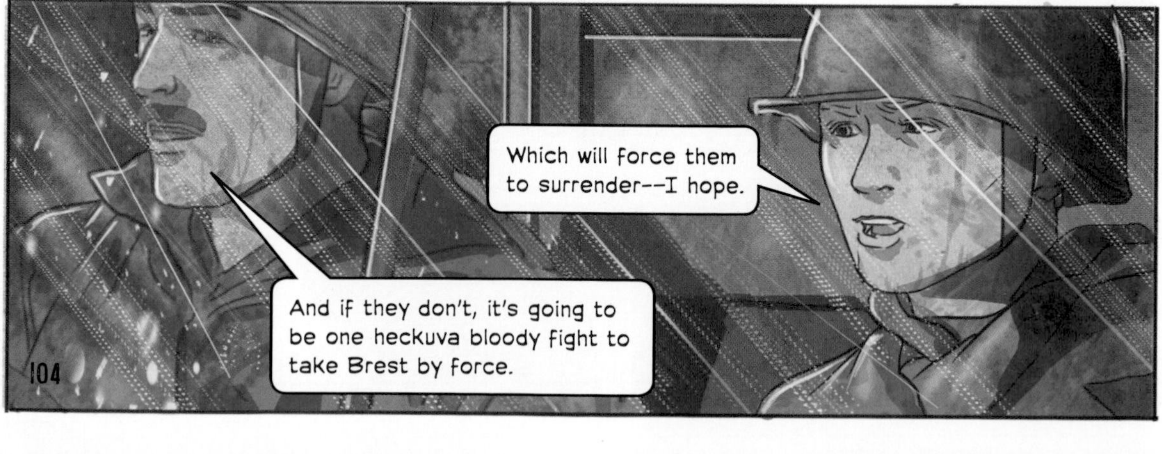
Which will force them to surrender--I hope.
And if they don't, it's going to be one heckuva bloody fight to take Brest by force.

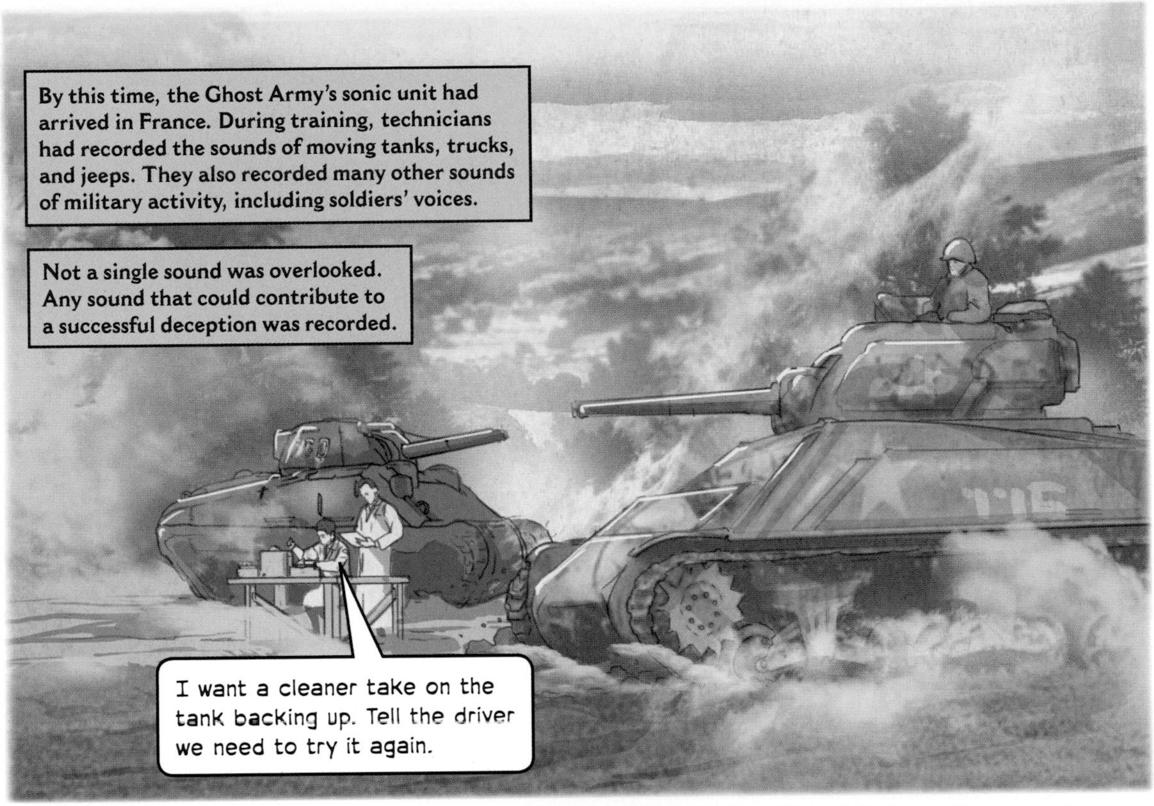
By this time, the Ghost Army's sonic unit had arrived in France. During training, technicians had recorded the sounds of moving tanks, trucks, and jeeps. They also recorded many other sounds of military activity, including soldiers' voices.
Not a single sound was overlooked. Any sound that could contribute to a successful deception was recorded.
I want a cleaner take on the tank backing up. Tell the driver we need to try it again.

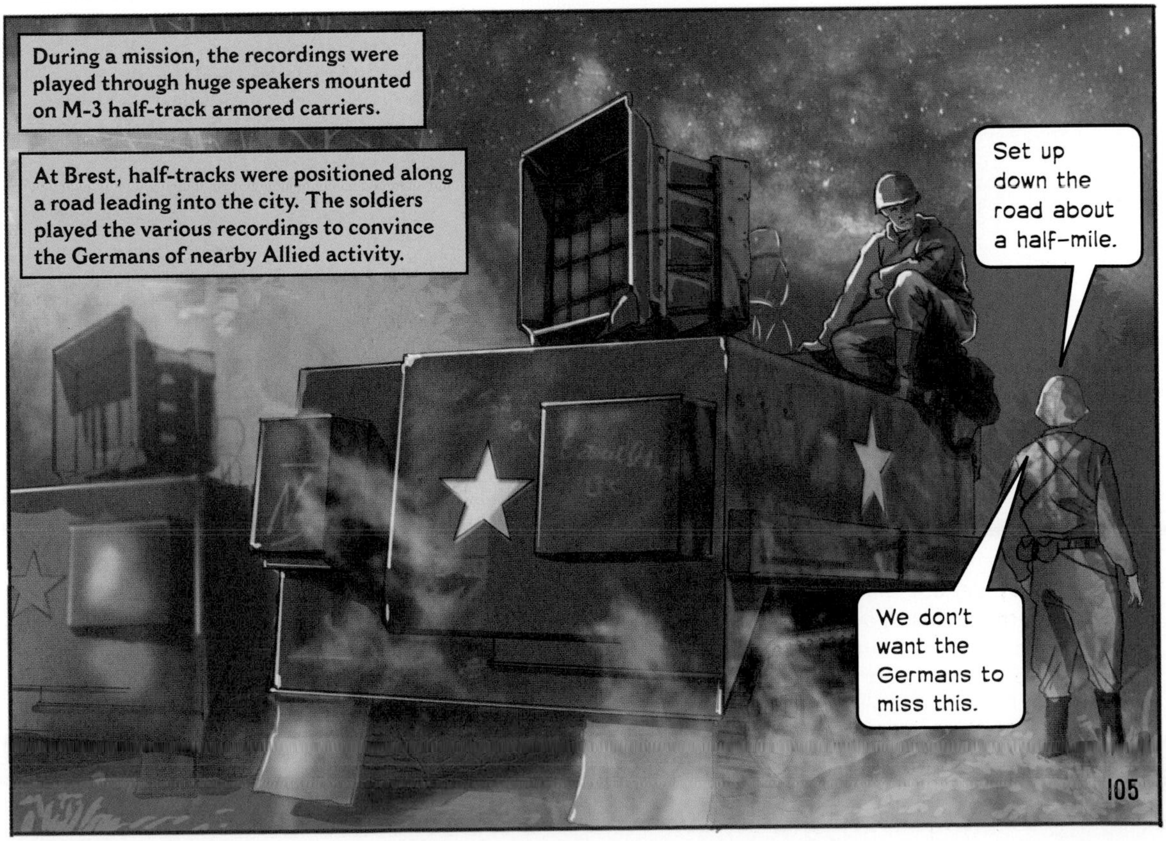
During a mission, the recordings were played through huge speakers mounted on M-3 half-track armored carriers.
At Brest, half-tracks were positioned along a road leading into the city. The soldiers played the various recordings to convince the Germans of nearby Allied activity.
Set up down the road about a half-mile.
We don't want the Germans to miss this.

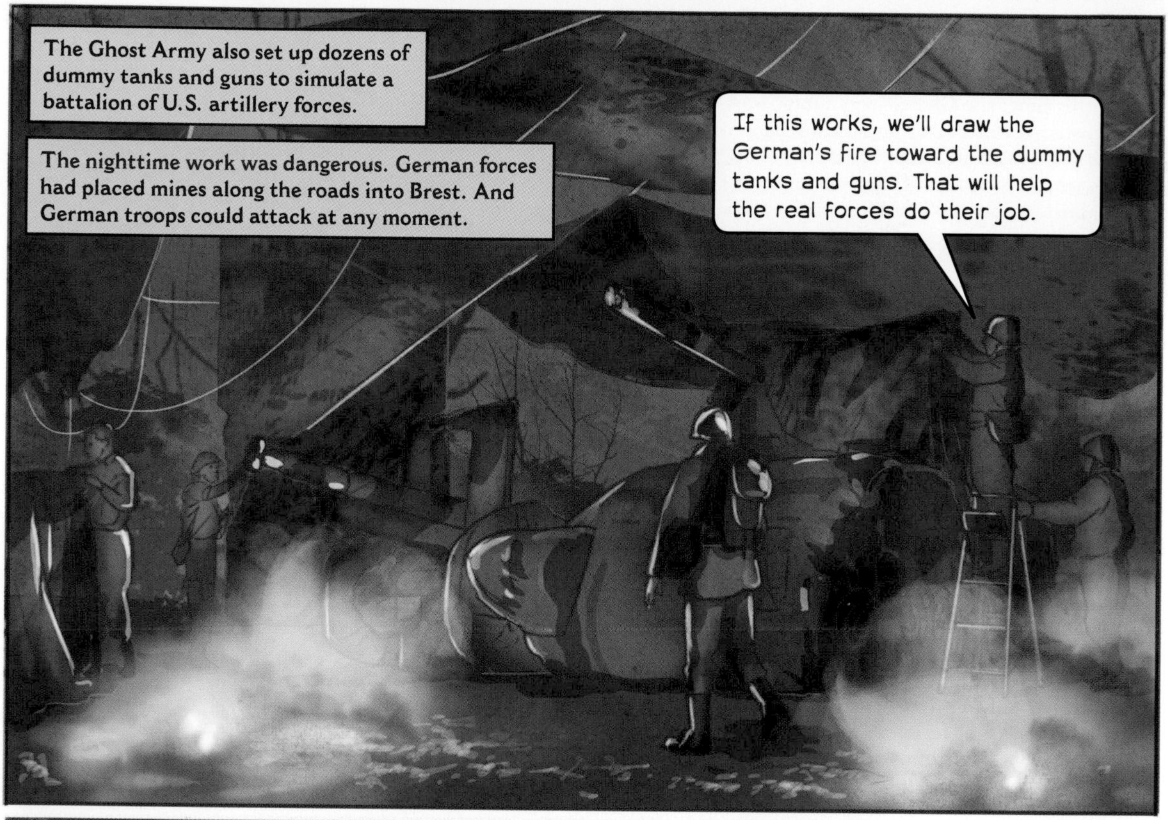
The Ghost Army also set up dozens of dummy tanks and guns to simulate a battalion of U.S. artillery forces.
The nighttime work was dangerous. German forces had placed mines along the roads into Brest. And German troops could attack at any moment.
If this works, we'll draw the German's fire toward the dummy tanks and guns. That will help the real forces do their job.

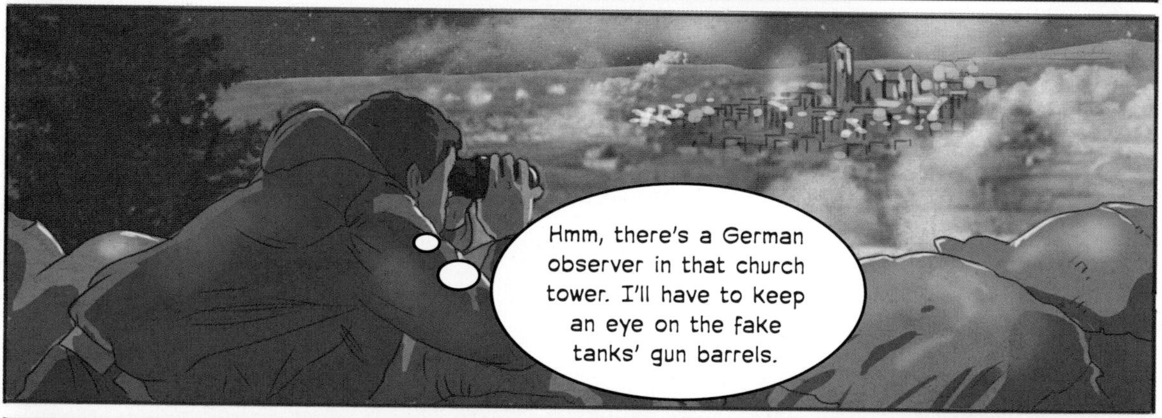
Hmm, there's a German observer in that church tower. I'll have to keep an eye on the fake tanks' gun barrels.

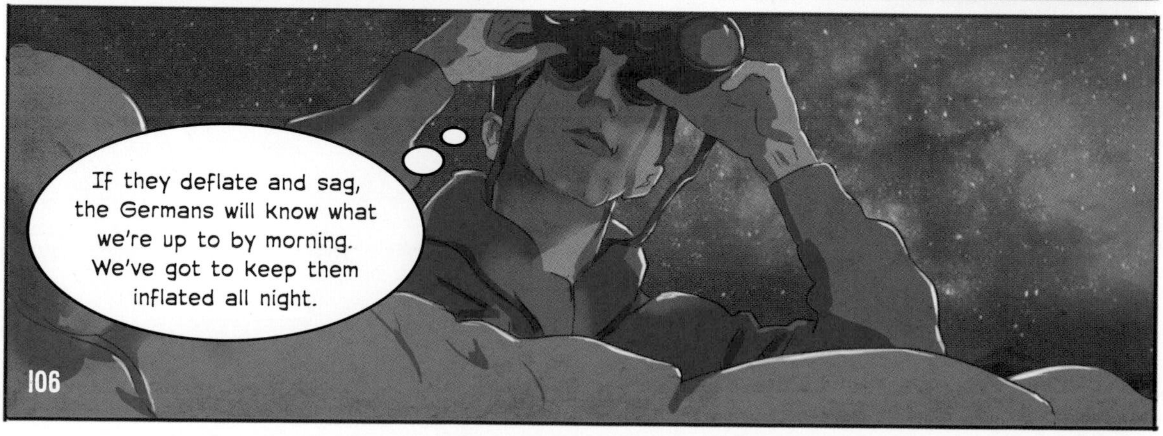
If they deflate and sag, the Germans will know what we're up to by morning. We've got to keep them inflated all night.

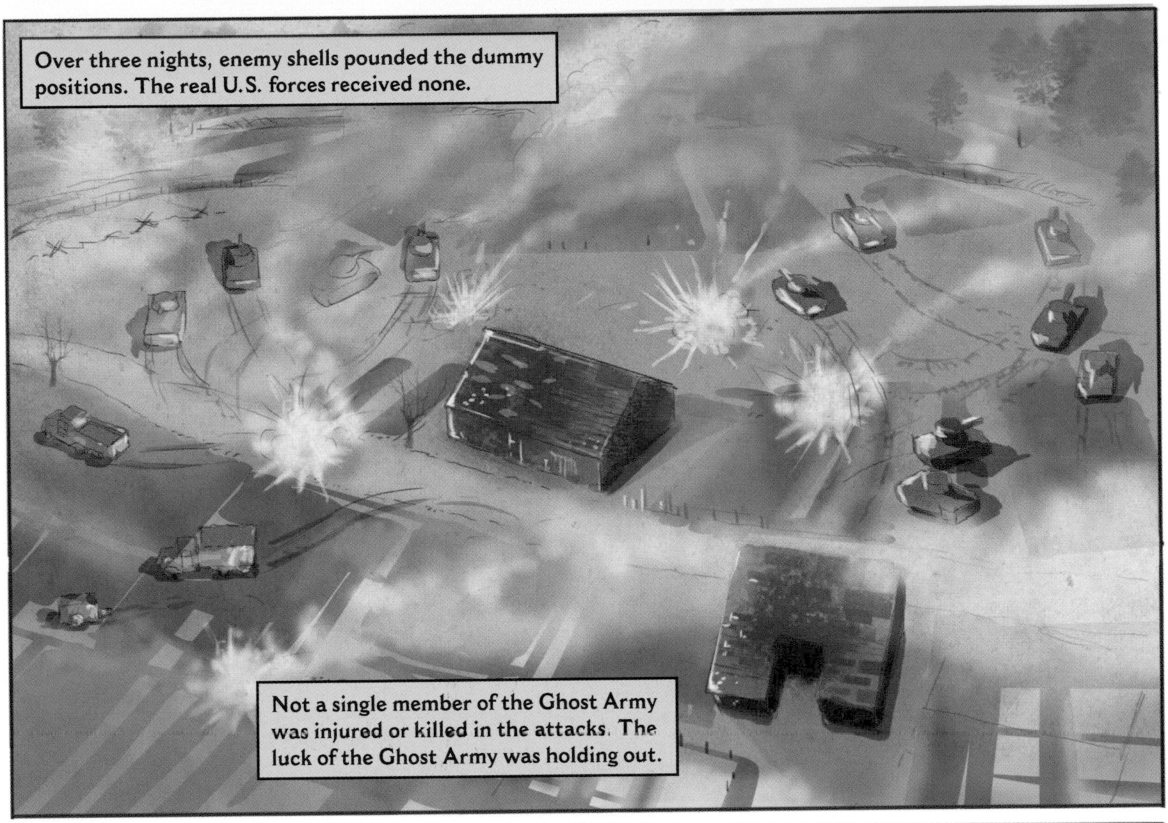
Over three nights, enemy shells pounded the dummy positions. The real U.S. forces received none.
Not a single member of the Ghost Army was injured or killed in the attacks. The luck of the Ghost Army was holding out.

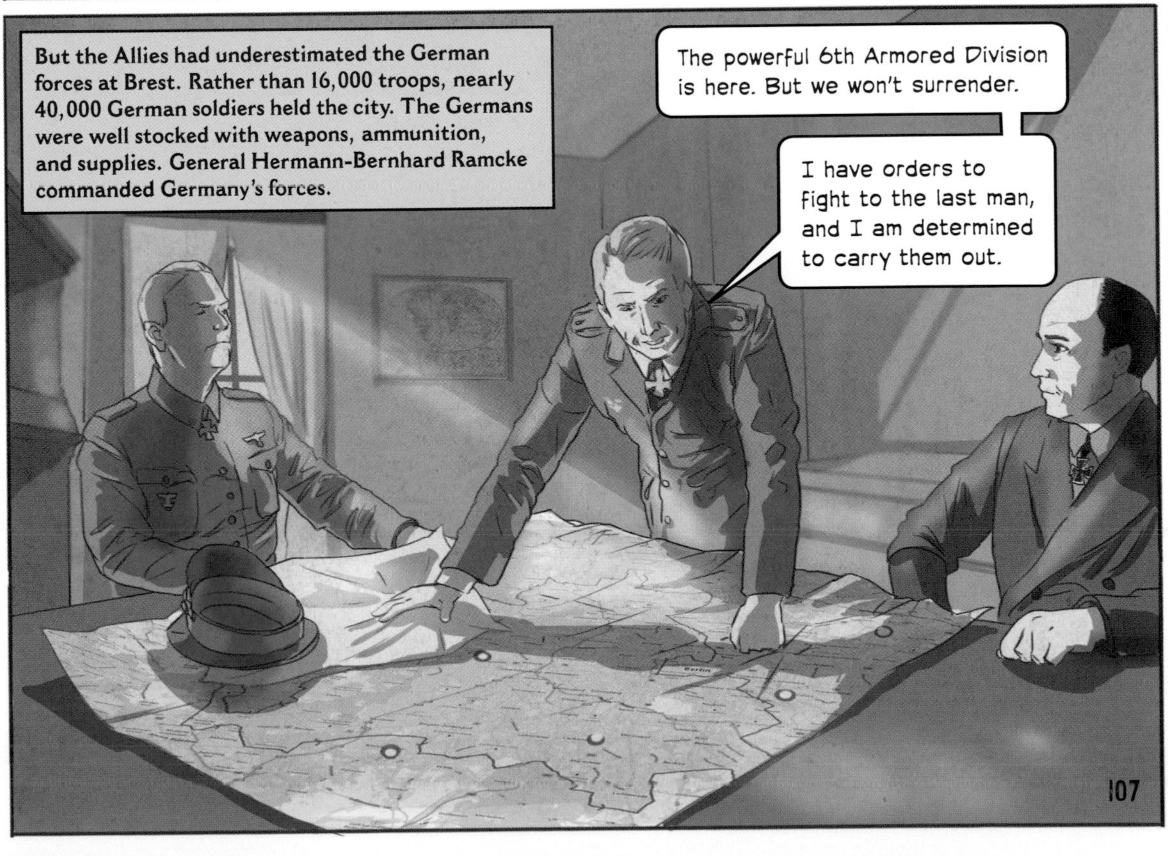
But the Allies had underestimated the German forces at Brest. Rather than 16,000 troops, nearly 40,000 German soldiers held the city. The Germans were well stocked with weapons, ammunition, and supplies. General Hermann-Bernhard Ramcke commanded Germany's forces.
The powerful 6th Armored Division is here. But we won't surrender.
I have orders to fight to the last man, and I am determined to carry them out.

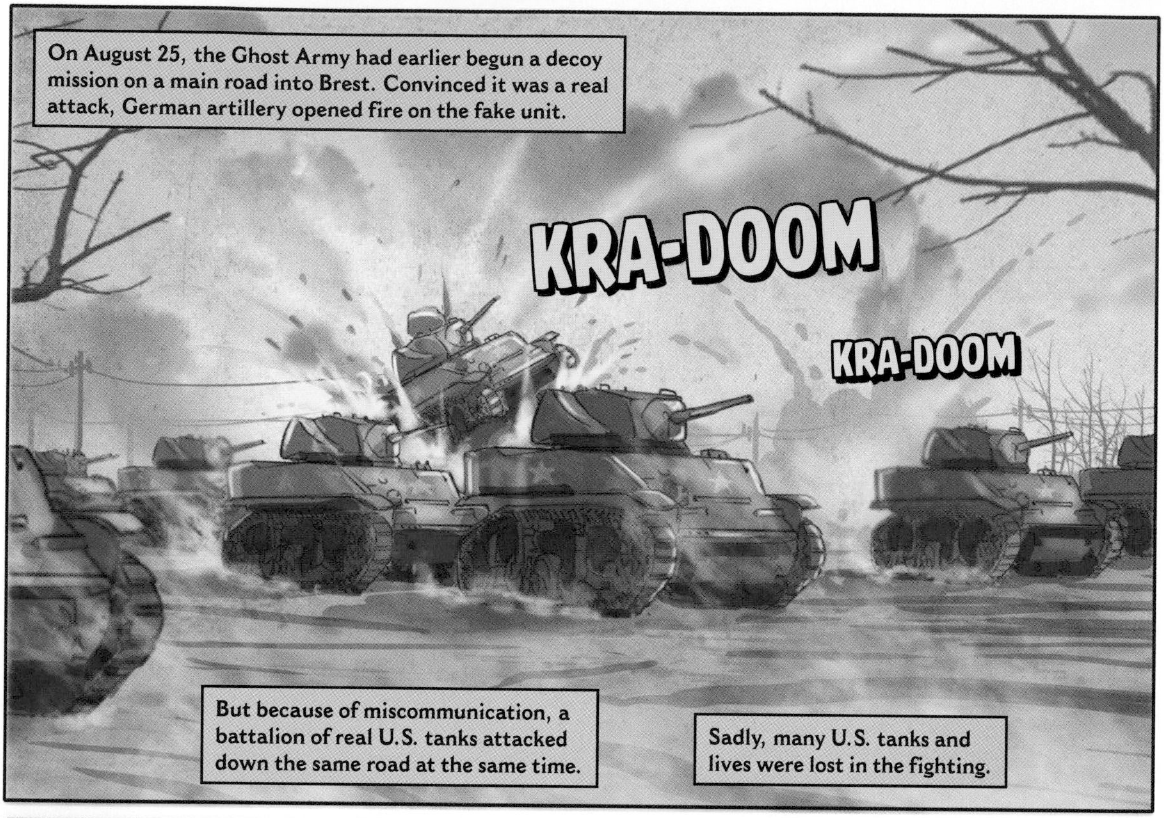
On August 25, the Ghost Army had earlier begun a decoy mission on a main road into Brest. Convinced it was a real attack, German artillery opened fire on the fake unit.
KRA-DOOM
KRA-DOOM
But because of miscommunication, a battalion of real U.S. tanks attacked down the same road at the same time.
Sadly, many U.S. tanks and lives were lost in the fighting.

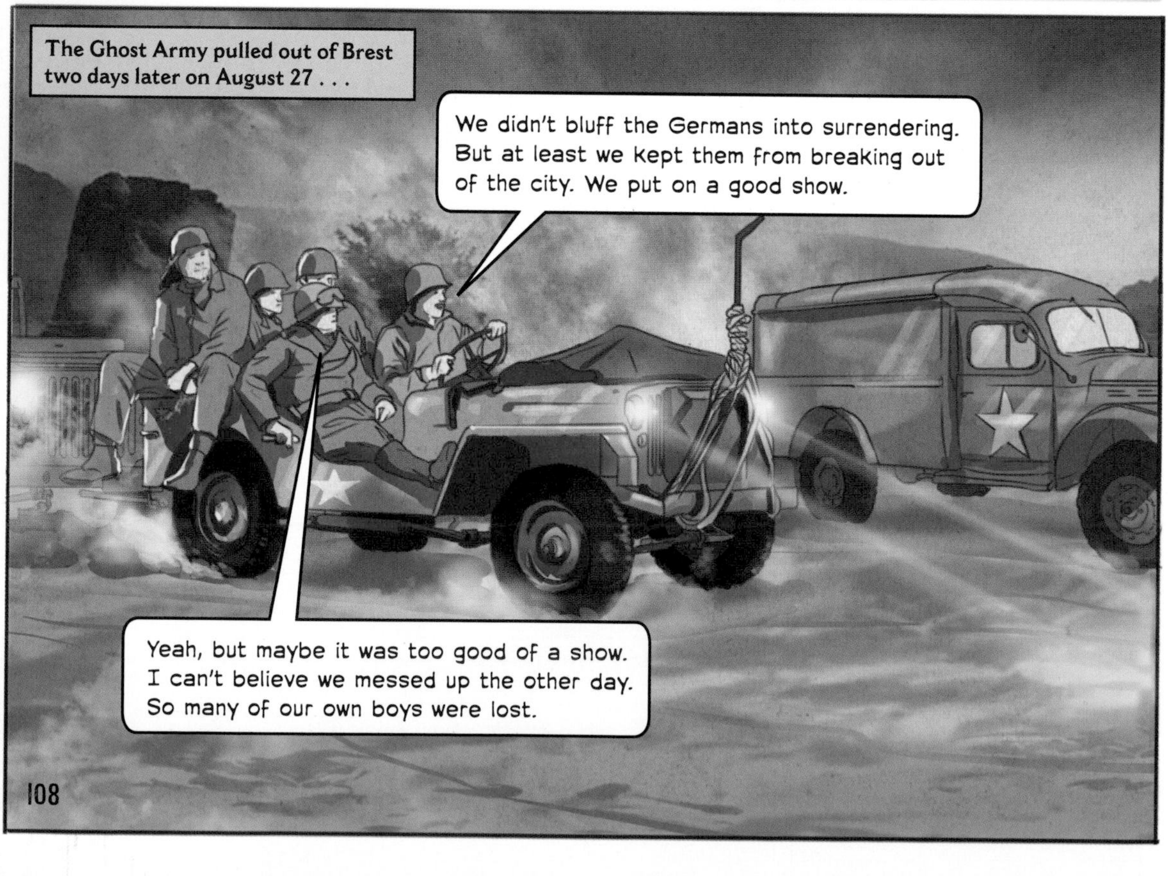
The Ghost Army pulled out of Brest two days later on August 27 . . .
We didn't bluff the Germans into surrendering. But at least we kept them from breaking out of the city. We put on a good show.
Yeah, but maybe it was too good of a show. I can't believe we messed up the other day. So many of our own boys were lost.

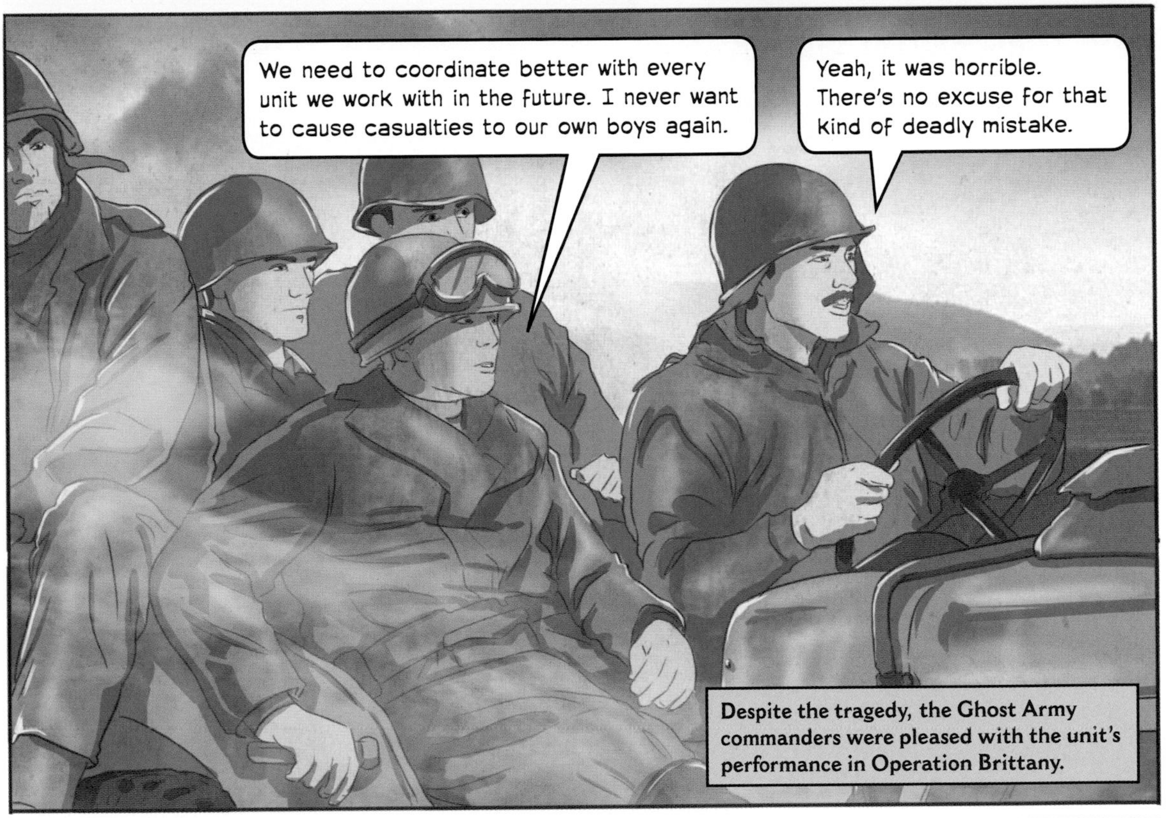
We need to coordinate better with every unit we work with in the future. I never want to cause casualties to our own boys again.
Yeah, it was horrible. There's no excuse for that kind of deadly mistake.
Despite the tragedy, the Ghost Army commanders were pleased with the unit's performance in Operation Brittany.

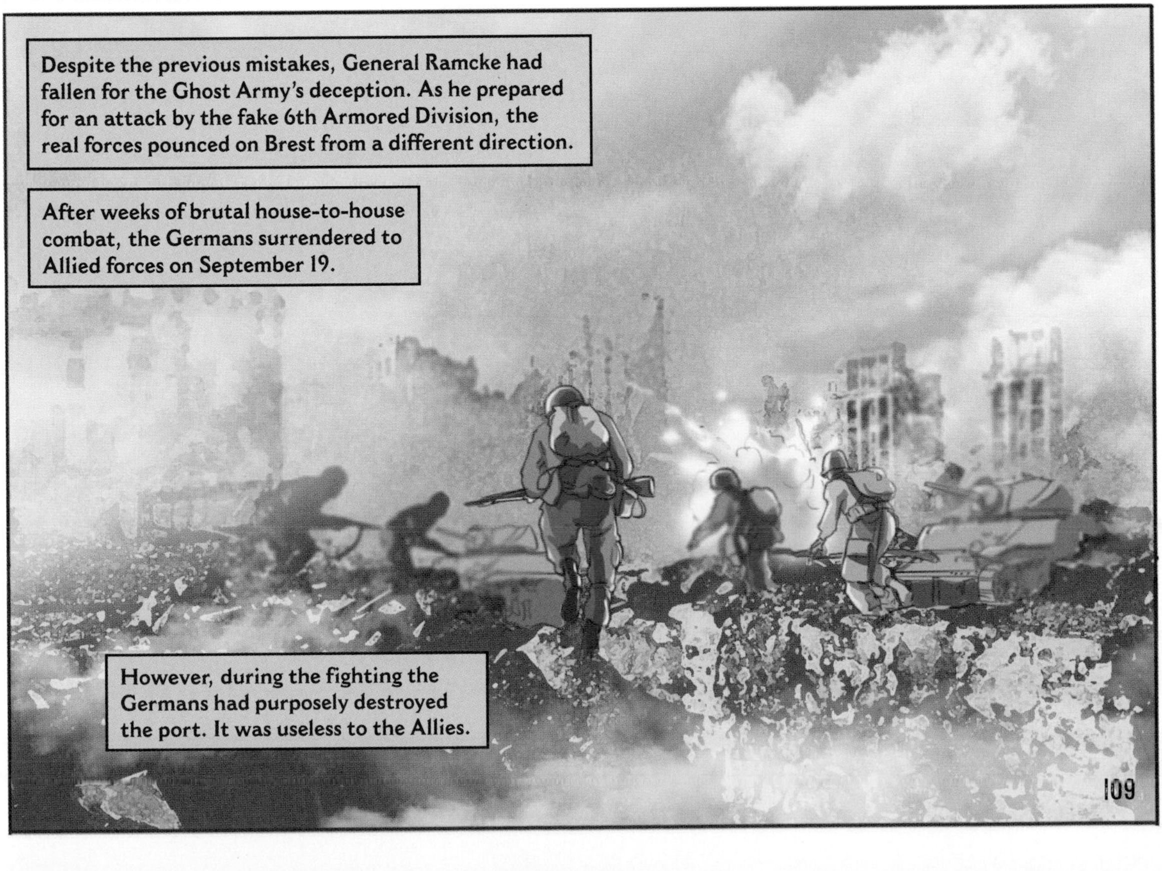
Despite the previous mistakes, General Ramcke had fallen for the Ghost Army's deception. As he prepared for an attack by the fake 6th Armored Division, the real forces pounced on Brest from a different direction.
After weeks of brutal house-to-house combat, the Germans surrendered to Allied forces on September 19.
However, during the fighting the Germans had purposely destroyed the port. It was useless to the Allies.

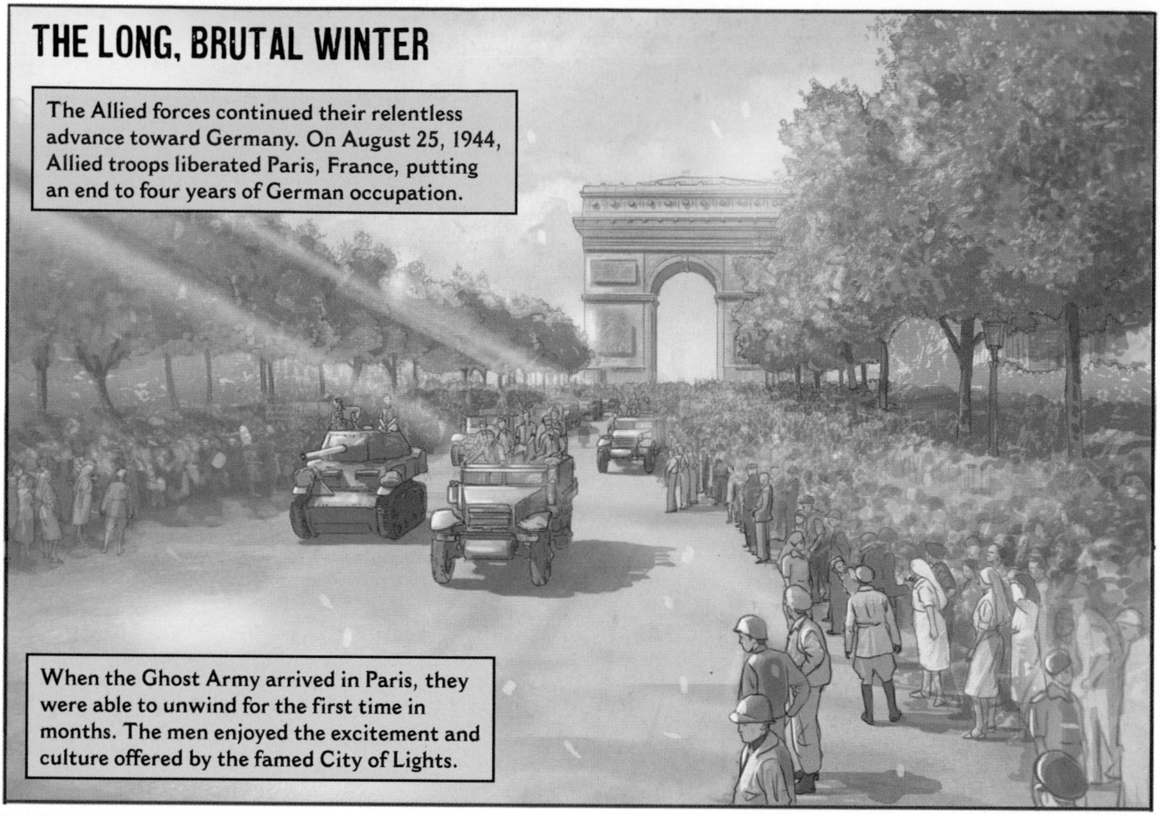
THE LONG, BRUTAL WINTER
The Allied forces continued their relentless advance toward Germany. On August 25, 1944, Allied troops liberated Paris, France, putting an end to four years of German occupation.
When the Ghost Army arrived in Paris, they were able to unwind for the first time in months. The men enjoyed the excitement and culture offered by the famed City of Lights.

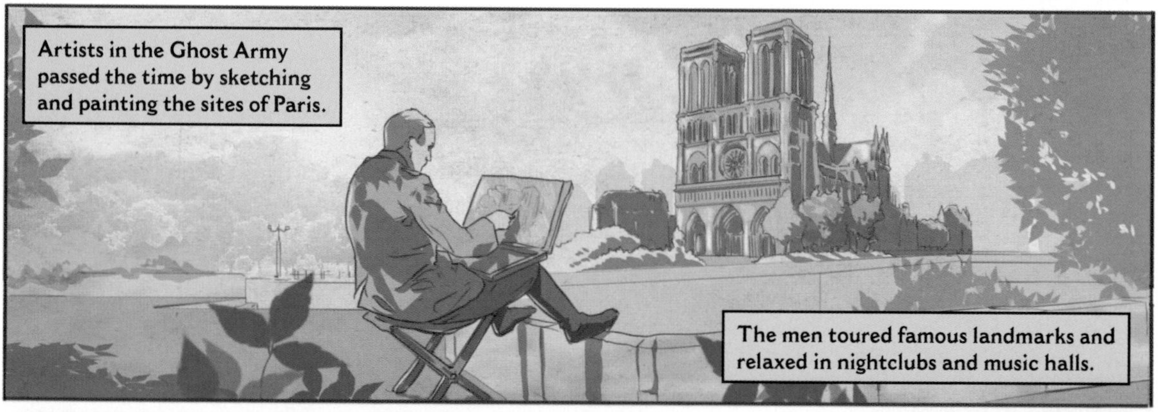
Artists in the Ghost Army passed the time by sketching and painting the sites of Paris.
The men toured famous landmarks and relaxed in nightclubs and music halls.

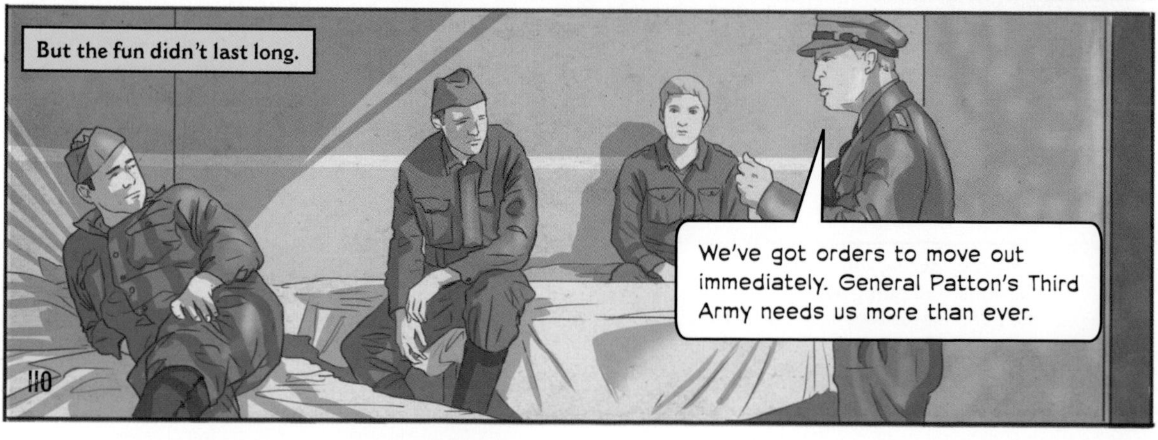
But the fun didn't last long.
We've got orders to move out immediately. General Patton's Third Army needs us more than ever.

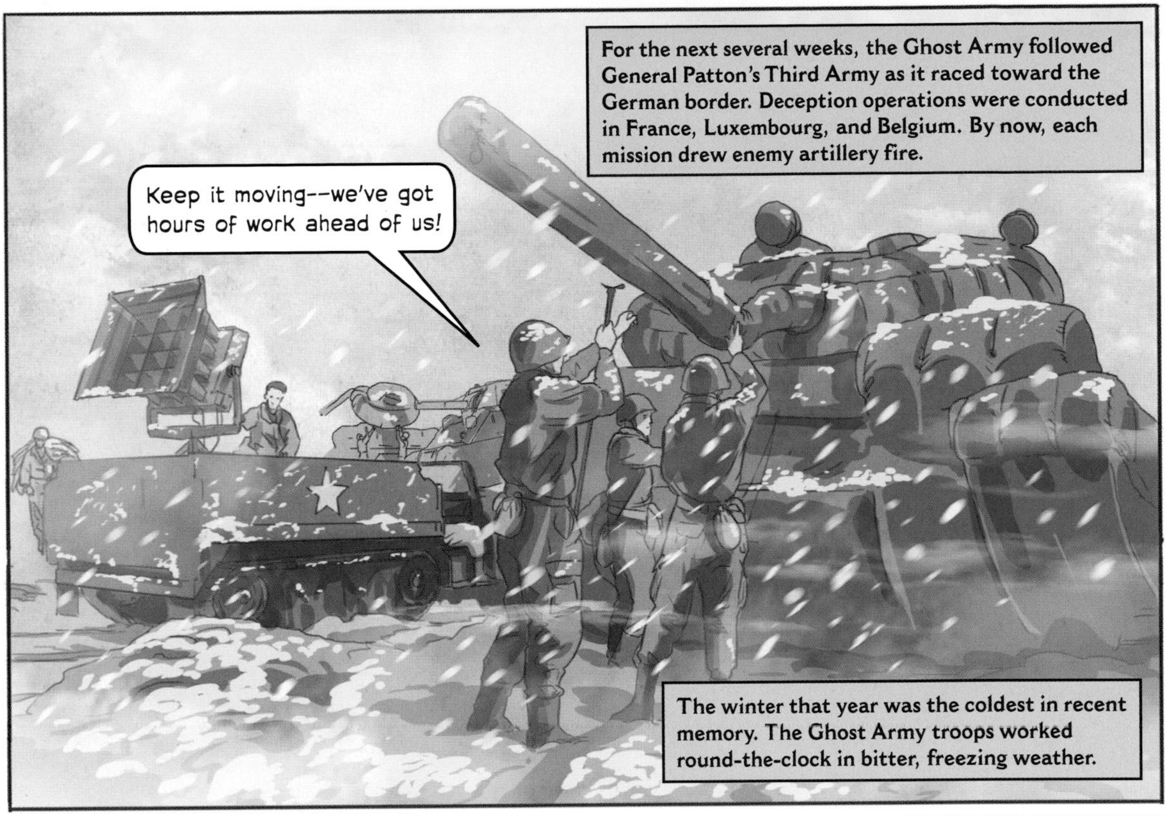
For the next several weeks, the Ghost Army followed General Patton's Third Army as it raced toward the German border. Deception operations were conducted in France, Luxembourg, and Belgium. By now, each mission drew enemy artillery fire.
Keep it moving--we've got hours of work ahead of us!
The winter that year was the coldest in recent memory. The Ghost Army troops worked round-the-clock in bitter, freezing weather.

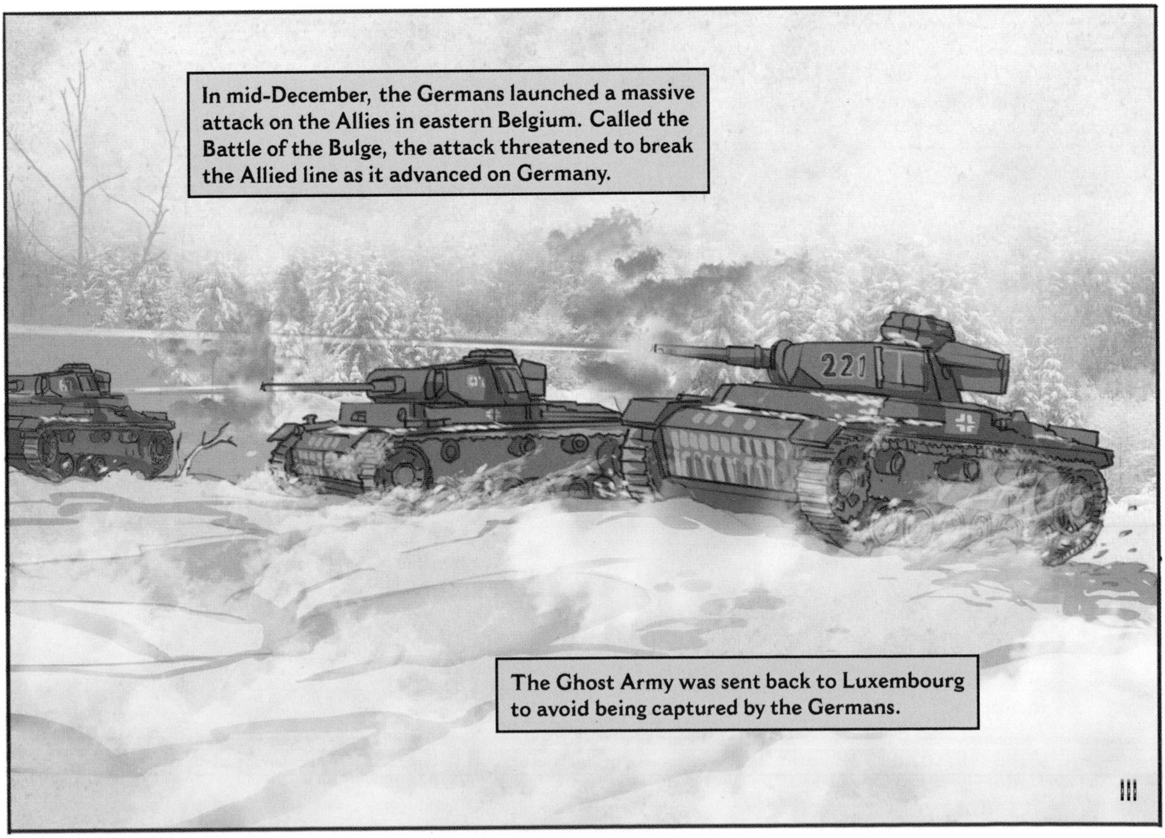
In mid-December, the Germans launched a massive attack on the Allies in eastern Belgium. Called the Battle of the Bulge, the attack threatened to break the Allied line as it advanced on Germany.
221
The Ghost Army was sent back to Luxembourg to avoid being captured by the Germans.

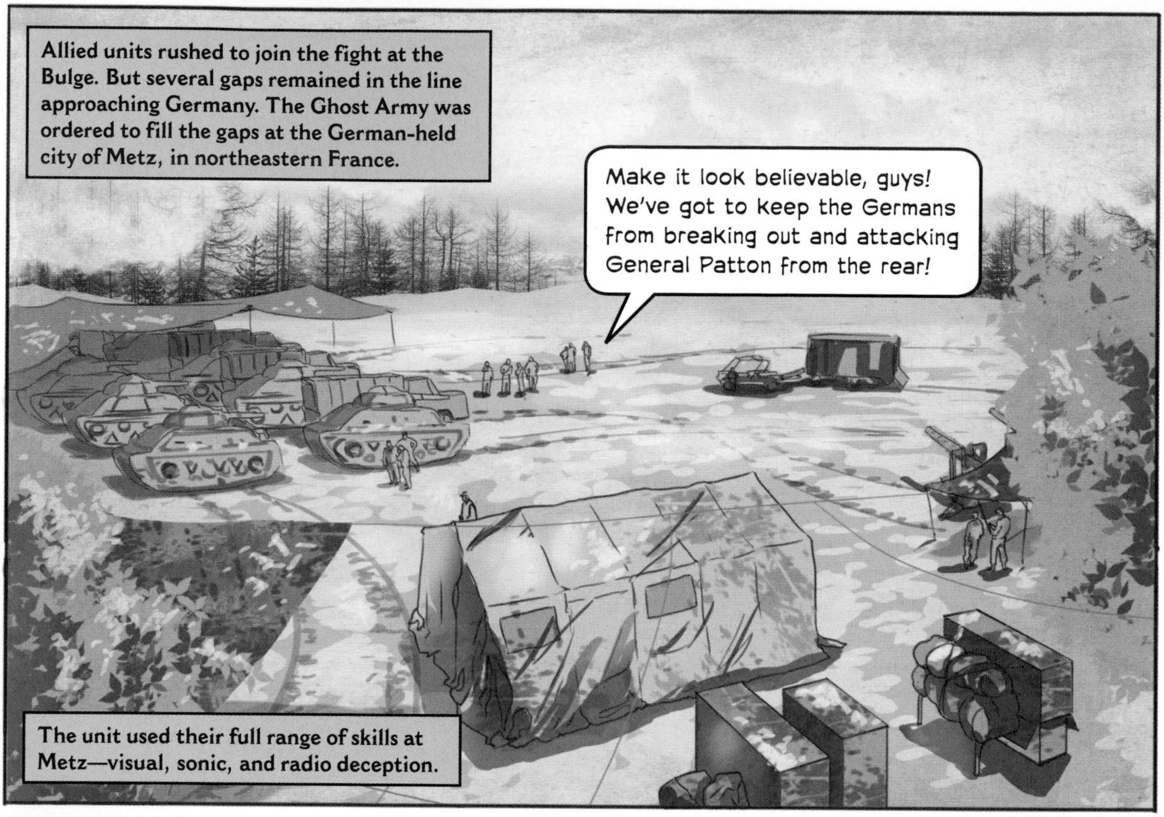
Allied units rushed to join the fight at the Bulge. But several gaps remained in the line approaching Germany. The Ghost Army was ordered to fill the gaps at the German-held city of Metz, in northeastern France.
Make it look believable, guys! We've got to keep the Germans from breaking out and attacking General Patton from the rear!
The unit used their full range of skills at Metz—visual, sonic, and radio deception.

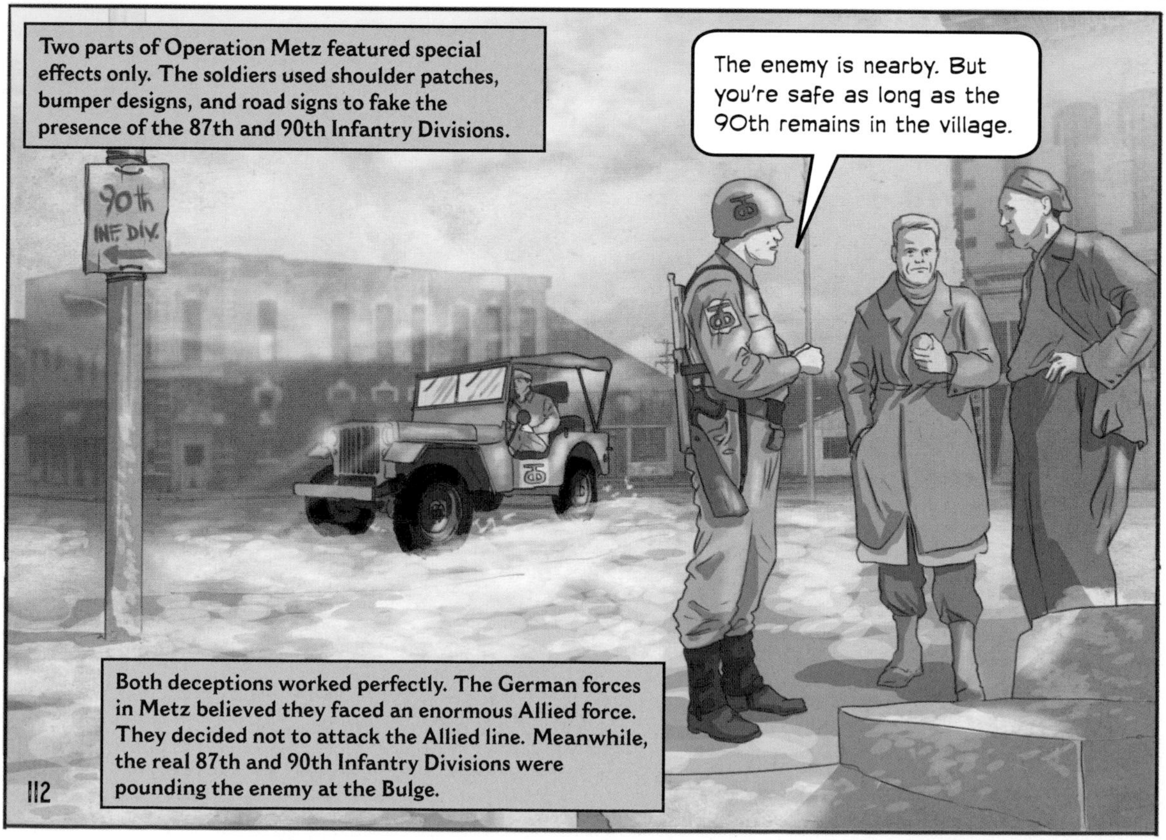
Two parts of Operation Metz featured special effects only. The soldiers used shoulder patches, bumper designs, and road signs to fake the presence of the 87th and 90th Infantry Divisions.
The enemy is nearby. But you're safe as long as the 90th remains in the village.
90th INF. DIV.
Both deceptions worked perfectly. The German forces in Metz believed they faced an enormous Allied force. They decided not to attack the Allied line. Meanwhile, the real 87th and 90th Infantry Divisions were pounding the enemy at the Bulge.

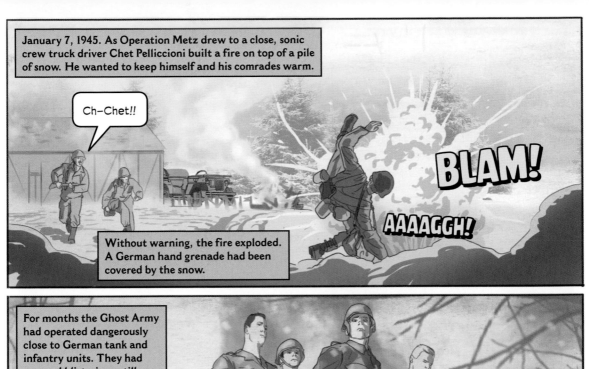

January 7, 1945. As Operation Metz drew to a close, sonic crew truck driver Chet Pelliccioni built a fire on top of a pile of snow. He wanted to keep himself and his comrades warm.

Ch–Chet!!

BLAM!

AAAAGGH!

Without warning, the fire exploded. A German hand grenade had been covered by the snow.

For months the Ghost Army had operated dangerously close to German tank and infantry units. They had escaped blistering artillery fire with no casualties. But now the first Ghost Army soldier was killed by simply lighting a campfire.

The luck of the Ghost Army had finally run out.

The Ghost Army had little time to grieve for their fallen comrade. Though the Allies won the Battle of the Bulge in late January, the war raged on.

The unit then set off on their most critical mission yet—Operation Viersen. It would be a dangerous crossing of the Rhine River directly into the heartland of Germany.

113

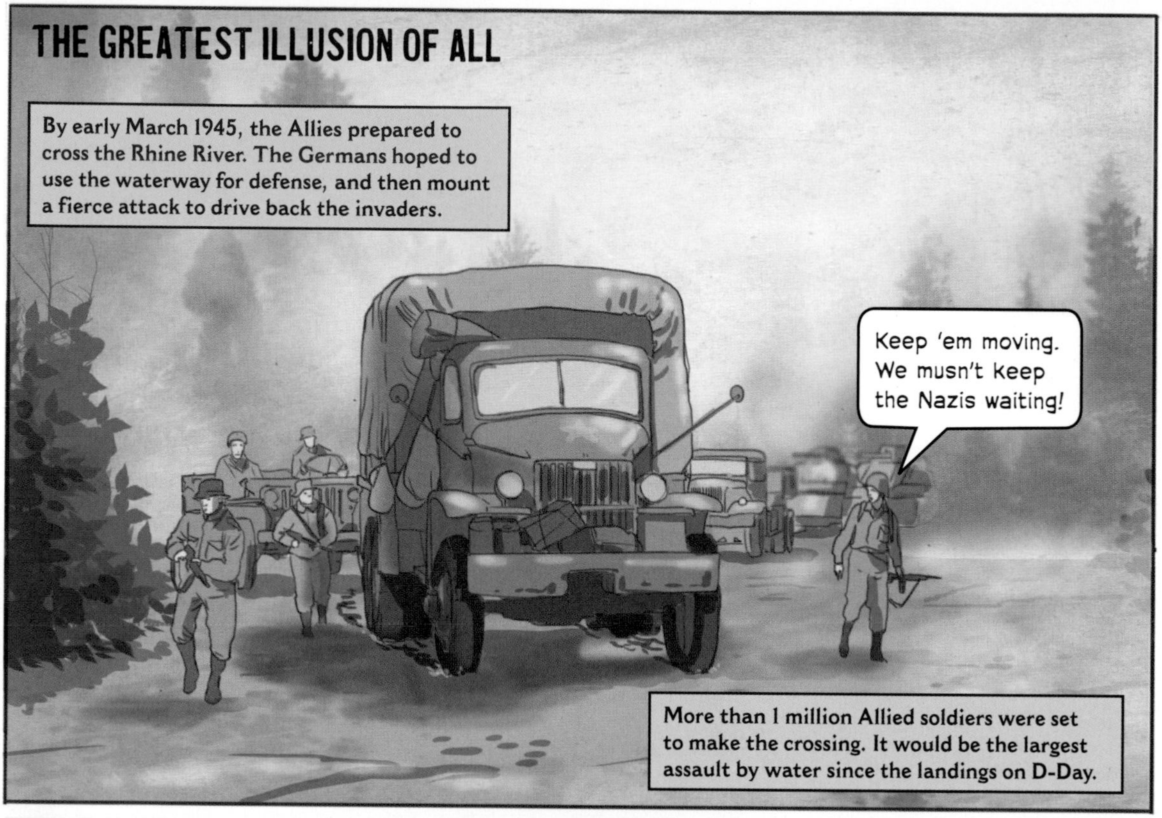
THE GREATEST ILLUSION OF ALL
By early March 1945, the Allies prepared to cross the Rhine River. The Germans hoped to use the waterway for defense, and then mount a fierce attack to drive back the invaders.
Keep 'em moving. We musn't keep the Nazis waiting!
More than 1 million Allied soldiers were set to make the crossing. It would be the largest assault by water since the landings on D-Day.

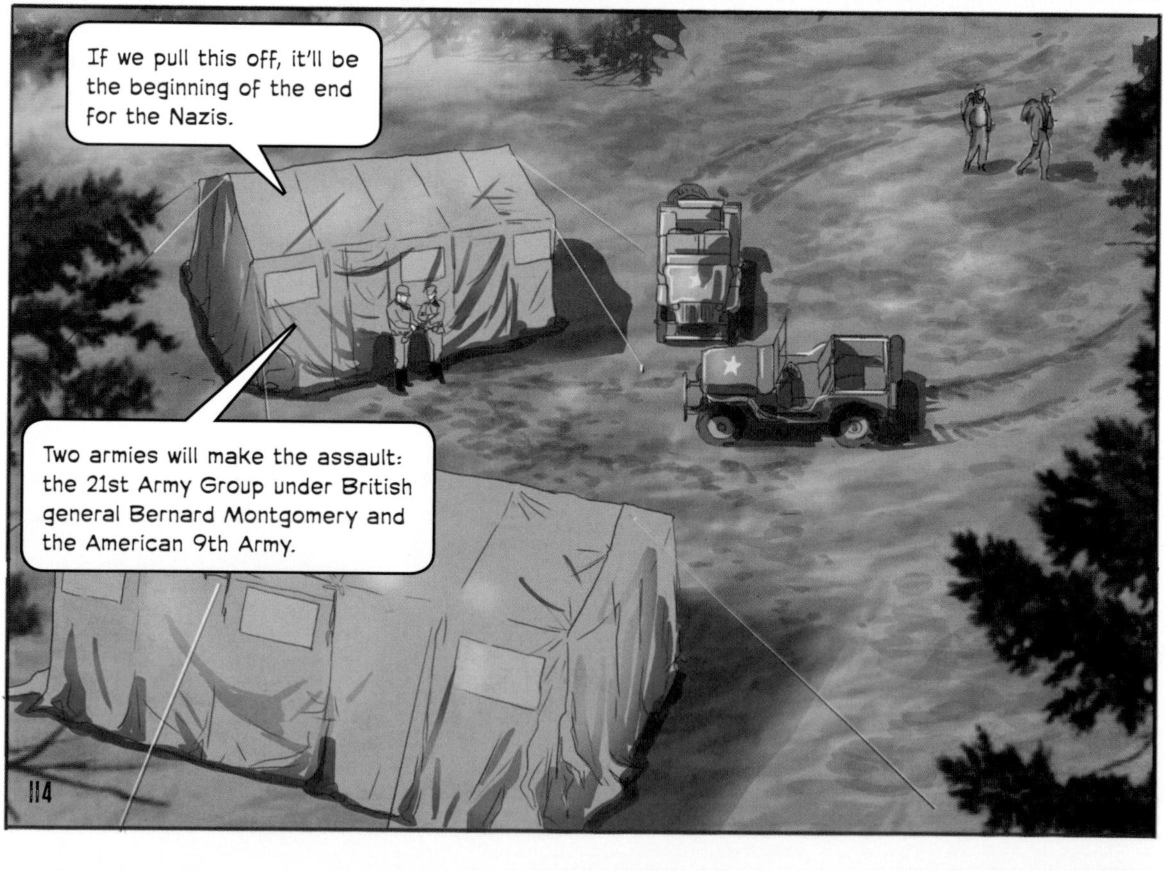
If we pull this off, it'll be the beginning of the end for the Nazis.
Two armies will make the assault: the 21st Army Group under British general Bernard Montgomery and the American 9th Army.

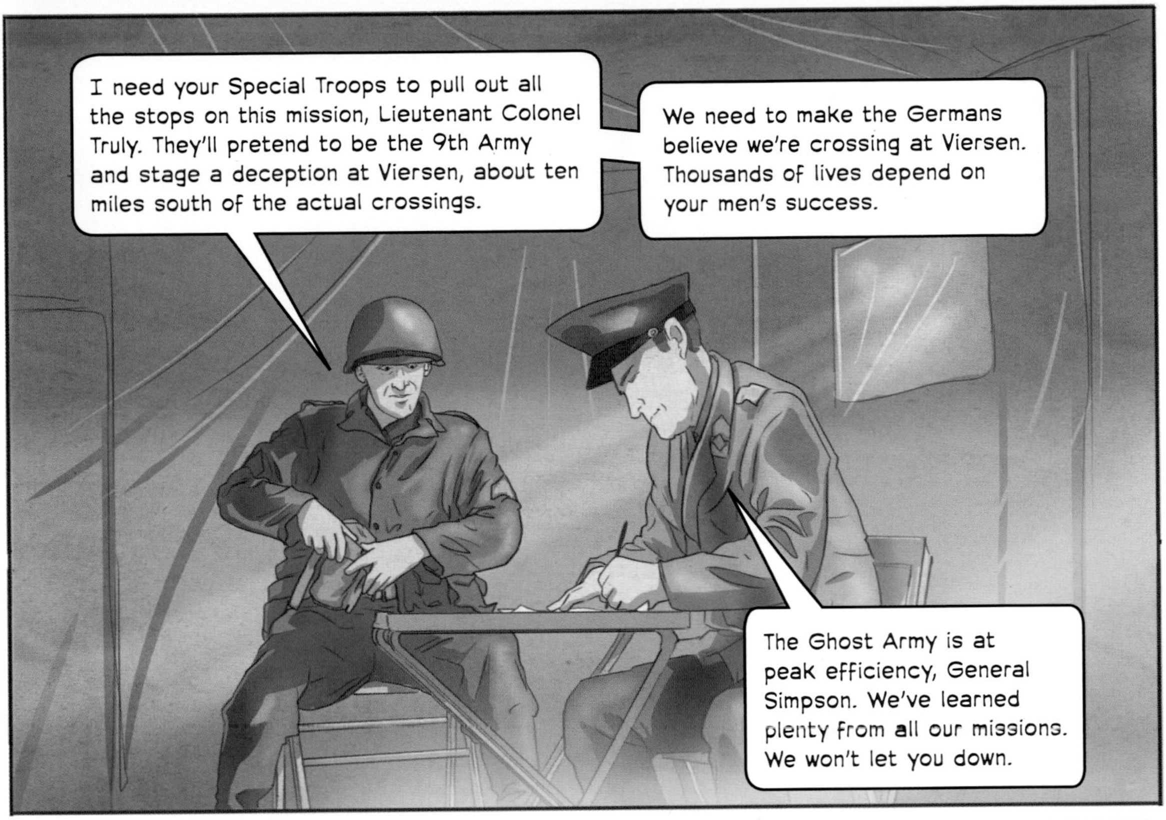
I need your Special Troops to pull out all the stops on this mission, Lieutenant Colonel Truly. They'll pretend to be the 9th Army and stage a deception at Viersen, about ten miles south of the actual crossings.
We need to make the Germans believe we're crossing at Viersen. Thousands of lives depend on your men's success.
The Ghost Army is at peak efficiency, General Simpson. We've learned plenty from all our missions. We won't let you down.

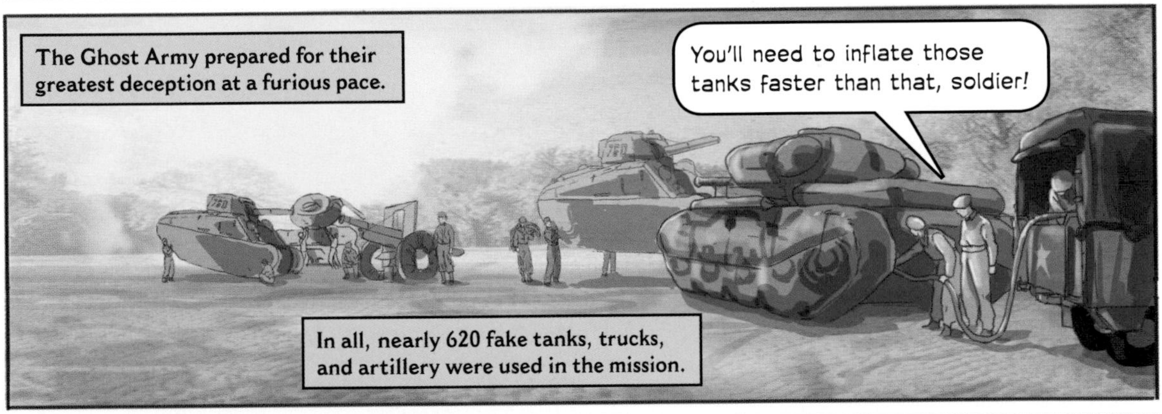
The Ghost Army prepared for their greatest deception at a furious pace.
You'll need to inflate those tanks faster than that, soldier!
In all, nearly 620 fake tanks, trucks, and artillery were used in the mission.

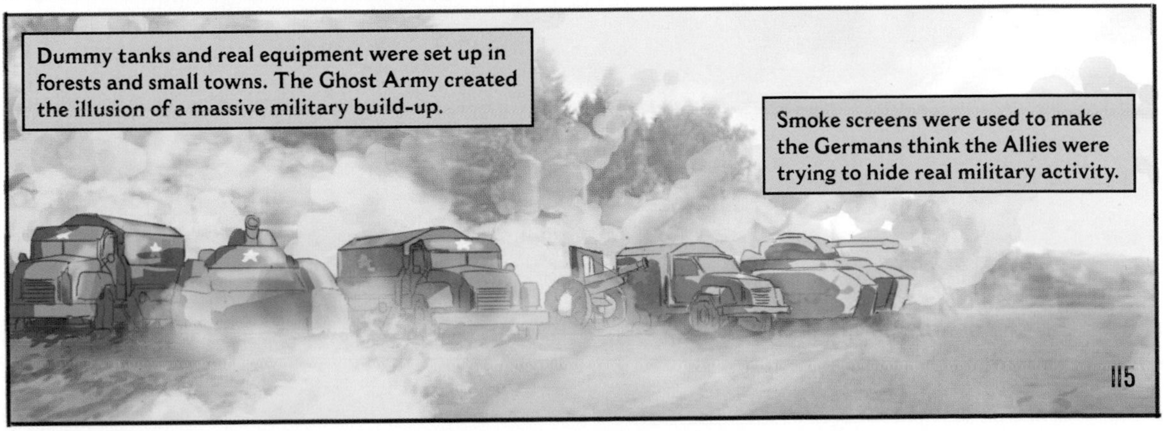
Dummy tanks and real equipment were set up in forests and small towns. The Ghost Army created the illusion of a massive military build-up.
Smoke screens were used to make the Germans think the Allies were trying to hide real military activity.

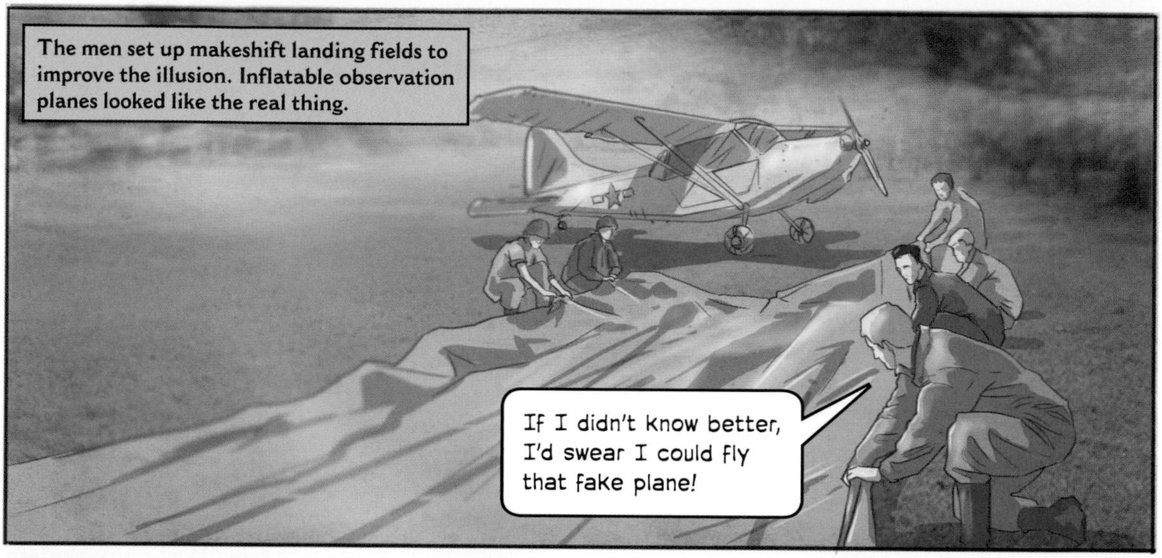
The men set up makeshift landing fields to improve the illusion. Inflatable observation planes looked like the real thing.
If I didn't know better, I'd swear I could fly that fake plane!

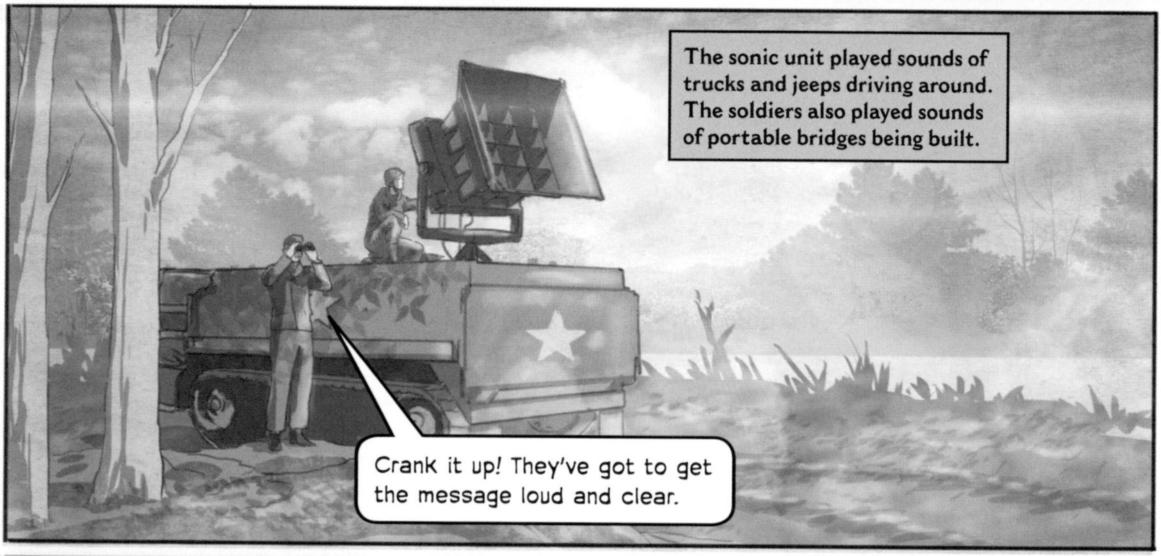
The sonic unit played sounds of trucks and jeeps driving around. The soldiers also played sounds of portable bridges being built.
Crank it up! They've got to get the message loud and clear.

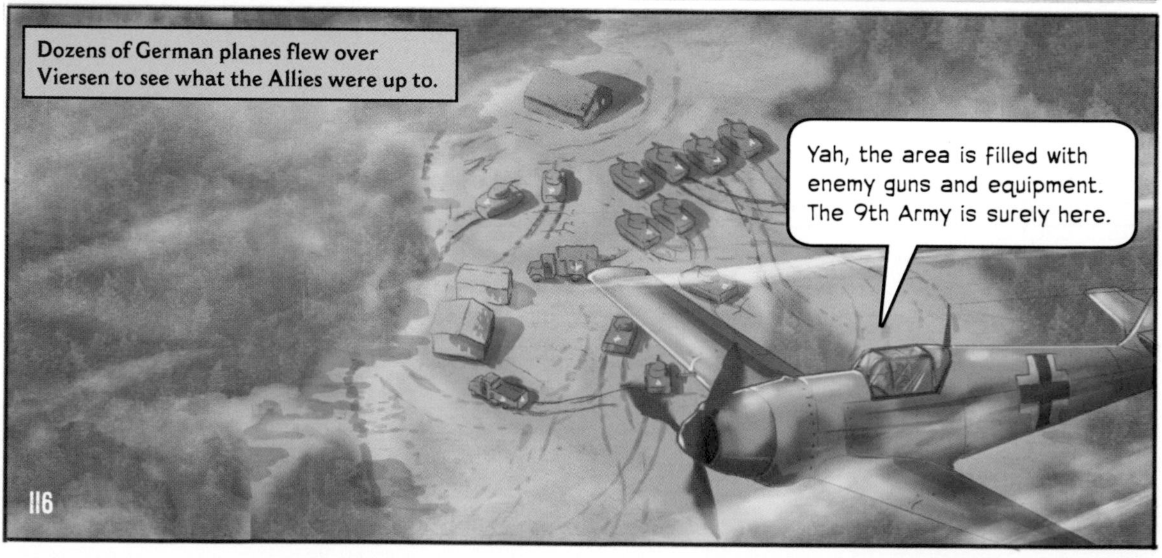
Dozens of German planes flew over Viersen to see what the Allies were up to.
Yah, the area is filled with enemy guns and equipment. The 9th Army is surely here.

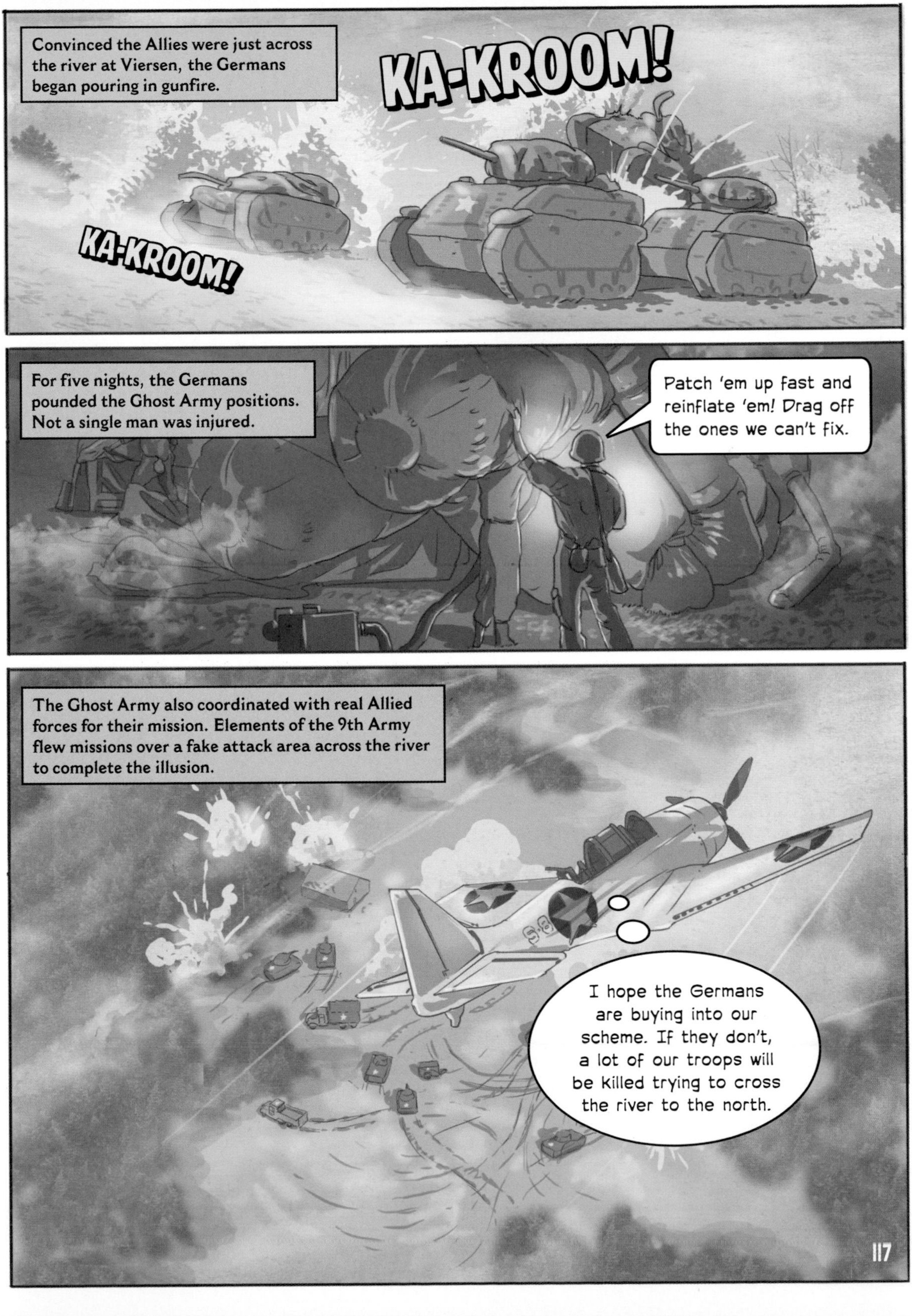
Convinced the Allies were just across the river at Viersen, the Germans began pouring in gunfire.
KA-KROOM!
KA-KROOM!
For five nights, the Germans pounded the Ghost Army positions. Not a single man was injured.
Patch 'em up fast and reinflate 'em! Drag off the ones we can't fix.
The Ghost Army also coordinated with real Allied forces for their mission. Elements of the 9th Army flew missions over a fake attack area across the river to complete the illusion.
I hope the Germans are buying into our scheme. If they don't, a lot of our troops will be killed trying to cross the river to the north.

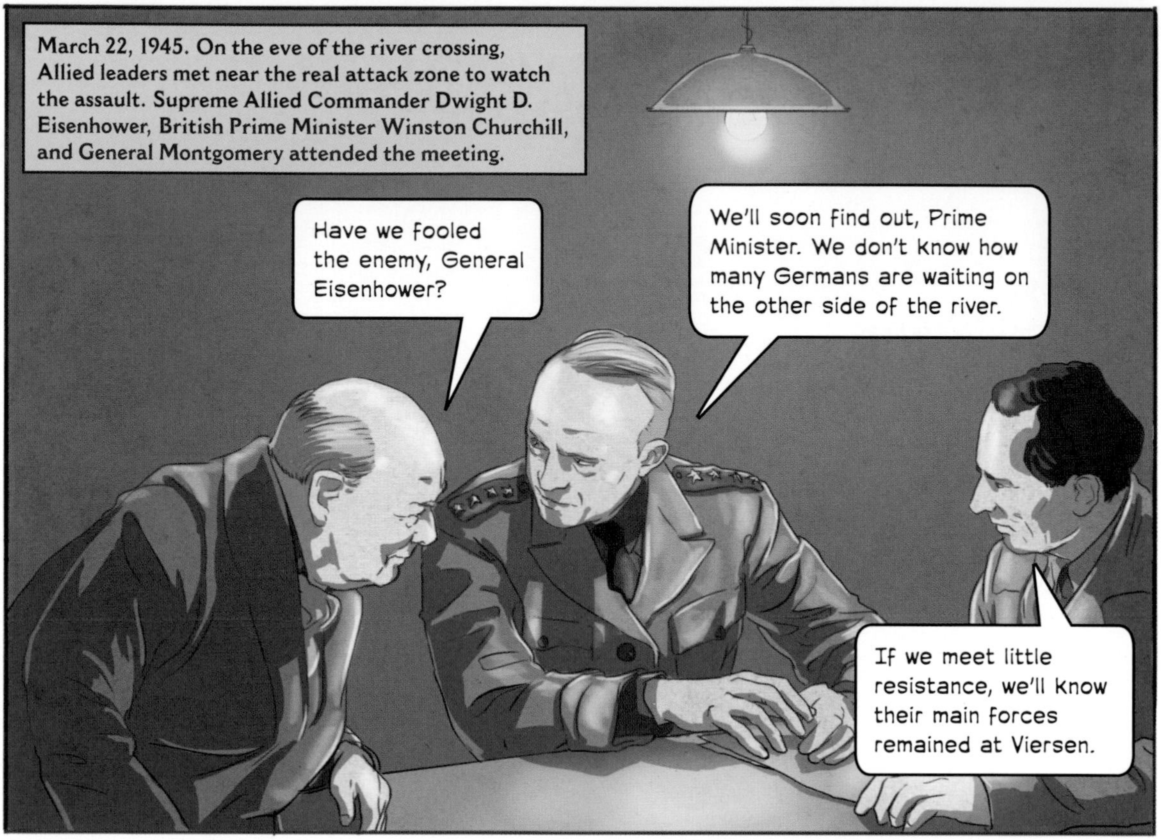
March 22, 1945. On the eve of the river crossing, Allied leaders met near the real attack zone to watch the assault. Supreme Allied Commander Dwight D. Eisenhower, British Prime Minister Winston Churchill, and General Montgomery attended the meeting.
Have we fooled the enemy, General Eisenhower?
We'll soon find out, Prime Minister. We don't know how many Germans are waiting on the other side of the river.
If we meet little resistance, we'll know their main forces remained at Viersen.

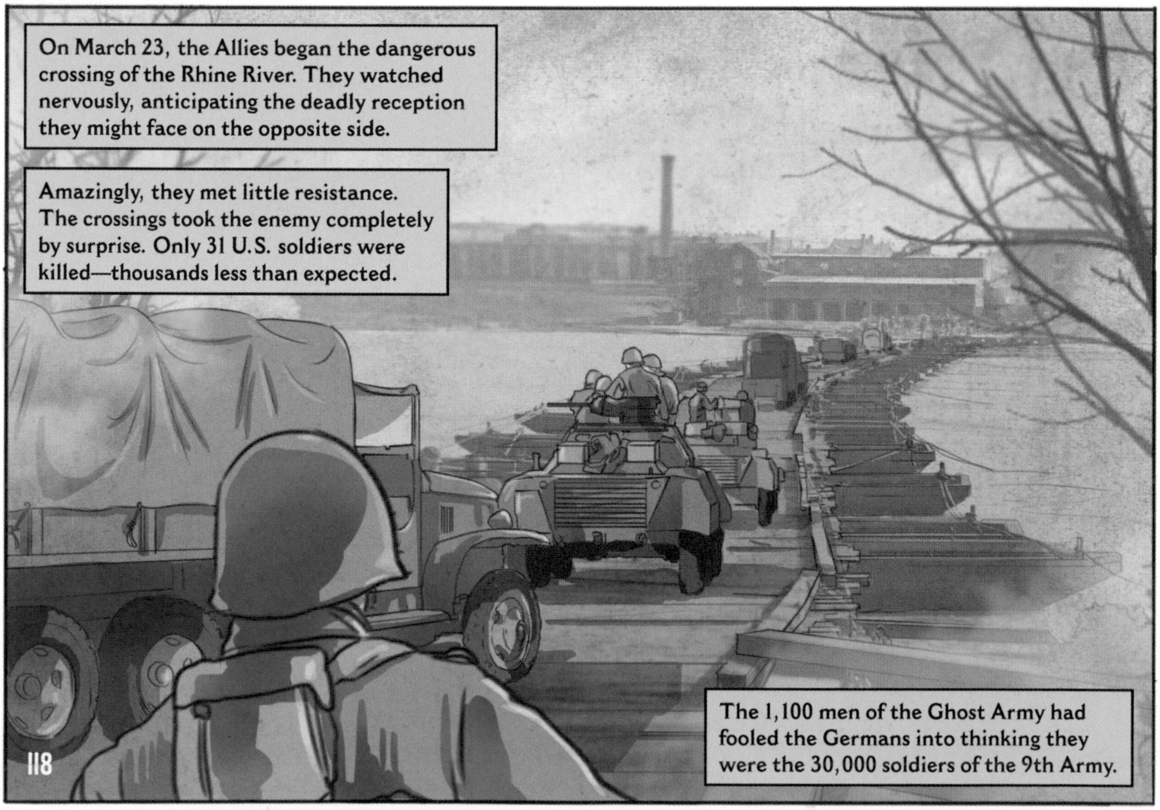
On March 23, the Allies began the dangerous crossing of the Rhine River. They watched nervously, anticipating the deadly reception they might face on the opposite side.
Amazingly, they met little resistance. The crossings took the enemy completely by surprise. Only 31 U.S. soldiers were killed—thousands less than expected.
The 1,100 men of the Ghost Army had fooled the Germans into thinking they were the 30,000 soldiers of the 9th Army.

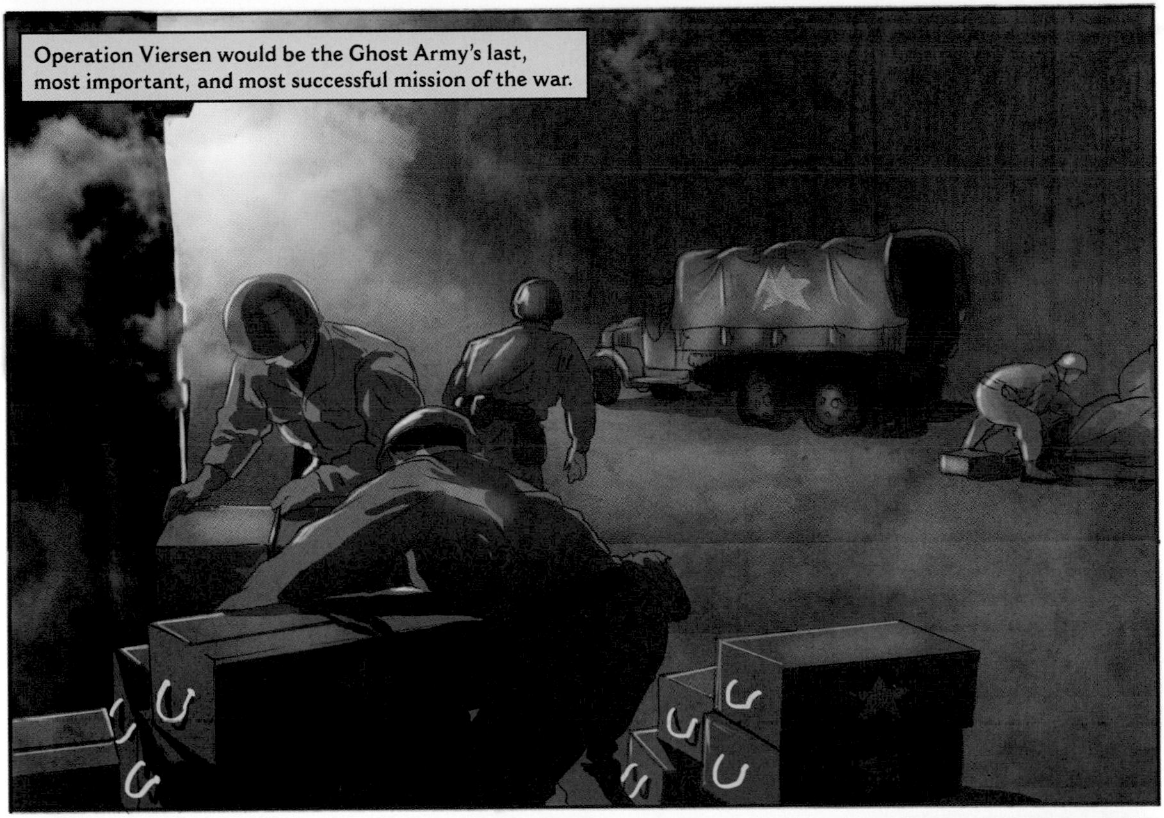
Operation Viersen would be the Ghost Army's last, most important, and most successful mission of the war.

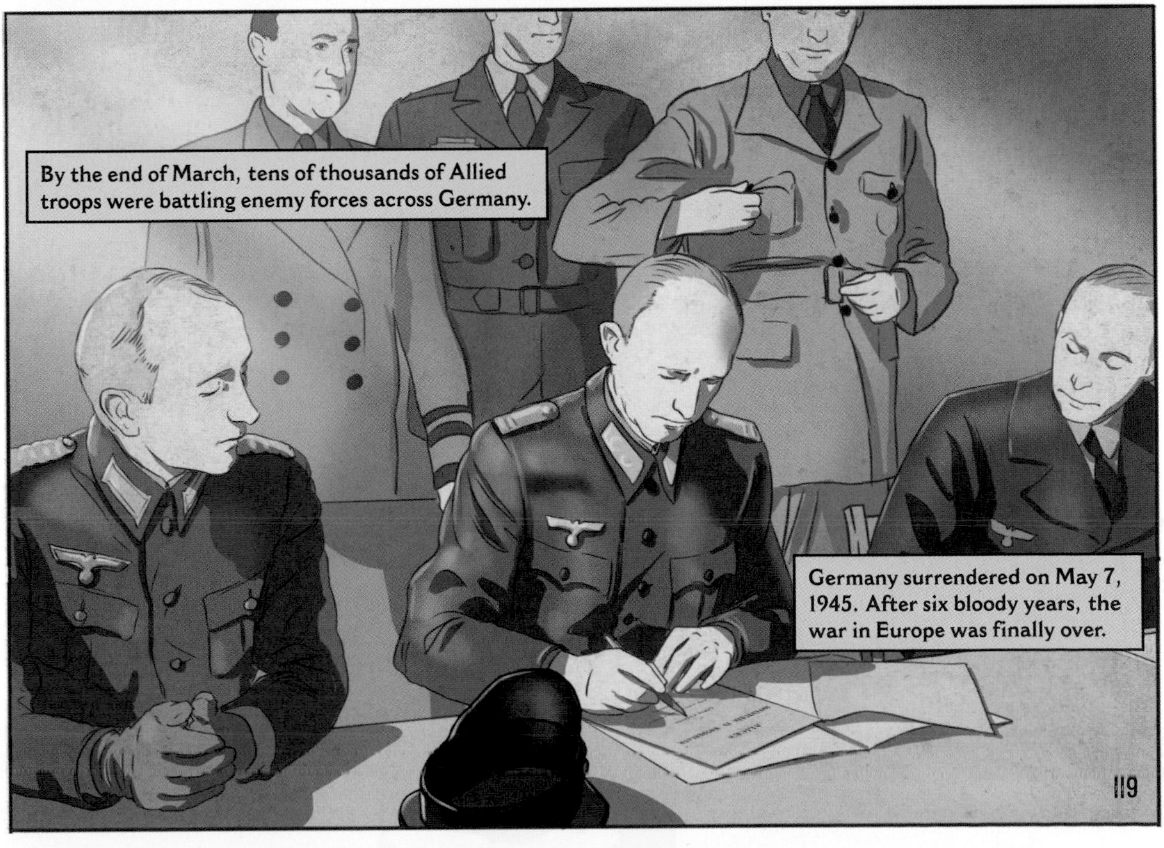
By the end of March, tens of thousands of Allied troops were battling enemy forces across Germany.
Germany surrendered on May 7, 1945. After six bloody years, the war in Europe was finally over.

HISTORY'S INCREDIBLE DECEIVERS

After Germany's surrender, the Ghost Army spent a few weeks helping guard refugee camps in Europe.

In late June 1945, the men of the Ghost Army returned to America aboard U.S. Navy transport ships.

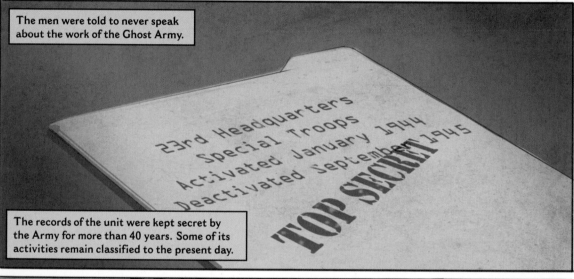

The men were told to never speak about the work of the Ghost Army.

23rd Headquarters
Special Troops
Activated January 1944
Deactivated September 1945

TOP SECRET

The records of the unit were kept secret by the Army for more than 40 years. Some of its activities remain classified to the present day.

By the 1990s magazines and newspaper articles began to reveal the remarkable story of the Special Troops.

The accomplishments of the Ghost Army—the army that never fired a shot—were finally written into the pages of history.

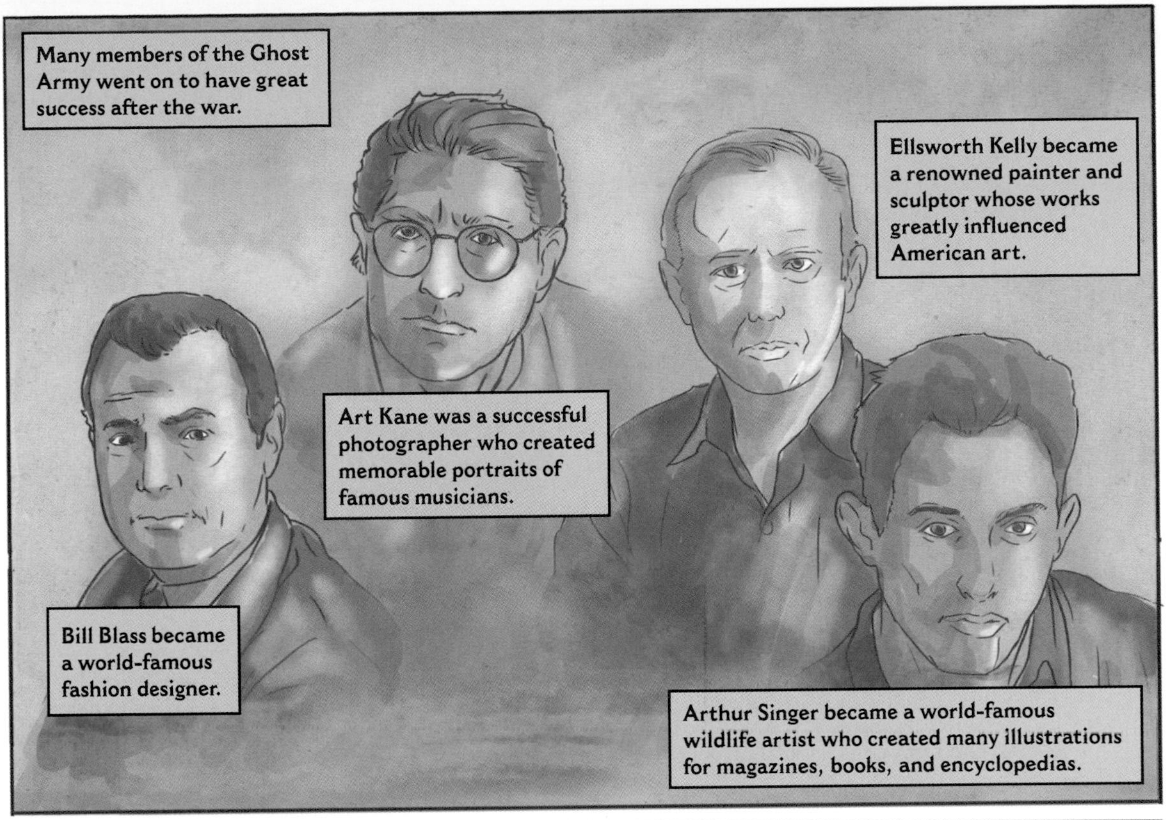
Many members of the Ghost Army went on to have great success after the war.
Ellsworth Kelly became a renowned painter and sculptor whose works greatly influenced American art.
Art Kane was a successful photographer who created memorable portraits of famous musicians.
Bill Blass became a world-famous fashion designer.
Arthur Singer became a world-famous wildlife artist who created many illustrations for magazines, books, and encyclopedias.

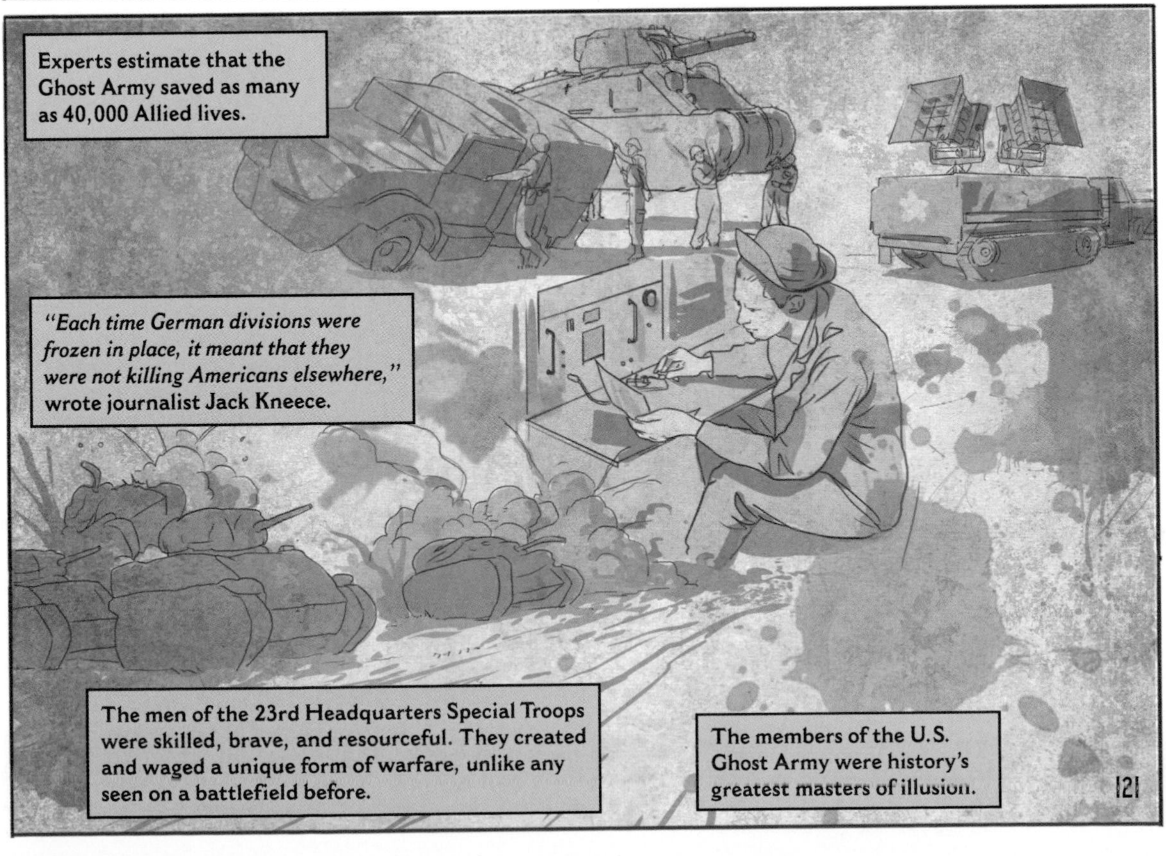
Experts estimate that the Ghost Army saved as many as 40,000 Allied lives.
"Each time German divisions were frozen in place, it meant that they were not killing Americans elsewhere," wrote journalist Jack Kneece.
The men of the 23rd Headquarters Special Troops were skilled, brave, and resourceful. They created and waged a unique form of warfare, unlike any seen on a battlefield before.
The members of the U.S. Ghost Army were history's greatest masters of illusion.

GLOSSARY

Allies (AL-eyes)—the group of countries that fought against the Axis powers in World War II, including the United States, Great Britain, France, and the Soviet Union

artillery (ar-TIL-uh-ree)—cannons and other large guns designed to strike an enemy from a distance

Axis powers (AK-siss POU-urz)—the group of countries that fought against the Allies in World War II, including Germany, Japan, and Italy

battalion (buh-TAL-yuhn)—a large unit of armed forces

bombardier (bahm-bur-DEER)—a bombing crew member who controls where and when bombs drop from airplanes

comrade (KOM-rad)—a good friend, or someone you fight with in battle; people in the Soviet Union often called each other "comrade" to show that they were working together for their country

coordinates (koh-OR-duh-nits)—a set of numbers used to show the position of a point on a map

decipher (di-SYE-fur)—to figure out something that is written in a code

dehydration (dee-hy-DRAY-shuhn)—a life-threatening medical condition caused by a lack of water in the body

flare gun (FLAIR GUHN)—a handgun that fires a brightly burning object; used as a signal to call for help

half-track (HAF-trak)—a military vehicle with wheels at the front and tanklike tracks at the rear

interrogation (in-ter-uh-GEY-shuhn)—the act of questioning someone about things in detail

Morse code (MORSS KODE)—a method of sending messages by radio using a series of long and short clicks

Nazi (NOT-see)—a member of the National Socialist Party, led by Adolf Hitler, that controlled Germany from 1933 to 1945

Pacific Theater (puh-SIF-ik THEE-uh-tur)—the area in the Pacific Ocean where several battles took place between the United States and Japan during World War II

propaganda (praw-puh-GAN-duh)—information that is spread to influence the way people think; often not completely true or fair

reservation (rez-ur-VAY-shuhn)—an area of land set aside by the U.S. government for American Indians

sadistic (suh-DIS-tik)—getting pleasure from causing pain, suffering, or humiliation on others

Soviet Union (SOH-vee-et YOON-yuhn)—a communist nation formed in 1922 combining Russia with fourteen other republics in eastern Europe and central Asia; it was dissolved in 1991

squadron (SKWAHD-ruhn)—a military unit; often a group of military pilots and aircraft

treaty (TREE-tee)—an official agreement between two or more countries to help each other and work together

INDEX

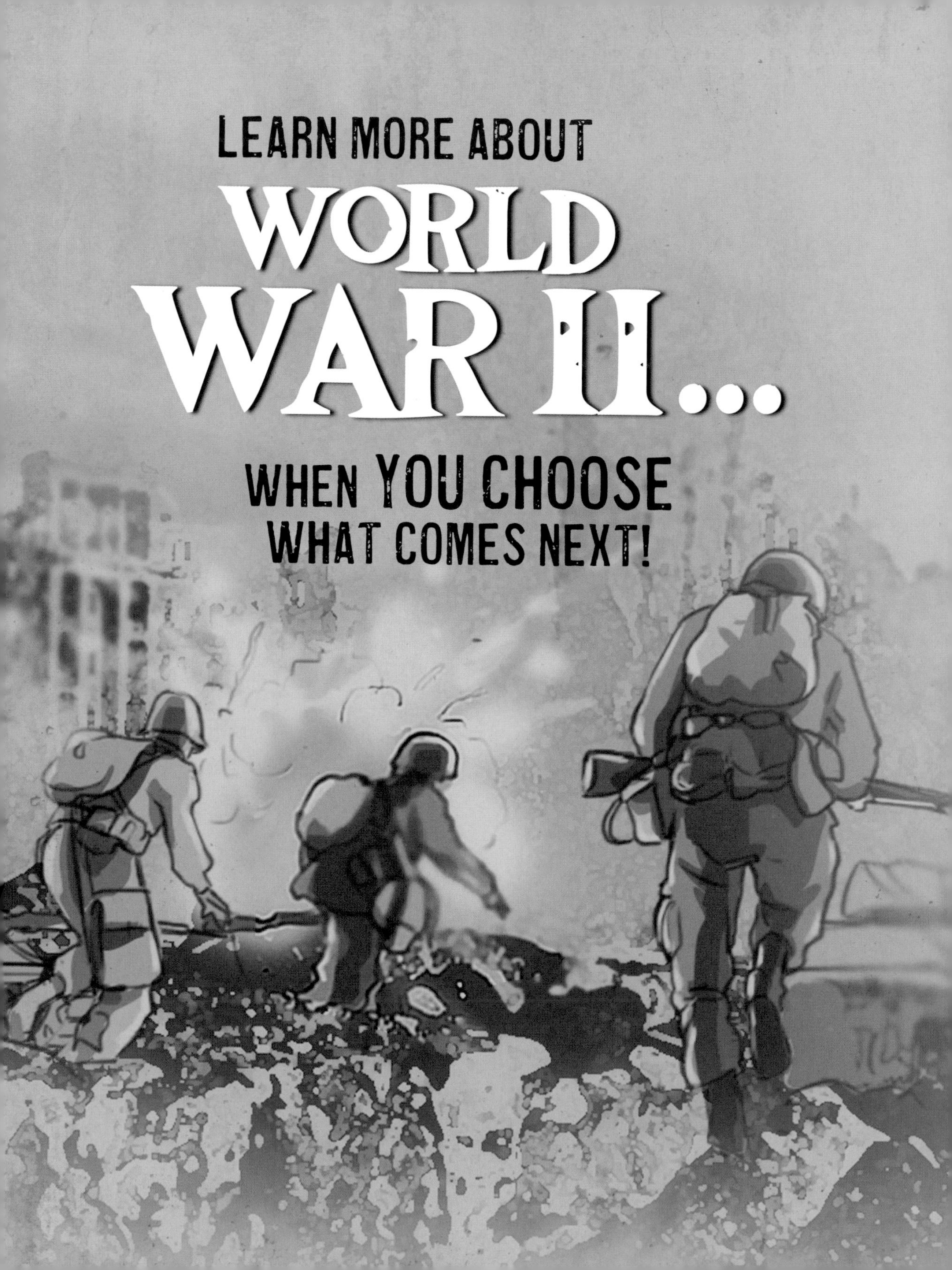

LEARN MORE ABOUT
WORLD WAR II...
WHEN YOU CHOOSE WHAT COMES NEXT!